SCOTTISH ISLAND HOPPING

Between them the four main groups of the Scottish Islands
encompass an enormous diversity in topography, tradition and
current life style, yet to the average traveller they are identified
only as the most remote and least known part of the British Isles.
Jemima Tindall describes the many methods of travelling around
the islands, whether by air, sea or road. She lists where to find the
best accommodation; an introduction to the history and mythology
of each island; and details their local crafts and specialities.
SCOTTISH ISLAND HOPPING is the first truly comprehensive
guide to the history, culture and practicalities of travel throughout
the four major groups of Scottish Islands.

Scottish Island Hopping

A Handbook for the Independent Traveller

JEMIMA TINDALL

SPHERE BOOKS LIMITED
30–32 Gray's Inn Road, London WC1X 8JL

First published in Great Britain by Sphere Books Ltd,
in association with Gentry Books Ltd, 1981
Copyright © Jemima Tindall 1981

To my parents for bringing me up in Scotland

Printed and bound in Great Britain by
Collins, Glasgow

Acknowledgements

I would like to thank the many kind people who found time to talk and point me in the right direction: the island tourist officers, the Scottish Tourist Board, the Highlands and Islands Development Board, and Dr Morton Boyd and the Nature Conservancy Council for their assistance in preparing this book; my travelling companions Liz Armitage, Catherine Goode, Susie Curtis, Peter Coates and Tess Canfield for their company and inquisitiveness; Alastair Gillies for his excellent maps; Pam Goddard for her dedicated typing; and my parents and brothers for their enthusiasm and encouragement.

Contents

Introduction

Accommodation

The Scottish Tourist Board has as yet evolved no system to grade
accommodation on the islands, and price gives little guidance. Hotels
carrying the name of a place tend to be the oldest, and are normally
fishing/family hotels with great atmosphere if not all modern conveniences. Guest houses have pulled themselves up in the world, and
some are now licensed. They tend to offer a more personalized
service, guests often eating around one table. Motels are ultra-modern
and out of keeping with the slow West Highland way of life, but
useful for catching ferries.

As a general rule, don't expect mainland standards and prepare to
be pleasantly surprised by a relaxed and friendly atmosphere. Most
hotels double as the local pub and take an active part in island life;
on ceilidh nights, it's worth asking for a room away from the bar if
you require a complete night of sleep. Licensing hours are unofficial-
ly different from those on the mainland.

If you want to meet the local communities, or have some peace,
B & Bs, the 20th century form of Highland hospitality, are the thing.
Although they can be disappointing occasionally, usually you will
find your hosts kind beyond belief, understanding wet clothes, the
need for a hot bath, and producing enormous breakfasts (and suppers
if asked), all for a reasonable price. Even incomers have a reason for
living on the islands, and they are often more interested in local

phenomena than those who were born to the island, although nobody can pull a yarn like an islander with a dram.

Camping is hazardous, as rain can fall with monotonous regularity, but it can be wonderful, perched under knolls with spectacular views. There are few official campsites and most are full of caravans and booked up. In general, camping is allowed everywhere except on farm land and on obviously unfriendly estates, but it is always a good policy to consult local knowledge as to pleasant spots and to ask permission before settling down. Crofters are sometimes incredibly kind, treating campers almost as family guests, so it pays to be polite.

There are only a few youth hostels, often full of noisy parties of French schoolkids. Scottish youth hostels give preference to their own members (you can join at most hostels) and insist on the three-night rule if the hostel is busy. It is best to book in advance for July and August. You can hire sleeping bags or bring your own, and most hostels are now self-catering.

Self-catering accommodation is usually in old croft houses, often with 'character' and ideal for families not wishing to rush on. Book early for July and August, as many return year after year to happy hunting grounds.

Transport

An essential companion for any island hopper is the compendium of timetables issued by the Highlands and Islands Development Board. Called *Getting Around the Highlands and Islands*, it is freely available and reprinted every spring.

Distances grow longer in the Highlands, not because the official Scottish mile is longer than the English one (it's redundant, anyway) but because the roads and railways seem to be influenced by the West Highland attitude of 'What's the hurry?'. Inter-City trains stop at Glasgow and Inverness, and the chances are that anyone coming from England will be told by their local BR Station that the Highland lines simply don't exist. Don't be put off: railway enthusiasts know that they do. Oban, Mallaig, Kyle of Lochalsh and Wick have at least three trains daily (Mon-Sat). The lines are single track, so passengers spend a great deal of time in the station teahouses, waiting for the one coming the other way. Local tradition attributes their lack of speed to the Scottish Tourist Board's policy of forcing all travellers to enjoy the countryside — the scenery is fantastic at all times of the year.

The eight-seat 'islander' plane that serves most of the islands is a great delight, far removed from modern airport protocol. Passengers are weighed in (if too heavy, the luggage is left behind) and then escape to the custody of friendly pilots and unbelievable views of fragmented coast and island landscapes.

The towns with ferry terminals tend to be glorious tourist traps, unpleasantly crowded in high season (July/August). Caledonian MacBrayne's breakfasts are no longer worth travelling for, but campers are always grateful for their endless supply of hot water. Berths on the early morning ferries are often available the previous night. In the summer, it is wise to make advance bookings for cars, to ensure a place on the boat of your choice (costs vary according to the length of the vehicle).

Some sort of local transport usually meets the ferry or plane, often a post bus which may circle the island, delivering the mail, before dropping passengers off at their final destination. It is best not to rely on public transport on the small islands, as the population is usually too small to justify a frequent service.

Most roads are single track with passing places: pull into the left to allow passing and overtaking. There is no point in being a road hog, and it can be dangerous.

Highland hospitality extends to cars and normally the only problem when hitching is the scarcity of traffic (though big packs are not popular). Many of the islanders have travelled more widely than most people could hope to, and have relations scattered to the four corners of the earth, but they are still curiously interested in other travellers' stories and impressions, and many a car conversation ends over a cup of tea or in the pub.

For the true island explorer, however, a bicycle is the ideal form of transport. Bikes are carried free by British Rail on most routes, are virtually impossible to fly with, and are cheap on ferries. A kit of spares is essential, as most islands cannot cope with 'fancy' bikes. Most distances are small and the lanes and tracks offer a panoramic variety of scenery, flowers, birds and other wildlife, often missed by those travelling in cars.

Walking

Very few limitations are imposed on the hiker who is expected to have due respect for the cultivated land, and for any notices forbidding access — these are usually because of stalking or rough shooting, when stray wanderers are both dangerous and a nuisance. (Between mid-August and mid-October, all hikers should check with the local tourist or estate offices as to whether it is safe and convenient to go on the hills.)

Distances become surprisingly long, especially around the coast lines and across the moors (usually heavy going). Any hiker should be properly prepared for rapid changes of weather, and should always carry maps, compass, whistle and extra warm clothes and food. Jeans are not suitable for rough walking for the cotton rapidly becomes waterlogged — a pair of knicker-bockers and good boots are a wise investment.

Those venturing onto the hills should leave details of their intended route and expected time of return, either at their hotel or clearly displayed on their car. Do not over-estimate your abilities: 3 miles (5 km) an hour is a good average over rough ground.

Diving

Diving is becoming increasingly popular around the coast, not surprisingly because of the vast numbers of wrecks. Before being tempted to explore these riches, ask the local tourist office to contact the local club or enthusiasts, and find out who holds the diving rights. The water is very cold and the weather may change suddenly. However, the clear views and many unexplored wrecks are a delight to the *experienced* diver. There are few facilities for the beginner except on Islay.

Fishing

Although the commercial fishing industries are now threatened by EEC regulations, fishing for sport or pleasure is still readily available from every island. Sea angling is not often organized, but a conversation in the pub or by the pier will invariably achieve a day's outing without any problems. Trout and salmon fishing, prized so highly by the Victorian Highland lairds, are still carefully maintained. The local tourist office will supply details about permits and advise which hotels offer special facilities.

Climbing

All potential climbers should consult the Scottish Mountaineering Club's guides.

Sailing

The Scottish islands provide some of the best sailing in Europe. However, it must be stressed that the rugged coastlines and compli-

cated currents can prove extremely hazardous, and all visiting yachtsmen should obtain the relevant charts. Most of these can be obtained
from:

Kelvin Hughes, Chart and Maritime Division,
Pegasus House, 375 West George Street,
Glasgow (tel 041 221 5452)
and
19 - 23 Featherstone Street,
London EC1Y 8SL (tel 01-250 1010).

It is also advisable to contact the local yacht clubs. These usually
extend a warm welcome to fellow yachtsmen, and can often supply
their own manuals of sailing directions and anchorages.

Shetland is a great place for regattas, with at least one every
summer weekend, but offers few boats for hire. Oban is a good
centre for chartering yachts to sail the Hebrides.

Supplies

The islands belong superficially to the 1980s, but low levels of
population mean that facilities are less sophisticated and far more
sparsely distributed than on the mainland.

Banks can be found in most towns but not in small villages. It is
unfair to ask the local shop to cash large cheques, so always carry
enough cash to cover your day-to-day expenses.

Shops are hard to find out of the towns. Mobile units behave like
the feet of rainbows, disappearing over the horizon. Village shops
carry limited supplies, keep extraordinary hours — without rhyme or
reason, and are to be found in caravans, old sheds, or even in the
back rooms of crofts. Shop whenever the opportunity arises, expect
everything to be shut on Sunday, especially on the 'Wee Free' isles,
and cater accordingly.

However relaxed the licensing hours may be during the week, the
Sabbath is invariably strictly observed.

Weather

Tiree holds the British sunshine record, but as a general rule you
should imagine that Scotland will be wet and windy even in the
height of summer, and be pleasantly surprised when summer clothes
are necessary. May is generally the sunniest month, the rain showers
increasing gradually thereafter until the October drenching.

The clear air and continuous breeze may prevent you from noticing the heat of the sun: wear suntan cream even on cloudy days, or

13

you will soon burn.

I do not recommend winter island hopping. Daylight hours are short, and the storms romp home from the Atlantic.

Midges

These get worse as the summer progresses, until they are killed by the cold of September. Rising in clouds from damp ground, they will suck blood from any and every bit of exposed flesh. Anti-midge sticks help to keep the tiny cannibals off, but smoke is the best screen. They are a particular menace on the Inner Hebrides.

Scottish Cooking

Images of endless fish and chip shops are most unflattering of Scottish culinary skills. Crofting women are renowned for their home baking and even if most cooking is simple, the standards are generally high, using local produce wherever possible.

Haggis: as you wander the islands, tales of this tartan-crested, one-legged monocled moorland bird will become more elaborate and whimsical. If you are invited to a midnight haggis hunt, don't go — they are pulling your leg. To make this culinary delicacy in true Scottish style, take a sheep's paunch, soak it in salt, turn it inside out and wash thoroughly. Boil the liver for ½ hour, add the heart and lights, and boil for a further ¾ hour. Chop finely and mix with ½ pint of oatmeal, two chopped onions, pepper, salt, half a grated nutmeg, 1½ pints gravy or stock, and the juice of one lemon. Stuff into the paunch (if too full, it will burst) and place in boiling water for 3 hours. Serve with mashed potatoes and neeps (turnips). (Jelly is a great help!) Feeds eight. Lazy cooks can save a lot of energy by buying ready-made haggis from a butcher.

Oatcakes: originally these were made from croft-grown oats, ground by the womenfolk on the hand quern, and baked over the open fire on the black cast-iron griddle. They can be revolting if made of coarse oatmeal and stale, as they then stick to the teeth and are quite unswallowable. Fresh and well made, they are quite a different story, and when spread with a little butter will melt in the mouth. It is best to buy small quantities of the locally made, daily. There is considerable variation from island to island.

Porridge: many Sassenachs are put off this delicious breakfast food by inconsiderately seasoned helpings in childhood. It does not have to be eaten with salt alone, the true Highlanders's meal, but is tasty with sugar and milk, treacle or even butter stirred in, and is the

14

best possible start to a long day tramping the hills, wading in streams or messing about in boats.

Kippers: NOT JUST A MOUTHFUL OF BONES! When skilfully dissected and freshly cooked in butter, these smoked herring are tasty beyond belief and should be recommended to all comers. The best varieties are smoked over a peat fire, but the flavour varies considerably from island to island. True old kippers are best avoided at all costs.

Language

English gets you most places, though island dialects tend to be broad and picturesque — story telling develops a magical air as mundane English words are transformed through evocative imagery. Most islanders are highly sensitive to the nuances of accents, and are always inquisitive as to where a stranger comes from.

Gaelic, the language of the original 'Scots' — invaders from Northern Ireland and colonizers of the west coast — was once spoken throughout the Hebrides, only a few of the educated islanders speaking any English. However, there is no need to be bilingual in the islands today, for the old language is now threatened by extinction, mainly as a result of education policies which until recently were out of sympathy with this Highland heritage. Many attempts are now being made to revive Gaelic, and visitors can enjoy the beautiful songs sung in local ceilidhs and broadcast on the radio. Some islanders have a disconcerting habit of switching into Gaelic should an outsider appear, but this is not done with any ill feeling.

In the northern isles, the Viking colonizers firmly established a variety of Old Norse, called Norn, which almost totally obliterated the language of the early Celtic settlers. However, when the islands were returned to the Scottish crown, the ruling classes began to use Scots, and by the end of the 18th century Norn had become redundant, except in songs. Today, it has disappeared completely. Nevertheless, many of these islanders continue to understand their Scandinavian cousins who pause to shelter in their harbours.

Placenames

Island placenames reflect the imaginations of their inhabitants and often reveal a great deal about the place, its appearance, occupants or peculiarities. Throughout the text the abbreviations of 'G' and 'ON' refer to those words whose origins are traceable to Gaelic and Old Norse, but many others come from old English, lowland Scots and older Scandinavian languages.

Gaelic names tend to describe the physical features of the land; specific references to the principal landowners or settlements have generally been eroded during centuries of habitation by Gaelic speakers. In contrast, the Vikings were very keen to establish ownership during their lightning occupation of the isles, often using a descriptive noun, such as village, pasture, or bay, to pinpoint the place in question; hence Rousay (Orkney) — Hrolf's island. Some of the more interesting Norse names record where their noble parliaments or 'things' met, eg Tingwall and Nesting (Shetland), or where there was good hunting, eg Jura — deer isle, and Laxdale (Harris) — salmon valley. Others record the tax paid on freemen's land — eg Pennygown (Mull), where the annual tax was one penny.

As yet there is no definitive dictionary of Scottish placenames and so the curious who insist on knowing all the derivations must rely on local knowledge or the few glossaries provided in individual island handbooks. Below is a short list giving some of the most common components of island names.

Placename Glossary

English	Gaelic	Old Norse
bay	camus/lag	ob, uig, voe, vagr
black	dubh	
big	mor	stora
chasm		geo
church	cill/kill	kirkiu
cow	buidhe	
fair/white	ban	
field	ach	
fort	dun	
grey	glas	
haven		hope
headland/point	ceann	ness/nish
height	aird	
hill	cnoc	hoi
hollow	coire	
island	eilean	ay/ey
islet		holm
little	beag	litla
long	fada	
mountain	ben/beinn	
old		ole
pasture		setter
priest		papa

English	Gaelic	Old Norse
red	dearg	
rock	craig	
salmon		lax
settlement		bost
shieling		shader
shore	traig	stround
short	gearr	
spotted	breac	
stone	clach	stein
stream	allt/struan	
town		burg
valley	strath	hope
village	bail	wick
well	tobar	
wood		vidr
yellow	buidhe	

Peat

Peat is formed on areas too wet and too cold to allow bacteria to break down the dead matter properly, but not too cold to prevent the bog plants, necessary to provide the dead matter, from growing. The water washes much of the goodness out of the humus and thus the soil becoms increasingly acid. When looking at peat banks, one can usually see a bed of clay above the rock, often containing tree roots, and scientists suggest that peat began forming only 9,000 years ago, after the Boreal Age.

The all-pervading blanket of peat occurs on those islands where there is inadequate drainage and no blown shell sand to counter the acidity. These conditions are illustrated most clearly in the Outer Hebrides, where the eastern ridge of hills provides drainage and the westerly wind blows the sand to form a band of fertile machair down the west coast: in between these two extremes, the peat rolls over the contours.

On average peat contains 93 per cent water, but once dried it burns superbly. Rights to cut the peat are firmly established by every croft and maintained vigorously, for a few days' labour supplies a year's fuel. In the spring the peat banks are cut with a 'tushkar' (a specially shaped spade) into bricks which are laid flat on the heather capping. Within a few weeks they are piled into pyramids of three, topped by a fourth, and left to be dried by the summer winds. Some years they never dry sufficiently and are left ruined in this state, but by August/September they are usually dry enough to be carried back to the crofts — once in 'kishies' (willow baskets), now in plastic sacks — where they are stacked close to the house. Even when the world's supplies of oil, gas and coal have been exhausted, there will still be peat to cut.

Tartans

May I be forgiven for explaining that most tartans are a post Culloden invention, glorified by the Victorians in their attempts to become true Highland lairds. Originally they were associated with areas, but gradually each area became associated with one particular leading family and the coloured cloths took on a dynastic significance. Nowadays, the number of different colours in a pattern indicates the rank of the chief; the royal tartans have nine colours, and a shepherd's tartan two.

Visitors should be careful to wear a tartan to which they are entitled — the islanders know. Do not expect to find your chief in full dress regalia — he's more likely to be mucking about with boats at the pier or behind the local bar.

History of Scotland — a very brief summary

Scotland was known to the Greeks and partially occupied by the Romans, but of the early inhabitants we know little. The skills of craftwork and metal manufacture were probably learnt later here than in most other barbarian states, but within years of the birth of Christ wonderfully effective fortresses, called brochs, had been constructed on the northern islands, far more complex than any found elsewhere in Europe. The Broch of Mousa is the most complete today; still standing to over 40 feet (though originally it was even taller), its circular walls contain galleries and stairs within, above head height. There is no definite explanation as to the reasons for this sophisticated development, although perhaps the advance of the Romans caused pressure for land on the tribes of the north.

The land continued to be invaded and settled by different peoples and by the 6th century four kingdoms had begun to evolve: the Picts in the north and north-east; the Scots (from Northern Ireland) in the southern Hebrides, slowly filtering inland; the Britons in the lowlands; and the Angles in the south and south-west. Genealogies trace convenient yet fictitious threads between leaders, relating them to great warriors and mythological creatures, but the lack of any records make this fabric difficult to unravel into 'historical truth'.

Contemporary to this was another wave of 'invaders' — the Christian missionaries. Although Christianity was first introduced to

England by the Romans, it retained only a tenuous hold there. In contrast, Ireland, which was never occupied by the Romans, rapidly emerged as a great Christian centre, with the founding and subsequent development of many large monastic settlements. Throughout Europe in the Dark Ages, monasteries such as these remained pockets of intellectual activity, where manuscripts were preserved and copied as things of value. Legend relates that the quarrel between St Columba and his teacher was caused by St Columba copying a manuscript without permission. He was advised to leave his homeland forthwith, and chose to settle in the island of Iona. Since Columba was related to one of Ireland's royal families, the dynastic politics of the day ensured that he was soon able to carve out a place for himself in Scottish politics.

It is important to remember that Columba was by no means the only Irish monk to settle in Scotland. Many were encouraged to leave behind family distractions and seek a lonely place for their contemplations, missionary zeal acting only as a secondary spur to this self-imposed exile. Great men attracted followers, and so formed the nucleus for the many monastic communities to be established on the islands.

At a time when the Scandinavian peoples were raiding the coastline of Europe, the Pictish kings began to emerge as the strongest rulers in Scotland. Their internecine quarrels, recorded with the inaccuracies of dramatic licence in Shakespeare's *Macbeth*, ended when Malcolm Canmore (G — Bighead) won the support of the English and finally emerged as the ruler of a unified Scotland — minus the isles and the fragmented west coast. The Norwegians had settled Orkney and Shetland in the 9th century and ruled these islands, and at times the western isles, for the next 400 years, while the Danes occupied Northumberland. The Scottish kings thus spent most of the 11th and 12th centuries trying to consolidate their territory against a background of frequent interference from the English and the Norwegians. By 1265, Alexander III had taken the Hebrides and by the Treaty of Perth, Norway ceded all her Scottish possessions except Orkney and Shetland. Marriage alliances firmly interlocked the fortunes of the Earls with those of the Scottish crown, but the death of the child Margaret, Maid of Norway and granddaughter of Alexander III, in 1290 left no obvious successor. Once again, Scotland was wracked by battles for leadership, well stirred up by the then powerful English monarchy, with no less than thirteen claimants to the throne, including John Balliol and Robert the Bruce. Eventually Robert the Bruce emerged victorious at the Battle of Bannochburn in 1314, independently of the English — a fact much commemorated in Scottish folklore.

Scotland was a poor country and the king's rule was not all powerful, being continually dependent upon clan feuds — as the development of the Lordship of the Isles bears witness. In the 15th and 16th centuries, the crown was weakened by an unfortunate succession of child rulers, all manipulated by greedy nobles for selfish ends, a process revealed most dramatically in the story of the reign of Mary Queen of Scots. Her grandmother had been the eldest sister of Henry VIII of England, and on the death of her cousin Elizabeth I, her son James VI of Scotland inherited the English crown to become James I of England, thus achieving the eventual union of the crowns.

Meanwhile, during the troublesome reign of Mary Queen of Scots, an eloquent preacher, John Knox, had led the Scottish people into the religious arguments then raging throughout Europe, and brought them out Protestant. The Jacobite issue revolved around an attempt to reinstate the Stuart family to their 'rightful' throne, exploiting the general Scottish discontent against the union with England. But many Scottish families were not prepared to risk their new found prosperity or their religion, for the 'Pretenders' were Catholics and by this time only a few Scots were fellow believers. The rising of the 'Old Pretender', James Edward in 1715, was badly organized and surrendered at Preston. Although the repercussions from the revolt were severe, 'the Redcoats' combing the Highlands for traitors, 30 years later a second rising supported James's son, Bonnie Prince Charlie, the 'Young Pretender'. He successfully captured Edinburgh and marched as far south as Derby before his supporters dwindled and he was forced north to a crushing defeat at the Battle of Culloden. He escaped but his followers paid dearly for their misguided loyalty. Many chiefs had their lands confiscated, and the new owners tended to look at their acquisitions from a purely financial viewpoint, evaluating people against sheep and finding them lacking. Hence the brutal clearances, whereby many highlanders and islanders were deported from their homelands to the barren rocks, or to the new lands of America and Australia. This issue was only satisfactorily resolved this century, with the crofting commissions.

During the First and Second World Wars, recruitment for the British army further exacerbated the problems of depopulation on the islands. The development of a materialistic society meant that many of the communities could no longer remain self-supporting, and even today the drain of the young continues, as they are forced to leave the islands for the towns of the mainland in their search for employment.

Scottish Kings

Malcolm Canmore III 1057-93
Donald Bane 1093-4 (brother)
Duncan II 1094 (nephew)

Donald Bane 1094-7
Edgar 1097-1106 (stepbrother)
Alexander 1106-24 (brother)
David I 1124-53 (brother)
Malcolm IV 1153-65 (son)
William I 1165-1214 (brother)
Alexander II 1214-49 (son)
Alexander III 1249-86 (son)
Margaret 1286-90 (grandaughter)
Interregnum
John Balliol 1292-6
Interregnum
Robert the Bruce (I) 1306-29
David II 1329-71 (son)
Robert II 1371-90 (nephew)
Robert III 1390-1406 (son)
James I 1406-37 (son)
James II 1437-60 (son)
James III 1460-88 (son)
James IV 1488-1513 (son)
James V 1513-42 (son)
Mary Queen of Scots 1542-67 (daughter)
James VI & I 1567-1625 (son)

Bibliography

Many books have been written about the islands, covering many different aspects —whether scientific study, historical research or traveller's impressions. Here is a list of books I have enjoyed and found informative through my own travels, combined with a small handful of 'highland and island' novels which evoke the atmosphere of the unique isles.

Frazer Darling, Morton Boyd, *The Highlands and Islands*
JB Sissons, *The Evolution of Scotland's Scenery*
Berry Johnson, *The Natural History of Shetland*
Heinzel, Fitter, Parslow, *The Birds of Britain and Europe*
Fitter, Fitter, Blamey, *The Flowers of Britain and Northern Europe*

Royal Commission of Ancient Monuments of Scotland:
  volumes on Orkney and Shetland; Outer Hebrides, Skye and Small Isles; Argyll
Lloyd, Laing, *Orkney and Shetland Archaeology*
Anderson, Anderson, *Adoman's Life of St Columba*
WD Simpson, *The Ancient Stones of Scotland*

21

L Harding, *The Celtic Church in Britain*
M Magnusson, *The Vikings*
JD Mackie, *A History of Scotland*
TC Smout, *A History of the Scottish People 1560-1830*
AJ Youngson, *After the Forty-Five*
J Hunter, *The Making of the Crofting Community*
Frazer Darling, *West Highland Survey*
T Steel, *The Life and Death of St Kilda*
Thompson, Derick, Grimble, *The Future of the Highlands*
A Fenton, *The Northern Isles: Orkney and Shetland*
IF Grant, *Highland Folk Ways*
S Don, *Fair Isle Knitting; Shetland Lace*

The Orkneyinga Saga
M Martin, *Description of the Western Islands of Scotland* (1695)
T Pennant, *A Tour in Scotland and the Western Isles* (1771)
Dr Johnson, *A Journey to the Western Islands of Scotland* (1775)
J Boswell, *The Journal of a Tour to the Hebrides* (1785)
J Sinclair, *The Statistical Account of Scotland* (1791-1798) - 21 vols
  compiled from reports from the parish ministers

I MacDonald, *A Family in Skye 1908-1916*
D Cooper, *Road to the Isles*
D Howarth, *The Shetland Bus*
Frazer Darling, *Island Years*
G Mackay Brown, *An Orkney Tapestry*
G Maxwell, *Ring of Bright Water*

N Gunn, *The Silver Darlings; The Butcher's Broom*
RL Stevenson, *Kidnapped; The Pirate*
Sir C MacKenzie, *Whiskey Galore*
J Buchan, *Sule Skerry*
M Stewart, *Wild Fire at Midnight*

THE ISLANDS

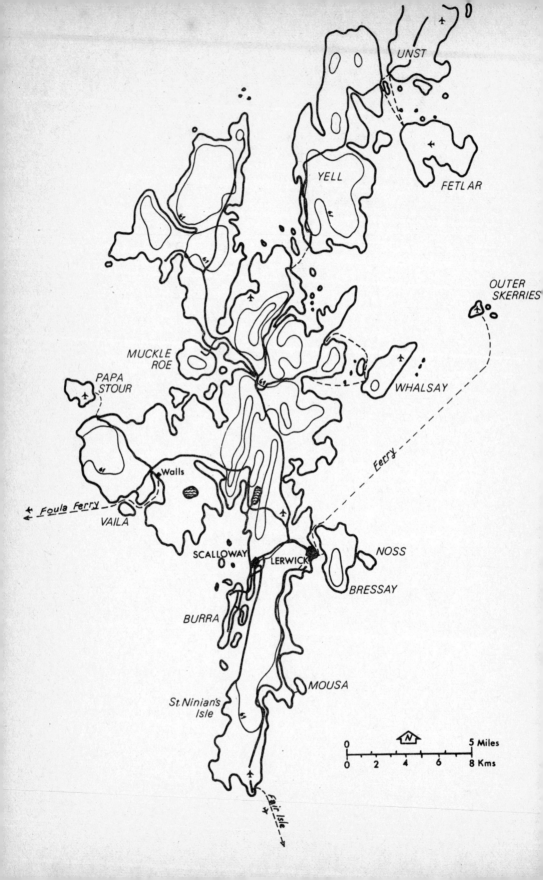

UNST

YELL

FETLAR

OUTER
SKERRIES

MUCKLE
ROE

PAPA
STOUR

WHALSAY

Ferry

* Walls

Foula Ferry

VAILA

NOSS

SCALLOWAY

LERWICK

BRESSAY

BURRA

MOUSA

St. Ninian's
Isle

Fair Isle

N

0   5 Miles

0   2   4   6   8 Kms

Part 1
The Shetland Islands

Connections:

By air: from Aberdeen to Sumburgh: four a day. From London to Sumburgh: Mon-Fri, two a day. From Birmingham to Sumburgh: Mon-Fri, two a day. From Glasgow to Sumburgh: Mon-Fri, one a day, except Sun. British Airways.

From Aberdeen to Tingwall: two a day, except Sun. From Edinburgh to Tingwall: one a day, except Sun. Loganair Ltd.

There are also direct flights from some north European countries.

By sea: from Aberdeen to Lerwick: three a week; cars; overnight crossing. P & O Ferries, Jamieson Quay, Aberdeen (tel Aberdeen 572615).

Shetland Life

One's first impression of Shetland, whether glimpsed by air or by sea, is of a land nibbled and carved by the all-dominating power of water. The sharp cliffs of Noss, Foula and Eshaness show what strength is needed to resist the constant attack of the waves, while the beaches of Sandwick and Spiggie are the grateful recipients of the finely ground sand rejected by these same forces.

The blanket moors of the spine of the land appear drained of all goodness, and few islanders continue to attempt to eke out a living there. But around the shore, where the lime of the seashell sand neutralizes the acidity of the peat, are wonderful herb-rich meadows, ideal for livestock grazing. Childhood memories recall sweet-smelling, delicate-tasting milk from such pastures, but sadly few crofters now prefer the hassles of maintaining cows in milk to the ease of shop-bought cartons. The summer months see families cutting and drying the wild flowers of these fields as hay. It is hard to believe that they belong to our time scale, but the fields and quantities are too small to warrant expensive modern machinery.

The smallholdings or crofts of Shetland were never intended to provide a complete livelihood for the families, but were a way of obtaining basic foodstuffs while the men earned a small income at haaf-fishing for the landlords. Oats and later potatoes were grown in the small fields in addition to the hay, while a few cows, ponies and sheep were kept on the common unfenced grazing lands of the moors, herded by the children with the help of a dog. Hens and perhaps a pig ate what scraps they could find around the house.

Enforced self-sufficiency through poverty meant that every minute of every day was precious. Before a man married, he collected stones from the moor and driftwood from the shore, and with the help of his neighbours built his own house, perhaps having saved from his fishing enough money to buy a few luxuries such as metal spoons or china plates. Once married, his wife and children would run the croft while he was fishing. She would never walk anywhere without her knitting, hence the knitting belts of leather (seen in the local museums) which held the needles steady and kept the garment out of the dirt. The long winter evenings brought the households indoors, the women to the spinning wheels to prepare the wool, either for their own knitting or for the local weaver to make cloth to clothe their families, the men to repair the fishing nets or to make straw ropes. Entertainment was provided by neighbours who would drop in to share the fire, recalling happenings of old, gossiping, or singing songs of their inheritance.

The waters around Shetland were first fished by the Dutch (see Bressay) and the 17th and 18th centuries witnessed many attempts by the English and Scots to dislodge them. They finally succeeded contemporaneously with the Clearances (moving the people to the shore in favour of sheep), by introducing a bounty in 1727 which encouraged the landlords to exploit this new source of wealth. The men were distrustful, but with no alternative means of earning a living, they soon won mastery of the sea, echoing their Norse seafaring ancestry. Along the shore (see especially West Mainland), many haaf-stations were built where the men lived and landed their catches in the summer months. Their boats and equipment were at first provided by the landlords, who also bought the catches at ridiculously low prices, until the initiative of Arthur Anderson (see Vaila) broke their stranglehold. The boats they used were directly evolved from Viking longships, double-ended timber-built yaols similar to those small craft found all round the shores of Shetland. They gave little protection to the men on their three- or four-day-long expeditions to the deep sea fishing grounds, in search of cod, ling or herring. The fishing industry today, with its fast, modern trawlers, is centred on Lerwick and Whalsay. The small boats are thus used mainly as pleasure craft, although a few are still taken out regularly in search of the lobsters to be found on the submerged rocky reefs.

Shetland knitting has become justifiably famous. Sheep have been kept on these isles since the Stone Age, and although there has been some inter-breeding since the 19th century (due to the increased emphasis on sheep farming which initiated the Highland Clearances), **Shetland sheep** have retained several characteristics intact — notably an intelligent look which defies most fences, and a fleece renowned for its softness and colour. In the summer months they look remarkably scruffy as they shed their fleeces naturally (vast quantities of wool can be collected from the heather by an ambling walker), although the crofters aim to shear them before too much is lost. The natural colours range from off-white through a series of greys and browns to Shetland black (a dark brown), the most sought-after shade being 'Moorit', a darker than fawn colour unique to this breed.

The incredibly soft but hardy wool makes long-lasting jerseys and many of the island knitters create and rework traditional patterns using the natural colours (see especially Fair Isle and Whalsay). Cobwebs of lace are still knitted into shawls (see Lerwick Museum), but this is a fast vanishing tradition, representing the more skilful aspects of knitting. Each family has its own patterns, passed down from mother to daughter and rarely written down. A few are still made on Unst and some of the simpler patterns have recently been recorded (see reading list).

Here, as elsewhere, community traditions have dwindled with the onset of television, but the local radio station (92.7mHz) does its best to broadcast local events and keep alive the old ways. Sometimes stories are recited in such broad dialect that an outsider will catch a bare handful of words. Frequent listening will enlighten and enchant the ear, as picturesque phrases throw new light on the ordinary. Shetlanders and Orcadians both spoke a dialect of Old Norse called Norn until the turn of the 18th century, but even today the language they speak among themselves is more comprehensive to Scandinavians than to other English speakers (although a visitor's English is kindly spoken for outsiders).

The old tradition of **Shetland fiddling** is regularly maintained in St Olafs Hall, Lerwick (Wed evenings 7 — 9) and at many local functions, but it is also easy enough to find a personal fiddler to play to you by asking around outside the towns. The origins of Shetland fiddle music are different to those of the rest of Scotland, being based on a Scandinavian instrument, the 'gue' (similar to the Hardanger fiddle), whose unstopped strings were used as drones. This led to a custom of ringing strings above and below the melody line, the instrument being held on the chest and moved against the bow (contrary to the classical technique). The fiddles were often taken to sea and so many reveal Nordic influences passed on as the fishermen met their fellows of common ancestry. Many Scots tunes have also been adapted and the tradition is maintained through the schools.

Many people still burn peat (see Introduction) as all other fuel has to be imported, and it is in collecting this that the famous Shetland ponies are most employed — traditionally carrying the peats from the moor back to the crofts, in an elaborate harness of straw and wood (of which there is a model in the Lerwick Museum). In the 19th century many ponies were reared to replace the children down the coal mines. Although allowed to roam wild, these short stocky creatures with watchful eyes and shaggy coats are all owned by someone. They are sold at the annual pony sales and often become excellent children's ponies when properly trained. (There are no organized facilities for riding in Shetland).

Getting Around: If transportless, the best solution is to hitch. The buses tend to go to Lerwick in the morning and return to the outlying districts at night, although there is a good service to Sumburgh Airport from Lerwick, and a daily (except Thu and Sun) overland and sea trip to Unst. Coach tours are organized by J Leask & Sons, 56 Commercial Road, Lerwick (tel Lerwick 3162). Hitching is easy and relatively safe. Crofters are more likely to pick you up than oilmen, so it is also a good way of learning much about old Shetland.

Mainland Shetland

Lerwick (ON leir vik — mud bay)
This, Shetland's capital, is best seen from the sea, the old stone houses rising in chaotic form up the steep hillside, most with their gable ends to the sea to gain slight protection from the wind, opening into dark wynds and stepped alleyways. Lerwick grew slowly from the 17th century, helping to supply the many Dutch fishing crews based at Bressay (see Bressay). Only in the 19th century, when the islanders began to fish their own waters, and when the gentry realized that the enforced winter isolation on their estates could be avoided if they invested in a town house, did Lerwick develop as the heart of Shetland. Typical early buildings can be seen at the

Lodberries where a tightly knit pack of houses and stores cluster round a small pier. The surviving sea-doors and crane speak of a more active age, for today the shipping business sprawls along the northern outskirts.

On the hill is **Fort Charlotte**, built by Cromwell during the Dutch wars, when the English were trying to exert their rights over the fishing. The actual fort, an approximate pentagon, is nondescript but it commands views across the sound to Bressay, and on the bustling town below. The light of midsummer's night is celebrated here by a costumed dance.

The harbour is alive with a babble of different tongues: Danish, Norwegian, Dutch, Russian, and of course the broad, unintelligible (almost) island dialect, emphasizing that even today Lerwick is still a major international fishing centre. The range of boats is equally impressive: cruise liners, cargo ships, car ferries (for Bressay), trawlers, fishery protection vessels, lobster boats, Shetland yaols, and surprisingly even a longship. There is a very active sailing club here as elsewhere in Shetland, and regattas are held frequently throughout the summer. The Viking longship (a modern replica) makes trips around the bay — enquire at the Tourist Office.

Lerwick was not a site of dynamic Viking settlement, but served as a resting place for several disastrous expeditions (eg that of King Hakon Hakonsson, who went on to be defeated by the Scots in the Battle of Largs in 1263). However, now the town has become the home of one of the nostalgic Viking festivals — Up-Helly-aa. Developed by Haldane Burgess in the late 1880s, out of the life-renewing fire festivals traditionally held at the end of Yule, the celebrations now take place on the last Tuesday of January. Burgess, a brilliant but blind son of Shetland, composed the soul-stirring songs and introduced the burning longship to replace the barrels of burning tar, rolled through the streets. Not really for tourists, the events begin when the 'guisers' place on display the longship they have built, and stick the 'Bill' up in the market square — a recap and distortion of the previous year's gossip and humour. The 'jarl' (leader) and his 'guisers' (men), dressed in their fantastical costumes, visit the communities, schools and homes to be admired and criticized before the evening, when they process the streets with lighted torches, singing Burgess's songs and leading the longship to its burning. The squads of 'guisers' outpace the night, entertaining the packed halls throughout the town, and only when each squad has played to each audience can the 'guisers' retire homewards. The efforts of a year's preparation and 24 hours of high spirits can be seen at the Up-Helly-Aa exhibition in the Galley Shed (Jun — Sep — 7 — 9 pm Tue and Thu).

Another notable son of Lerwick is Sir Robert Stout, born to a merchant family in what has been renamed **Stout's Court**. He emigrated to New Zealand in 1863, worked as a teacher and a barrister, and by 1884 had become the prime minister of his adopted country.

The townhall, crowning the crest of the hill in true Scottish baronial style and built in 1882, is a powerful statement of the civil pride felt by Shetland. Although rather forbidding, it is worth penetrating during the summer months for the mouth-watering coffees and teas served by the SWRI on Tuesdays, along with the demonstrations of wood crafts, ie carding, spinning, and knitting, held in the Great Hall. The hall itself is a splendid Victorian fantasia of a Viking drinking hall with vast fire places, stained glass windows portraying the Norse leaders and slightly incongruous armorial shields.

Close by is the swimming pool (closed Thursdays) and opposite is the excellent **Museum and Library** (open 10 — 1, 2.30 — 5, 6 — 8, Mon, Wed, Fri; 10 — 1, 2.30 — 5, Tue and Sat; 10 — 1 Thu). The library has a very comprehensive room on Shetland and reveals many gems from local life and history — a good place for a rainy day. The museum holds in safe keeping many finds from local archaeological sites, Pictish hammers and knives, Viking combs and artifacts, and Celtic stones, including the famous Monks Stone from Papil, with its shallow carving of four priests and a rider. There is a display of the types of stones found in Shetland, many of them semi-precious. Many of the household objects from last century are explained, eg the pundlar and bismar — wooden steelyards for weighing, and Norway bosts, boxes used for carrying 'messages' (supplies) home in the boats – so preventing them from being soaked. Here too are examples of straw-work, a craft sadly dying out now but once practised in every household for making baskets, bags and mats. Some fine examples of Shetland lace, such as wedding veils and shawls, bring back memories of Queen Victoria, for she was given some by another of Lerwick's successful sons, Arthur Anderson (see **Vaila**), and soon created a trend for them in Victorian London. It is hard to believe that such cobwebs of thread were knitted by the women, as they walked around their crofts. An exhibition in **Isleburgh House** (open June — Aug — 7.30 — 9 pm, Mon — Fri) demonstrates the various crafts, and also includes a thought-provoking collection of old photographs of how life was, even within a lifetime.

On the outskirts of Lerwick, being rapidly swamped by ugly new housing, is the **Broch of Clickhimin**. The site was first settled by a late Bronze Age farmer, whose trough quern for grinding corn can still be seen, and was then taken over by an Iron Age community. Quite why the complex defence rings were built is unknown, the identity of any possible attackers being lost in the mists of legend, but the fortifications were rapidly developed into a broch (see also **Mousa**), a high drystone circular tower. The site is slightly difficult to understand but there is a comprehensive guide book available, tracing the several periods of development. The galleries and stairs within the two layers of walls can be seen easily, although a later 'wheelhouse' was built inside the broch, so called because its chambers were set within a circle, making up the shape of a wheel (open Apr — Sep — 9.30 — 7, Mon — Sat; 2 — 7, Sun; Oct — Mar — 9.30 — 4, Mon — Sat; 2 — 4, Sun). The surrounding loch was a popular corner for wintering wildfowl, but recently the area has been built up and the loch is now being reclaimed.

Lerwick is the main shopping centre in Shetland (if uninspired), so it is best to stock up here. The *Shetland Times* produces a remarkably balanced and far-sighted newspaper (weekly) and runs a comprehensive bookshop. There are numerous knitwear and craft shops, but it is sensible to remember that if you have time you can visit the factories. If inspired to knit yourself, you can obtain proper Shetland wool from Jamieson & Smith Ltd, 90 North Road.

Accommodation:
Kveldsro House Hotel (tel Lerwick 2195)
Lerwick Hotel (tel. Lerwick 2166)
Queens Hotel (tel Lerwick 2826)
B & B and self catering — details from Tourist Office
Youth Hostel, Islesburgh House (tel Lerwick 2114)
Camping: there used to be an idyllic site next to Clickhimin broch and loch, but this has since been closed as it occupies the site of a proposed leisure centre. No unofficial sites can be recommended near the town, as the threat of vandals is real. Eventually the campsite will be reopened near the leisure centre.
Tourist Office:
Market Cross (tel Lerwick 3434); 9 — 5, Mon-Fri; 9 — 3, Sat.
Car Hire:
Bolts Motor Garage, North Rd (tel Lerwick 2855)
J Burgess, 20 Commercial Rd (tel Lerwick 2896)
J Leash & Sons, Esplanade (tel Lerwick 3162)
Macleod & Maclean, Commercial Rd (tel Lerwick 3313)
Station Garage, North Rd (tel Lerwick 3315)
Bicycle Hire:
Eric Brown, 7 Commercial St (tel Lerwick 3733) (will not repair any but his own bicycles)
Harbour Master:
Capt Poleson (tel Lerwick 2991)
Banks:
Clydesdale
Bank of Scotland
Royal Bank of Scotland
Trustee Savings Bank
Sea Angling:
G Laurenson, 3 Water Lane (tel Lerwick 2309)

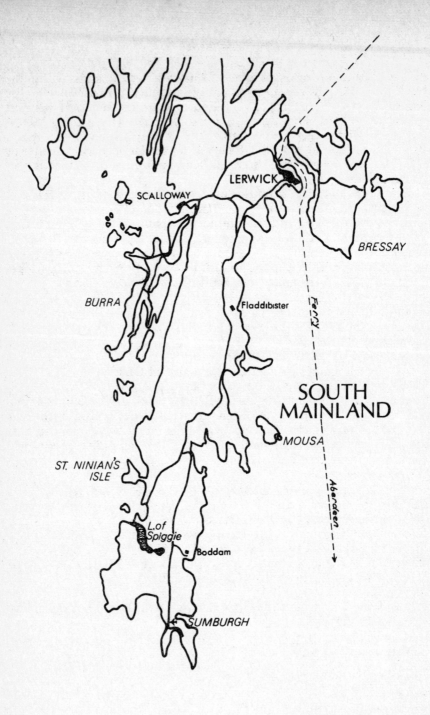

SCALLOWAY

LERWICK

BRESSAY

BURRA

Fladdibister

SOUTH
MAINLAND

MOUSA

Ferry

Aberdeen

ST. NINIAN'S
ISLE

L.of
Spiggie

Boddam

SUMBURGH

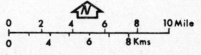

0   2   4   6   8   10 Mile

0   4   6   8 Kms

A Simpson, 115 North Rd (tel Lerwick 3781)
E Manson, 80 Commercial St (tel Lerwick 3488)
Detailed information from M Mullay, Tourist Office, Market Cross
(tel Lerwick 3434); open 9 — 5, Mon — Sat; 9 — 3, Sun.
Events:
January: Up-Helly-Aa
June: Johnsmas Fair
August: Lerwick Regatta
          Sea Angling
September: Viking festival
October: Pony sales
Early closing:
Wednesday.

South Mainland
The long leg of Shetland leading due south is a mixture of flat peat
moorland capping the hills and crisp meadows lining the shore. Every
turn of the road brings magic views of water, crofts and hill. Even in
the heaviest of light, a bright patch of cut grass or foaming waves
conjure up views that demand a camera; on a fine day the hazy vistas
of cliffs and sand, islands and ocean are of incomparable beauty,
while rainy days merge the tones into a constantly changing
watercolour. The broad and empty white beaches of sand are
tempting to swimmers but should be treated with care: some are
swept by a dangerous undercurrent, and it is best to find one
sheltered by an island, eg at Spiggie. Every township has its own
charms, and all need time to explore, but here are some thumb-nail
sketches of a few.
    Fladdibister, nestling below the road, seems many years removed
from Lerwick, with the remains of many old thatched crofting
buildings. Its carpet of wild flowers is scythed as hay, and beside the
pebbled beach are the ruins of lime kilns, used for exploiting the vein
of limestones that so encourages the flowers.
    Cunningsburgh is a similar little community, now sprouting new
houses, with good views north and south from Helti Ness along the
coast.
    Sandwick is the ferry point for Mousa (see Mousa) and an easy
place to find common seals hauled out on its shore.
    In the neighbouring village of **Hoswick** is a weaving and knitwear
factory (open 10 — 1, 2 — 5.30, Mon — Fri) making, among other
things, rugs from Shetland wool in its natural colour. This village,
piled up on itself in a similar way to Lerwick, was a major fishing
centre. Whenever the boats spotted a school of 'caain' whales (pilot
whales), they would attempt to drive them on to the shore, as the
blubber was a very valuable source of light fuel before electricity was
installed. Frequently there were disputes over the division of the

catch, the landlords claiming a third for the use of their beach, the royal representative claiming a third if the whale was too large to be dragged up the beach by four oxen, whereupon it was considered to be a royal beast, thus leaving only a third for the men who landed them. Not until 1888, when 300 whales were landed on the beach of Hoswick, did the whalers manage to claim the whole catch.

At **Levenwick** (ON hloe-vang-vik — bay of the warm, sheltered garden), there is a long sheltered beach and a craft shop (open 10 — 1, 2 — 6, Mon — Fri), making domestic pottery with some pleasant experimental glazes.

The loch at **Clumbie** is a favourite spot for the wintering wildfowl, and for divers and grebes, as they are undisturbed by the now abandoned surrounding township. Rapidly disappearing into piles of rubble, this still gives some indication of the density of the population in the last century.

2 miles (3 km) further south at **Boddam**, a **croft house** has been rethatched and furnished as if the date was 1850 (curator — William Manson; open May — Sep — 10 — 1, 2 — 5, Tues — Sat). Notice how the straw thatch is placed over cut turfs laid on straw ropes. Many an evening was whiled away twisting straw and then carefully rolling it into balls — there is one hanging from the rafters. As there were practically no trees on the island (and there are not many more today), all timber had to be imported, and so driftwood was carefully hoarded for the beams and furniture. The chairs occasionally had straw backs (like the style in Orkney) but more frequently had wooden backs and sides to keep out the draughts, often, as on one here, with a shelf above the head in which to keep the family Bible. Winter food was a great problem — fish were dried above the fire, a practice which still continues today: watch out for clothes lines adorned with these sad corpses!

Knitting has always been a way of life here, but one of the problems with Shetland wool is that it is inclined to shrink (be warned); hence the characterful jumperboard, on which the jerseys were placed for drying. Many little details in this croft house press home how ingenious the islanders were in compensating for the lack of modern technology. By the local burn is a reconstructed Norse mill, used for preparing the household flour (ask for a working demonstration which is dependent on the water supply). Nowhere in Shetland is there a major flow of water, and so several Norse mills were often built in line, the burn water being stored in a small pond and let out to give the necessary momentum for turning the horizontal wheels, through a complicated system of waterways which allowed any mill to be bypassed if not in use.

Sumburgh (probably 'the swain's castle') is a curious area, once the site of a small airstrip, where the local oystercatchers would walk up and down in formation on the football pitch. Now it has been turned into an international airport and the main supply station for the North Sea rigs (buses to Lerwick), squashed between the sea and the hills.

Just beyond this 20th century monstrosity is one of the most famous British archaeological sites — **Jarlshof**. Six distinctive periods of habitation lasting over 3,000 years were first tentatively revealed when a violent storm exposed the southern end of the site. It has since been beautifully excavated so that every distinctive form of house, although superimposed upon each other, can be seen in isolation. A guidebook is essential to lead both the novice and the expert through this potted archaeological history. The excellent anchorage in the bay, fresh water springs of the hillside and green pastoral land, as well as its proximity to the vantage point of Sumburgh Head, account for the popularity of this site.

The earliest building — an oval hut — dates from the Stone and Early Bronze Age, but little is known of these people, except their eating habits — shellfish, as deduced from the midden piles (eg the limpet shells!). Then came a pastoral people, of the Late Bronze Age, who kept cattle and sheep similar to the Soay breed, and soon afterwards the people of the Early Iron Age, who built larger circular huts and the famous earth houses for larders. A small broch similar to Clickhimin was built for protection against raiding parties. Even at this date, around the birth of Christ, they were still using stone and bone implements as well as a few more 'modern' ones of iron. In the 2nd and 3rd centuries wheel houses were built — here in a very good and comprehensible state of preservation; on the threshold of one is an incised cross, taking us into the time of the Celtic monks and recorded history. Two phases of Viking settlement can be seen. The long houses similar to those all over the Viking lands, were later replaced by a more elaborate medieval farm complex, before a castle was built by the unpopular Stewart earls in the 16th century, only to be sacked by Earl Patrick in 1609 after a siege against the immigrant Fife laird William Bruce.

This ruin caught the imagination of Robert Louis Stevenson who made it the home of his Mr Mertoun in *The Pirate* and renamed it Jarlshof. Stevenson's grandfather built the lighthouse of Sumburgh Head (open 2 pm to 1 hour before dusk; tel Sumburgh 60375 in advance) where the enormous lens floating on mercury is lit by a 250 watt light bulb! Still kept glowing and polished, the fitments will be fluently explained by an enthusiastic keeper.

Loch Spiggie (Swedish spigg — a stickleback) is a large eutrophic loch, a good place for water plants and a great favourite with fishermen (for this and all other freshwater fishing, contact the Shetland Anglers Association, 3 Gladstone Terrace, Lerwick, tel Lerwick 3729), as well as with whooper swans and other wildfowl. From here there is a pleasant drive back to the main road past St Ninians Isle (see St Ninians Isle). Foula can be sighted on a clear day, standing alone in the Atlantic.

Accommodation:
Barclay Arms Hotel, Sandwick (tel Sandwick 226)
Spiggie Hotel, Scousburgh (tel Sumburgh 409)
Meadowvale Hotel, Virkie (tel Sumburgh 240)
Sumburgh Airport Hotel, Sumburgh (tel Sumburgh 201)
B & B and self-catering — details from the Tourist Office, Lerwick.
Car Hire:
Boots Self-Drive Service, Sumburgh Airport (tel Sumburgh 60331)
A J Eunson (tel Sumburgh 60209)
Sandwick Transport Co, Swinister (tel Sandwick 214)
Sea Angling:
D Black, Tolob, Virkie (tel Sumburgh 243)
J Harper, Meadowvale Hotel, Virkie (tel Sumburgh 352)
Bank:
Sumburgh Airport (11 am — 2.30 pm)
Mobile unit on Wednesday.

Scalloway (ON skaalr vagr — bay with shielings around)
Until 200 years ago, Scalloway was a very important centre for
Shetland, the home of many of the fish merchants who salted the
catches and sent them south to Scotland to be sold. As Lerwick
grew, Scalloway declined, and even the new wealth from the oil has
done nothing to avert this trend. Once the islanders of Tronda and
Burra rowed across the water to buy their supplies, but with the new
bridge connections they drive directly to Lerwick, and so Scalloway
no longer supports even a shop!

Dead on a Sunday the town seems barely awake on weekdays, as the
locals move sleepily around the harbour — there is still a boat
building yard here, and a fish processing factory (visitors welcome,
9 — 3, Mon-Thu). Waders can usually be seen amongst the jetsam on
the shore. Here an attempt has been made to grow flowers despite
the fierce wind and these gardens are the best in Shetland — a
welcome change from the bleak moor.

The town is watched over by a gaunt **castle** built by Andrew
Crawford for the unpopular Patrick Stewart, the legitimate son of
the illegitimate son of James V. The gateways and windows were
taken by Sir Arthur Mitchell two centuries later to furnish his own
house at Sandsting. Patrick Stewart was the man who heavy-
handedly imposed feudalism on the Northern Isles, ignoring the
traditional Norse law and thus changing the islanders' status from
freemen to bondmen, an act for which he has never been forgiven.
There are good views from the top of the castle (key from the
cottage opposite).

Near the castle, on a pretty row of two-storey houses, is an
intriguing plaque expounding on the 'German theory of waves'.

Accommodation:
Bona Vista Hotel (tel Scalloway 648)
Scalloway Hotel (tel Scalloway 444)
B & B — details from the Tourist Office, Lerwick.
Bank:
Open 10 — 12 Tue, 2 — 4 Fri.
Early Closing:
Thursday
Festivals:
August: Scalloway Regatta

West Mainland

Forming a motley pattern of water, moor and meadow, its hills and
dales traversed by the recently improved road, this is one of the
prettiest areas of Shetland, even on the dreariest of days. Take time
to enjoy the views across watery landscapes and the little islets
scattered in profusion — most were never inhabited by man but used
for sheep grazing. Here too can be found herds of Shetland ponies,
similar in colours to the sheep, and sometimes losing their coats in
exactly the same way. By midsummer both look scruffy, with wool
and hair dangling around their ankles (the sheep were traditionally
plucked, not sheared).

The road from Scalloway to Tingwall (can you spot the buried oil
pipe line?) passes the large quarries that provided foundations for the
road improvement scheme and **Gallows Hill**, before following
Tingwall loch northwards. This is one of many sites on the island
that was used for rough justice up until the 18th century. The last
two victims were two women accused of witchcraft, cruelly burnt to
death. For the archaeologist, there is a two-storeyed cist near **Asta**,
and of more obvious interest a solitary standing stone by the
roadside. The little holm at the northern end of the loch christened
the area, for it was thought to be here that the Norse elders held
their parliament (or Thing). Either they chose fine weather, or more
probably they used this spot to enact the holmgang, a ritual duel of
trial by ordeal.

Tingwall (ON:þingvold — fold of the Thing, ie local assembly) has a
fascinating **Agricultural Museum** (open May — Sep: 10 — 5, Tue,
Thur, Sat), totally unsterilized and laid out in an old farmyard. The
old crofting tools, collected by the owner, Mrs Jean Sandison,
require her vivid explanations to make any sense in this mechanized
age. The tushkar, the traditional peat cutting tool, is still used in the
spring; but the threshing machines, ploughs and rakes belong to the
past. There are also old cooking pots from peat fires, butter churns,
cowskin shoes (remembered as most uncomfortable by the owner's
mother-in-law) and a collection of old photographs. Two long black
poles evoke the days when coffins had to be carried many miles to a
graveyard. It is worth spending many hours here for an insight into

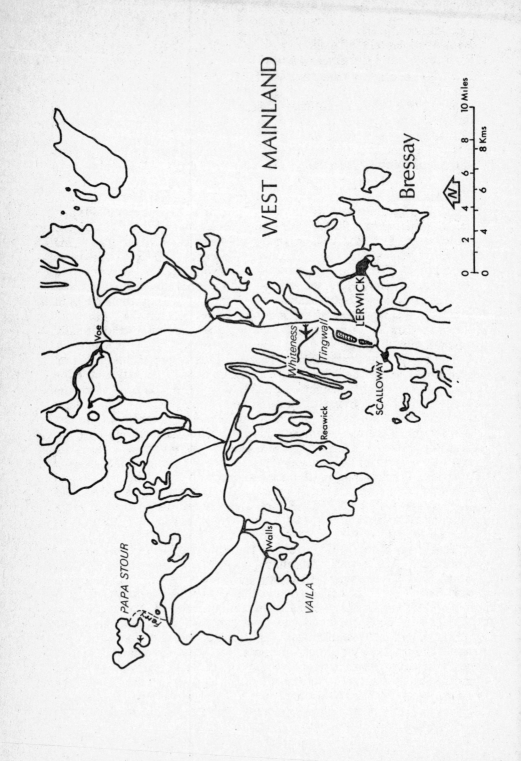

WEST MAINLAND

Bressay

LERWICK

Whiteness

Tingwall

SCALLOWAY

Voe

Reawick

Walls

VAILA

PAPA STOUR

N

0   2   4   6   8   10 Miles

0   4   6   8 Kms

the less romantic side of crofting life.

At **Whiteness** there is a stone-polishing workshop — Hjaltasteyn (open 9 — 1, 2 — 5, Mon — Fri). Semi-precious stones collected on beaches throughout Shetland are cut and polished before being secured in hand-made silver settings. Ask to see the workshop, as it is hard to believe that these gems come from dull rough rocks.

Along the road (A971) at Weisdale is the Shetland Silvercraft factory (open 9 — 1, 2 — 5, Mon — Fri) where traditional Shetland designs of birds and ships are worked in silver and gold. Here again, a visit to workshops is interesting. The old **Aamos church** was believed to have been built with divine aid in response to a dream. Every morning the stones and timber necessary for the day's task would be waiting for the builders. Once the church was finished, a custom of laying alms developed, ensuring safe voyages, good health and success. John Clunies Ross, born in Weisdale in 1786, certainly had a successful, if curious, life. Joining a whaling ship, he worked his way up to become the skipper of an East Indies brig, only to fall foul of the Press Gang while docked in an English port. Dashing into a house to elude the ensuing chase, he fell in love with the daughter of the family and married her, but the problems of supporting a family soon turned his thoughts to emigration. They left for one of the Cocos Islands where he was soon regarded as the unofficial king. His sovereignty lasted until his death in 1854, and was even acknowledged by Queen Victoria. North of Weisdale, at Kergord, is the largest plantation of trees in Shetland. Although in no way thriving, it still provides good shelter for small birds.

Reawick (ON — red bay) is slightly unnerving with its red sands, a very unusual feature in Scotland. At **Sand**, there is an arched ruin of St Mary's chapel close by the pier. Local legend records that this chapel was erected as a thanksgiving by the crew of one of the galleons of the Spanish Armada, wrecked in 1588. Although no trace of the craft has yet been found, the story is not implausible, for many ships of that ill-fated expedition came to grief on these northern isles.

A possible temple from an older civilization can be found at **Staneydale**. On the open moor is an unusually large heel-shaped cairn, dating from c 1600 BC. It has been suggested that this was a neolithic meeting place or temple, especially as a similar structure at Mnaidra in Malta is known to have possessed religious significance. The neolithic cairns of Shetland are completely different to those of Orkney, and no stalled cairns have yet been found here, indicating that the two island groups were inhabited by different tribes (or sects) — but the windswept Shetland moorland gives away few secrets of the past.

Over the hill at **West Houlland** there is an abandoned township, the grey stone dykes measuring out the boundaries of long-forgotten ownership of this rocky slope, empty houses deserted for possible

39

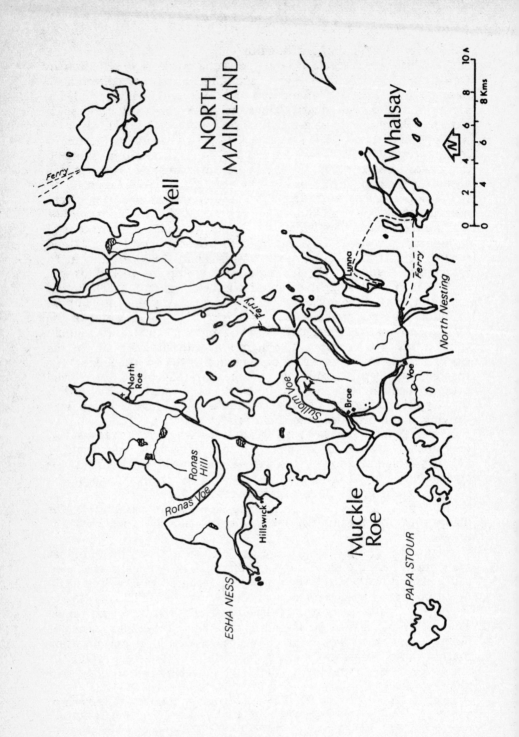

fortunes in the New World.

The small town of **Walls** (ON vagar — voes, bays) once knew great prosperity. Boats from Aberdeen and Leith would dock regularly at the pier to collect the salted barrels of fish, in the harbour sheltered by the island of Vaila. Much folklore grows up around fishermen, from how to recognize the 'eighth wave' — the one that always reaches the shore no matter how far out to sea, to the superstition about the unluckiness of returning home with dry clothes — one Walls man was renowned for leaping into the sea to avert such a disaster.

Accommodation:
Westings Hotel, Wormadale (tel Gott 242)
B & B and self-catering — details from Tourist Office, Lerwick.
Bank:
Mobile unit on Thursday.
Events:
June: Angling competition, Walls
July: Walls Regatta
      Walls show, Tingwall Grand Summer Foy
August: Walls Agricultural Show
       Angling Competition, Walls
September: Angling Competition, Tingwall

North Mainland
The hamlet of **Voe** (ON vagr — little bay) comes as a surprise, for although the visitor can never forget that these are northern shores, still tied by language and blood to the Viking peoples, nowhere else in the Northern Isles can one stumble across a corner of Norway, with little wooden houses nestling around the pier at the head of the 'fiord'. There are excellent views of the flooded valley on the steep hill dropping down to Voe, by the disused limestone quarries. As the haaf fishing dwindled, a boat family had the novel idea of setting up a weavers' workshop, now slightly run down but charmingly old fashioned, above the village store (open 9 — 1, 2 — 4, Mon — Sat, except Thu and Sat afternoons; tel Voe 332 first, if a tour of the looms is desired). This is a very good place to get warm Shetland tweed at reasonable prices.

Brae (ON breio eio — broad neck or isthmus) is an unfortunate village, the victim of the planners' decision not to allow it to develop with the coming of the oil wealth. It grew anyway in a hideous fashion, and is best passed with the window blinds down!

Just off the main road is Busta House, now a high quality hotel with pleasant wooded gardens (booking is necessary). It was originally built as the laird's house, for the 18th century landlord, Thomas Gifford, who did much to help the haaf fishing industry to the benefit of his own pocket. Even in those days Busta House had a solid reputation for hospitality, Gifford himself maintaining a large household including fourteen of his own children. A curious and never satisfactorily explained story is linked to his sons. In 1748 all four went seal hunting. On their return journey no matter how much effort they made, the boat refused to move until their chaplain, who accompanied them, began to pray. As they returned to shore they saw three monsters or seal people. The following day, in fine weather, they again set out by boat (the normal means of transport in those days) to their uncle's house. After a convivial evening, they made for home, never to be seen again, except for the body of the eldest. He had been married in secret by the chaplain to a poor relation living in the house, who was found to be pregnant. Although the alliance was never recognized by the parents, the baby son was acknowledged as their heir, but there were numerous law suits during the 19th century concerning his legitimacy and inheritance.

Mavis Grind (ON maev eids grind — the gate of the narrow isthmus) has great curiosity value. No more than 100 yards (90 m) across, it is nibbled on one side by the North Sea, and on the other by the Atlantic. The need for stone for the enlarged road foundations has turned this once renowned beauty spot into a quarry and an eyesore, but further north some of the old crofting township is still intact.

Hillswick (ON hildiswik — battle bay) spreads out along the shore, misty and soft even on a sunny day. It was developed as a haaf fishing station by Thomas Gifford of Busta, who supplied the fishermen with all their equipment in return for all their fish — the standard practice in the early 19th century. The local hotel, St Magnus Bay Hotel, an ideal setting for a John Buchan mystery and now popular with oilmen, has very fine art nouveau furnishings, unchanged from the First World War. The ultimate Edwardian family hotel, it is quiet at lunchtimes when it provides a hospitable retreat from the rain, livening up in the evenings. Close by is a small craftshop selling an imaginative range of local artefacts, including crisp line drawings of old villages and boats which challenge one's own draftsmanship. This is a good starting point for a picturesque walk around the headlands, where the sea is populated by fantastically carved stacks and arches — rough spikes of old red sandstone called **The Drongs** (ON drangr — stacks).

Further west at another haaf station, **Stenness** (ON steinn — stone ness), the curtain of cliffs touches the shore on a pebble beach where once 85 boats were based and their catches dried on the rocks. Now only the ruins of the lodges remain, their turf roofs long fallen in. The ground tilts up again and at **Eshaness** the cliffs, stacks and arches, cutting into the faults, take on an animate character: a wild place, ideal for watching guillemot and kittiwake, puffins and fulmars, breeding on the ledges and in the turf. There is also a cormorant colony on a stack — known as the **Runk**. Mind the slippery grass and thrift edges, for the boiling sea will eat humans as well as local rubbish.

Not without good cause have the **Holes of Scrada** been attributed to the devil, who supposedly carved them out in punishment for wrecking ships on the Vee Steerries.

At **Hamnavoe** (ON hamna vagr — bay of the haven), a storm beach of pebbles can be found 60 feet (18 m) above sea level. This great whaling and fishing station celebrates its son, Jonnie Notion. Born John Williamson in 1740, and probably never receiving any schooling, he became a jack of all trades — weaver, blacksmith, joiner, clock repairer and bone setter, and in response to the smallpox epidemics of that century he developed a highly successful technique of innoculation. While contemporary doctors advocated bleeding and starvation, he innoculated patients with vaccine, taken from the vesicles produced by the disease, dried by the peat fires, and buried for several years. It was inserted just under the skin and the wound was covered with a cabbage leaf — elastoplasts were not yet invented!

Ronas Voe is the only proper fiord in Shetland. Its U-shape is clearly defined, so that the crofters' pastures run steeply uphill. It is now empty and quiet and a favourite spot of the great northern divers in April. During the Dutch war against the English in 1624, a crippled Dutch East India ship, the *Wapan van Rotterdam*, trusting the time-honoured friendliness of the Shetlanders, hid in the voe, but some official sent information to Scotland and the ship was caught unaware. A little knowe called the Hollander's Grave, east of **Heylor**, is where the massacred Dutch seamen are supposed to be buried. In the 19th century there were six fishing communities spread along the shores of the voe, and until the First World War it also boasted two whaling stations. These were abandoned because not enough whales deigned to swim past Shetland, hence making the occupation uneconomic. Today few traces remain of its former glory except hints of piers.

Ronashill, the highest of Shetland hills (1,470 ft/448 m) and capped by a watchtower, is an easy place to find alpine flowers while commanding views of the island groups. The snowy owl and ring ouzel may be sighted here, as well as the blue (or mountain) hare, recently introduced but now thriving due to the lack of predators.

Beyond North Roe, an easy walk due north leads to **Fethaland**, another deserted haaf station, the ghost town of old huts and bothies now appreciated only by the seabirds. The rich limestone meadows make a nice summer picnic spot with views of the **Ramna Stacks** (an RSPB nature reserve). The island of **Gruney** is one of the few places where the grey seals pup on grass (in November).

Sullom Voe was once a quiet bay, the salt marshes surrounding it popular with wintering duck. Now it is the main origin of Shetland's wealth. The vast oil terminal (not open to visitors) employs an enormous labour force as it is still in its construction period, and looks totally incongruous in its heather surroundings. Huge cylindrical oil drums are filled by pipelines from the Brent and Ninian fields, only to be emptied daily by tankers which ship the oil south and abroad, for although it is equivalent to two-thirds of Britain's consumption, most is exported to be blended with the more treacly Arab oil. Camps at Toft and Mossbank house 3,500 men in dormitory cabins, while another 500 live in the ships moored close to the site. The bright night lights of this alien plant with its science fiction atmosphere, are enjoyed for novelty value by the crofters across the water.

Lunna House, built in the 1660s and immortalized in David Howarth's story of *The Shetland Bus*, was the centre of Norwegian resistance during the Second World War. Fishing boats left frequently from the small pier, using the old Viking routes to transport arms, ammunition and freedom fighters, to harass the Germans. Their incredible feats of daring represent the modern folklore of Shetland and many Norwegians caught the Shetland Bus to safety. Now a quiet country hotel, the grey building seems to meditate on its past history, the unusually gay, painted interior chapel of 1753 offering a happier welcome to the sightseer. Close by is the ruin of a 12th century chapel: built into its side is a 'leper-hole' where the afflicted could follow the service and participate in communion, without risk of spreading the disease — at one time rampant in Faroe and much feared in Scotland.

The townships of Nesting are so called not because of their rural apathetic air, nor even because of their undoubted attractions for breeding birds, but in commemoration of the Norse parliament or 'Thing'. Here the archaeologists have found indications of many heel shaped cairns waiting to be explored. With these are associated countless legends of fairies and trows who would spirit away talented fiddlers for years at a time, swap their children with human babies, and play numerous tricks on the simple crofters, all remembered with good humour. A less lucky 17th century fisherman discovered an ideal spot for catching fish in foul weather at **Luggies Knowe, Dale Voe**; unfortunately his ability to catch the fish ready cooked caused him to be burnt as a wizard at Scalloway. The golf course at Dale must be one of the most scenic in Scotland (visitors welcome; clubs for hire).

Accommodation:
Brae Hotel, Brae (tel Brae 456)
Busta House, Brae (tel Brae 209)
St Magnus Bay Hotel, Killswich (tel Hillswick 209)
Lunna House Hotel, Vidlin (tel Vidlin 237)
B & B and self-catering — details from Tourist Office, Lerwick
Banks:
Sullom Voe — Wed, Thu, Fri by local arrangement

Mobile unit — Mon (except Nesting and Vidlin)
Mobile unit for Nesting and Vidlin — Tue fortnightly
Festivals:
July: Brae Regatta
      Hillswick Sheepdog Trial
      Angling Competitions
September: Angling Competitions
Dale Golf competitions — most summer weekends.

Unst

(perhaps meaning 'erns isle' — eagle isle, or outermost isle, but the variations in spelling defy the scholars of Old Norn.)

Connections:
By air: from Tingwall: Mon — Fri, four a day (via Feltar and Whalsay by arrangement). Loganair (tel Gott 246).

By sea: from Gutcher: frequent service; cars; 30 min crossing. From Oddsta: two or three a day; cars; 40 min crossing (booking advised). Shetland Islands Council Ferry Office (tel Burravoe 259).

Unst is the most northerly island of Britain. John o'Groats has nothing on this, yet it is surprisingly green and populated, the two hill ridges sheltering active crofting and fishing communities. The outermost skerry, **Muckle Flugga**, with its tall white lighthouse built by D Alan Stevenson, is further north than Leningrad or Labrador, but although the highest (unofficial) windspeeds of the British Isles have been recorded here (177 mph/285 kph), the climate is in general surprisingly mild, being tempered by the gulf stream. At least all the insects are blown away!

The Nature Conservancy Council runs an important nature reserve at **Hermanness** (stout boots needed). It has a resident summer warden and its cliffs house thousands of gulls and auks, especially fulmars. These represent a great Scottish success story, for since arriving on Foula around 1876 they have multiplied to such an extent that they are now a common seabird. During the last decade a gannet colony established itself on the cliffs around the Point of Saito, and now numbers about 6,000 pairs. Recently, a lone black-browed albatross has pathetically been making his nest among them, though he still lacks a mate. The grassy tops are perforated with puffin burrows, while the bonxies (great skuas) viciously dive on anyone approaching their moorland chicks. To appreciate this reserve to the full, it is necessary to spend days scouring the 600 ft (185 m) high cliffs with binoculars. If you feel you have seen a surfeit of birds, you can usually spot a few common and grey seals playing off the northern shores.

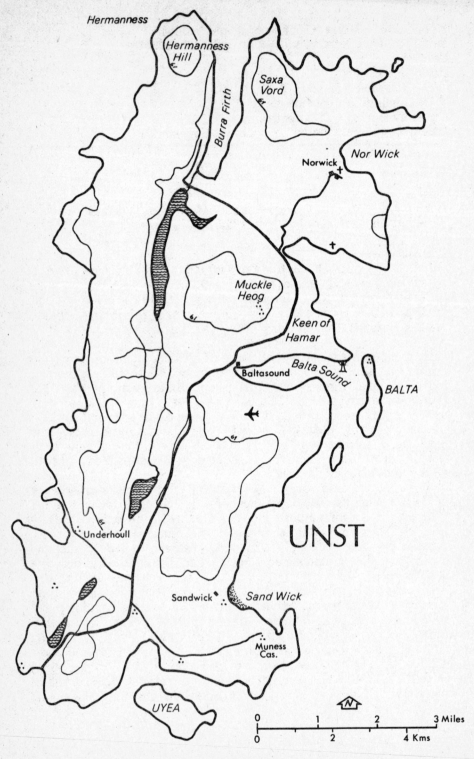

MUCKLE FLUGGA

Hermanness

Hermanness
Hill

Saxa
Vord

Burra Firth

Nor Wick

Norwick

Muckle
Heog

Keen of
Hamar

Balta Sound

Baltasound

BALTA

UNST

Underhoull

Sandwick

Sand Wick

Muness
Cas.

UYEA

N

| 0 | | 1 | | 2 | | 3 Miles |
| 0 | | 2 | | 4 Kms | | |

While the prefix 'sand' in these northern isles is normally honest, indicating lovely beaches, so too is the prefix 'wood', for **Woodwick** bay has been filled up with sea-driven wood — a freak of nature's sea currents and a wonderful asset in the past to the islanders' building aspirations. Reddish semi-precious garnets can be found here, and indeed Unst is generally an exciting place for the geologist.

With its latitude and rough hilly landscape, it is not surprising that Unst inherited some of the Norwegian giants, and much of the local folklore revolves around Herman and Saxi (based on the hills bearing their names — **Hermanness Hill** and **Saxa Vord**). These two rivals threw numerous boulders across Burra Firth at each other, quarrelling at the slightest provocation — eg when Saxi refused to cook a whale caught by Herman in his 'kettle', a boiling gully in the cliffs of Saxa Vord. The general situation was not happy, and so when by chance they both fell in love with the same mermaid, she decided to rid the island of this troublesome pair, by promising herself to the one who followed her to the North Pole without touching land. Giants cannot swim. (At Norwick, among the ruins of the chapel, can still be seen a standing stone with a hole, used by Saxi to tie up his horse.)

This corner of Unst has been taken over by the RAF, but the islanders have cause to be grateful for the added employment possibilities, even if Saxa Vord is now capped with a giant radar scanner (the views are still breathtaking). While not a nature reserve, the area around Norwick supports an astonishingly wide range of breeding birds. The northernmost post office at **Haroldwick** will frank your stamps specially, while you have time to admire this charming old crofting community scattered over the valley. South of the village on **Muckle Heog** is the chambered cairn known as 'Harald's Grave', after Harold the Fair-haired, who supposedly sailed here from Norway in 875. The road and surrounding slopes are covered with dust from the talc quarries, which mine the stone mainly for supply to the roofing felt industry. Litter from old and disused serpentine mines can also be seen on this hillside, which supports an interesting collection of Arctic alpine plants. The nature reserve of **Keen of Hamar** (consult the Nature Conservancy Council Warden before entering) displays a similarly wide botanical range and also has some interesting glacial features.

Baltasound is the industrial centre of Unst and the export port for talc. There is an oil rig helicopter supply base here, and — more interestingly for the visitor — a seal-skin factory (tel Baltasound 444 for appointments for visiting), where bags and knick-knacks are made from leather and skins. In the bay, here as elsewhere, are many of the Shetland 'jaols' — double-ended descendants of the Viking longboat which conquered the Atlantic. Size and useage varies from fishing to pleasure boats, and although the boat-building yard has been forced out of production by escalating costs, nearly all the boats are still made locally by the crofters in the long winter evenings as their needs and impulses dictate. While Unst could no longer be described as isolated, somehow the old crafts have survived. This is the place to search for a Shetland lace shawl, knitted into incredibly intricate patterns, of such fine wool that a 6 ft (180 cm) square can easily pass through a wedding ring. It seems almost beyond belief that lace is still being made here to a comparable quality to that displayed in the Lerwick Museum, and while it is not cheap, it cannot be considered expensive in view of the amount of work involved. The best way to trace a knitter is to chat to the locals.

At **Underhoull** a 9th century Viking house has been discovered and excavated, built on top of an earlier Iron Age site. The artefacts have been placed in the safekeeping of the Lerwick Museum. On the opposite side of the island, down on the beach at **Sandwick**, a similar but later settlement has been explored and is now being allowed to become reburied by the sand. It is hard to believe that this is 8 centuries old, and not just a ruined but and ben of the last century — the Viking heritage remains dominant in island life.

From this wonderfully wide white beach, approached across the moorland, it is a pleasant walk around the coast up to **Muness castle** (open weekdays Ap — Sep: 9.30 — 7; Oct — Mar: 9.30 — 4; key from the white cottage opposite). Although the castle is relatively small, it undoubtedly possesses a direct relationship with those of the unpopular Stewart Earls, and indeed it was built by Laurence Bruce, half-brother of Earl Robert (the illegitimate half-brother of Mary Queen of Scots). Although it is hard to think of it as a Renaissance castle, the regular plan of the oblong block and diagonally opposed circular towers, with the simple but strong stone dressings detailing the windows, must date it to the late 16th century. Over the entrance is a much weathered inscription reading:

LIZT ZE TO KNAW YIS BUILDIG QUHA BEGAN LAURENCE THE BRUCE HE WAS THAT WORTHY MAN QUHA ERNESTLY HIS AIRIS AND OFSPRING PRAYIS TO HELP AND NOT TO HURT THIS VARK ALVAYIS

THE ZEIR OF GOD 1598

Local tradition does not remember Laurence kindly, nor his children, the cause of the castle's ruinous state being blamed on a Bruce who abducted a girl named Helga. Helga escaped by a rope from an upstairs window and helped her rescuer burn the castle down. Certainly within a century it had fallen into disuse.

Uyeasound is another quiet crofting township, the road being flanked by a band of white daisies. In general, although the wild flowers are not exotic, they produce a magnificent display throughout the summer. The literary may note that the map of Unst has distinct resemblances to that of Robert Louis Stevenson's *Treasure Island*, probably explained by the fact that he had been on the island just before he began his novel. Unst is the actual setting for one of John Buchan's stories, *Sule Skerry*, and he himself preached in Uyeasound Kirk. From Uyeasound can be visited the now uninhabited island of **Haaf Gruney**, a national nature reserve, and a favourite haunt of seals. (Transport is not easy: ask the summer warden at Hermaness.)

This is a very picturesque, quiet island, and an ideal holiday retreat — watch out for a snowy owl.

Accommodation:
Baltasound Hotel (tel Baltasound 334)
Uyeasound Hostel (contact Mr Frazer Crosbister, tel Uyeasound 237): booking necessary as this is understandably popular.
B & B and self-catering — details from Tourist Office, Lerwick
Fishing:
Details from Shetland Anglers Association: Mr A Miller (tel Lerwick 3729).
Sea Angling:
J Cluness, Uyeasound
Bank:
Mobile unit, alternate Tuesdays
Specialities:
Lace knitting. Also a good place to hear the Shetland fiddle — locally, by request.
Event:
October: pony sales

Yell
(ON gall — barren)

Connections:
By sea: from Toft: frequent service; cars; 30 min crossing. From Belmont: frequent service; cars; 30 min crossing. From Oddsta: two or three a day; cars; 40 min crossing.
Shetland Islands Council Ferry Office (tel Burravoe 259): booking advised.

Yell is a gloomy island, covered by a blanket of peat bog, described by the 16th century traveller George Buchanan as 'so uncouth a place that no creature can live therein, except such as are born there', and aptly dismissed by a local as 'a dreary place'. This is very much an island of the past, unconquered by modern ways. While roads may score its back, the only houses perch uncomfortably on the little green corners, by the seashore. Of all the main Shetland isles, Yell is the one most threatened by the ills of unemployment and depopulation, threats which the oil industry has done little to avert, and although there is a fish factory at Mid Yell, and a knitwear centre at **Aywick** (visits can be made to see the finishing stages — 8.30 — 5.00, Mon-Fri), the population is still basically dependent

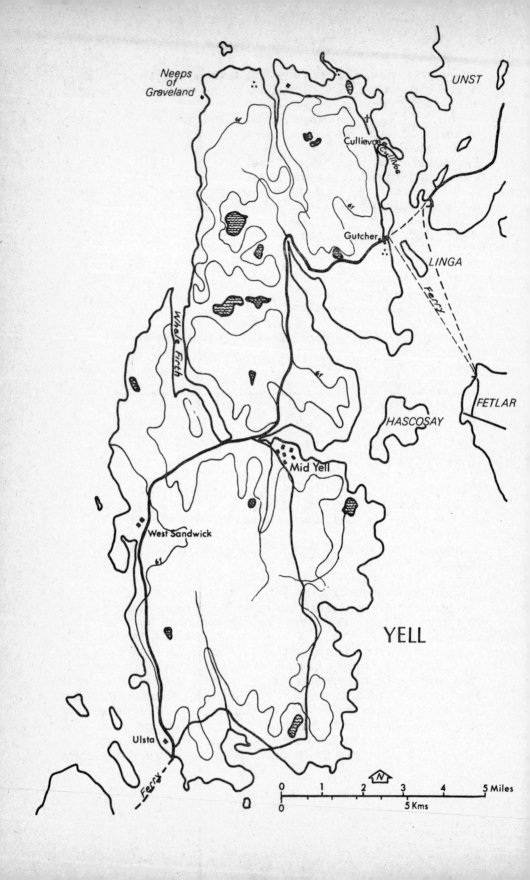

Neeps
of
Graveland

UNST

Cullivoe

Gutcher

LINGA

Ferry

FETLAR

Whale Firth

HASCOSAY

Mid Yell

West Sandwick

YELL

Ulsta

Ferry

N

0   1   2   3   4   5 Miles

0   5 Kms

on crofting and fishing, neither of which are organized into efficient units.

Having cast the gloom, light can be found in small patches. In the north, the village of **Cullievoe** is typical of the charms of rural Shetland, a small careful community using everything available (eg old boats providing roofs for sheds). Many old folk can tell tales that seem to come straight out of the Middle Ages — childhoods of earth floors and bare feet, open hearths as stoves, and no coinage; no wonder they are dazzled by modern conveniences. At **Papil Ness** there is an old ruined chapel dedicated to St Olaf, and close by a Viking settlement. Local folklore claims this to have been the spring board for Leif the Lucky's expedition to America, although this is not supported by the Viking sagas. Gloup became famous in 1881 when a sudden gale hit all of Shetland, carrying away many of the small fishing boats, and leaving widows and children to destitution. Gloup was hit particularly hard: six boats and crews were lost in a sudden storm, bringing incredible hardship to the community.

There is a fine walk along the western moorland cliffs from the **Neeps of Graveland** towards West Sandwick, through a neglected wilderness of wild life, and past Whale Firth, supposedly an unloyal harbour for German submarines in the First World War — it's quite understandable why they were not discovered! Erne Stack of the tip of **Nev of Stuis** was the last recorded nesting place of the sea eagle. Grey seals can be seen all along this coast — a bearded seal was first recorded in Yell in 1977. West Sandwick is a tidy crofting village with long sandy beaches sheltered from the wind. Yell Sound provides protection for many wintering birds, while the moorland lochs and the east side are popular with the divers and waders. This side has been nibbled by the sea, broken up by voes into more interesting patterns, but even so there is little worthy of note.

Accommodation:
B & B and self-catering — details from the Tourist Office, Lerwick.
Bank:
Mobile unit: alternate Wednesdays.
Sea Angling:
D Robertson, Guddon, East Yell (tel Burravoe 242).

Fetlar
(ON — fat isle)

Connections:
By air: from Tingwall and Unst by prior arrangement. Loganair (tel Gott 246)
By sea: from Belmont & Gutcher: two or three a day; cars; 40 min

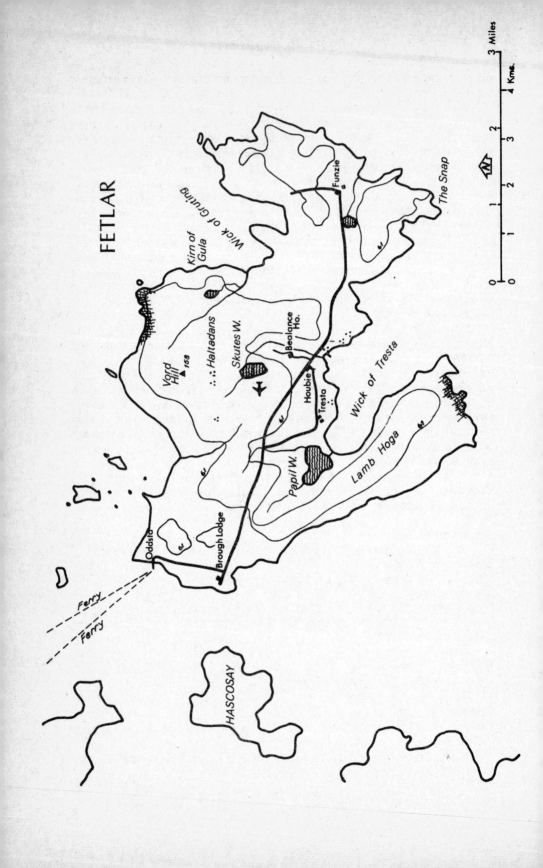

crossing. Shetland Islands Council Ferry Office (tel Burravoe 259): booking advised.

In character very much an outlier, although situated only 2½ miles (4 km) east of Yell and 3 miles (5 km) south of Unst, Fetlar is very different from its close neighbours in both geology and mood. This feeling is heightened by its lack of a safe harbour; even the reckless Norse King Harald the Fair-haired could not find a suitable bay and, during his pursuit of Viking pirates in the 9th century, although he landed here, moved on to Unst. Up until 1974 the island was supplied weekly by boat from Lerwick, the mv *Earl of Zetland* being anchored offshore and met by flit-boats. Today, with the ferry service to Oddsta, Fetlar has been gently brought into line with the other crofting isles.

For a while it even had a thriving tourist trade, for it was here that the snowy owl successfully bred from 1967 to 1975. These large white birds can be seen hunting in the summer evenings in the twilight, but sadly the territorial aspirations of the old father drove out his sons, and since his death the three or four females have been without a mate. However, for the ornithologist there are still many attractions — red throated divers breeding on the shores of the small lochs, a very large population of whimbrels, and a small number of protected red necked phalaropes, while merlins may be seen hunting overhead. Before attempting to see these birds, please consult the RSPB Warden at Bealance (tel Fetlar 246) who will guide you to suitable spots where you may watch without disturbing these decorative species.

The gneiss rocks of Lamb Hoga (sheep pasture) house Britain's largest colony of storm petrels, as well as Manx shearwaters, puffins, kittiwake and guillemots, and the inevitable diving bonxies (great skuas). On the Lamb Hoga can be seen the remains of 'peat hoosies' made from turf and wood, used by the 'flitters'. After the men had cut the peats in May, and left them to dry, the whole family would move onto the moor with their ponies to carry the peats to the shore, from where boats would transport them back to the townships — a laborious method of securing fuel but one which must have been fun if the tales told have any grain of truth. In the summer this moor is white with a dusting of bog cotton, and the small Shetland ponies roam freely. The Nicolson family, the lairds of Brough Lodge, did much experimental breeding, crossing local stock with Norwegian to eradicate the dangers of inbreeding. Below Brough Lodge is a likely place to spot otters. Over 200 different species of flowers have been recorded on Fetlar, including the northern gentian and frog orchid.

As you travel east into the rich green crofting valleys, the fields became dappled with colour. The beaches of **Tresta** and **Houbie** (ON hopr — light) will provide many delights for the shell collector. One of Fetlar's famous sons, William Watson Cheyne, an Edwardian surgeon who helped Joseph Lister in the pioneering of antiseptic surgery, was knighted and returned to Houbie to build 'the big house' of Leagarth. The little lochans attract wintering wildfowl (eg whooper swans). A walk north towards Vord Hill (ON valdhald — keeping watch) leads to the Haltadans, a circle of low stones with two in the centre, of uncertain date or function, and explained away as a fiddler and his wife dancing with the trows or the little folk and caught by the rising sun and petrified. The view from the hill is of a magic play of water and land and the old township dyke separating the pasture from the common grazing can clearly be seen to the east. Legend records that the tenant of Culbinstoft, annoyed by the wanderings of his neighbour's cattle, vowed to give up his best oxen if a wall was built by the morning. He awoke to the wall and a dead oxen. Due east from the summit is the Kirn of Gula, a blow-hole where the fishermen of the 18th century were said to have hidden to evade the Press Grang. Across the bay are the rocks that brought down a Danish trading ship, the *Vandela*, while she was carrying large quantities of silver bullion. Although most was immediately salvaged, a diving team recently found a diverse collection of international coins, explained by the fact that Denmark did not have a strong national currency in the 18th century.

At Funzie many empty buildings speak of past activity and the declining population, but this township remains one of the most picturesque in all of Shetland.

Accommodation:
St Rognvald's Guest House (tel Fetlar 240)
Tresta Lodge Guest House
B & B and self-catering — details from the Tourist Office, Lerwick
Camping is forbidden on the Links of Tresta.
Car Hire:
C Thompson (tel Fetlar 225)
Bird Sanctuary:
RSPB Warden (tel Fetlar 246)

Out Skerries

Connections:
By air: charter only — enquire at Sumburgh Airport.
By sea: from Lerwick: Tue and Fri; 3 hour crossing. Shetland Council, Ferry Office (tel Lerwick 2024).

At first sight, it is hard to believe that anybody could still, in the 20th century, want to live on this tiny archipelago of rocky islands. However, once ashore, the rich green meadows dispel all doubts, in

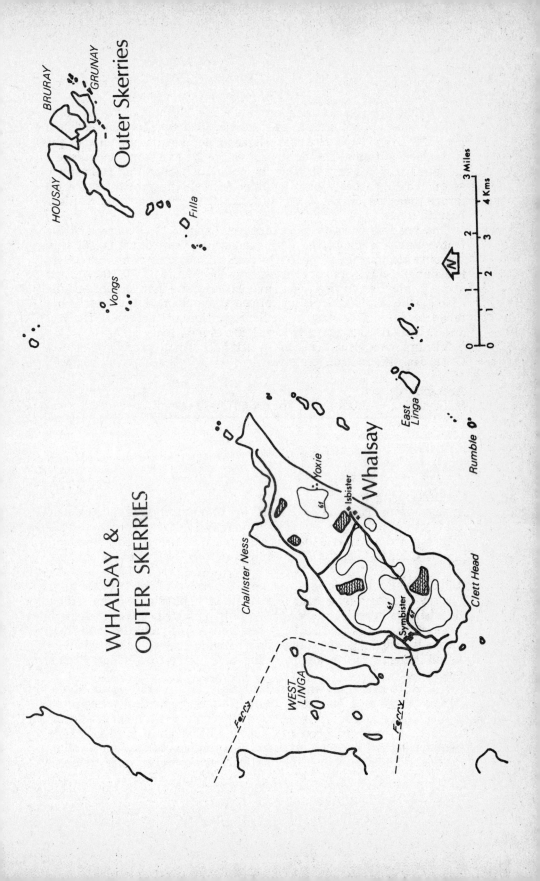

WHALSAY & OUTER SKERRIES

Outer Skerries

BRURAY

GRUNAY

HOUSAY

Filla

Vongs

Challister Ness

Yoxie

Isbister

Whalsay

61

Symbister

61

61

WEST LINGA

Ferry

Ferry

East Linga

Rumble 0°

Clett Head

N

0   1   2   3 Miles
0   1   2   3   4 Kms

the summer at least; in the winter it is a completely different story, described as 'like the underside of a wave' by one islander.

The Out Skerries are not rich in bird life, although there are some small colonies of seabirds, as everywhere else in Shetland; but like Fair Isle, the archipelago catches a large collection of migrants in the spring and autumn. The rich pastures on the limestone encourage a carpet of wild flowers. The thriving population of around 100 people, as on Whalsay (see Whalsay), prefer to reap the profits of the sea rather than toil on the land, although they maintain their gardens beautifully.

One possible treasure trove not yet exposed is the wreck of the Dutch East Indiaman, the *Carmelan*, which went down in 1664 on her outward journey from Amsterdam. All but four of her crew were lost but the survivors brought ashore tales of the 3,000,000 guilders aboard, intended to buy spices and clothes. The then landlord of the islands, the Earl of Morton, immediately claimed the wreck, but failed to find more than a small proportion of the coins. The rest awaits treasure seekers ready to risk the moody sea.

Visitors can visit the silver workshop which produces tasteful Celtic designs at reasonable prices.

Accommodation:
Self-catering — details from Tourist Office, Lerwick.

Whalsay

Connections:
By air: from Tingwall and Unst by prior arrangement, Loganair (tel Gott 246).

By sea: from Laxo: at least six a day; cars; 50 min crossing. Shetland Islands Council, Ferry Office (tel Symbister 280); booking advised.

Called the 'Bonnie Isle' by the Scots fishermen of the 19th century, Whalsay is blessed by excellent green pasture, but this is dismissed by the islanders in active preference to farming the silver fish of the sea. It is hard to accept that the large new houses of Symbister, with their unusually fruitful gardens, over-flowing with flowers, bear no debt to the oil industry, but result from the toils of the town's large fishing fleet.

This potential trade was realized early on. To the north of the harbour there is a Hanseatic trading booth, pathetically neglected with a decaying roof, where the 17th century German merchants stored their linen, tobacco and salt, and other rareties, to exchange them for herring and cod. The wooden windlass of that era is still in position. The harbour is full of all manner of vessels, large trawlers, smaller boats for lobster and crab (cheap here), and little Shetland yaols for pleasure craft. No son of the island contemplates being a farmer.

Looking down on the activity is a severe Victorian fantasy building, the second home of a Shetland laird, who preferred to sink £30,000 rather than leave the money to his presumptuous relations. Now it is the main school on the island. The grounds are said to be haunted by an old seaman who was murdered by the gardener after a game of cards.

The **Standing Stones of Yoxie**, about half a mile (.8 km) north of Isbister, are considered to be the remains of a temple of c 2000 BC, and close by stands the roofless **Benie House**, a typical neolithic house neatly ascribed to be the dwelling of the officiating priests of the temple.

Everybody in Whalsay wears ornamental jerseys, often 'panelled' and with all-over patterns. These are far more elaborate than the typical Fair Isle designs, and come in a wide variety of colours. If you are tempted, it is no good looking for them in shops: you must ask the locals to find someone who will knit to commission. They are not expensive.

Accommodation:
Difficult, but this island makes a good day trip.
Sea angling:
Ask around at the harbour.
Specialities:
'Panelled' jerseys.

Bressay

Connections:
By sea: from Lerwick: frequent service; cars; 30 min crossing. Shetland Islands Council Ferry Service (bookings on actual vessel).

Across the water from Lerwick, Bressay's position has always ensured that the sound was a safe harbour for shipping, as was recognized as early as the 15th century by the Dutch fishing fleet, which made Bressay their headquarters.

By the 17th century there were as many as 1,500 boats based here after the midsummer Johnsmas festival, the islanders taking the chance to earn a few pennies by knitting socks and providing Shetland ponies for the crews to ride. As the boats passed the **Bard of Bressay**, a crew member from each would throw a silver coin overboard for luck, towards the **Orkneyman's Cave** (the reason for its name is lost in history).

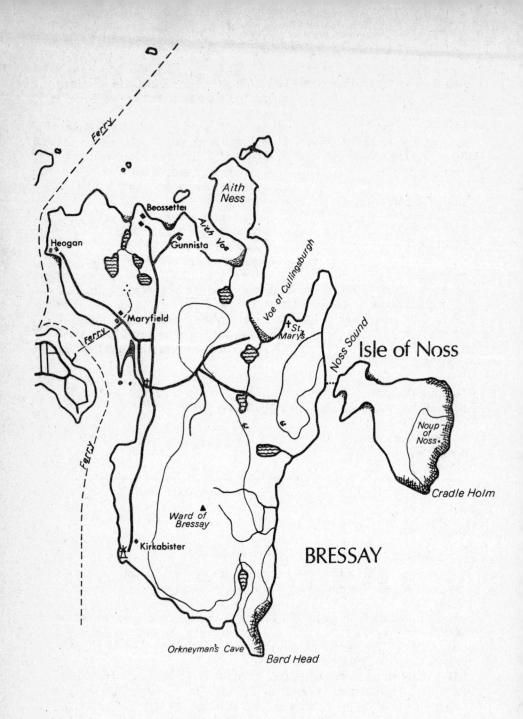

Aith
Ness

Beossetter

Heogan

Gunnista

Aith Voe

Voe of Cullingsburgh

Maryfield

Ferry

St.
Mary's

Isle of Noss

Noss Sound

Noup
of
Noss

Cradle Holm

Ward of
Bressay

BRESSAY

Kirkabister

Orkneyman's Cave

Bard Head

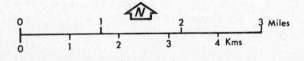

0   1   2   3 Miles

N

0   1   2   3   4 Kms

From here there is a good cliff walk, resonant with the echoing calls of the high-rise colonies of seabirds on the rocks. Waders can be seen by the moorlands lochs but beware of the bonxies (great skuas). To the north is St Mary's Church and the tombstone of a heroic Dutch captain, Claes Bruyn. He was buried in 1665, having steered his ship through a foray with the Portuguese off Mozambique, only to be delayed by gales at the Cape of Good Hope, forcing him to limp north with a seriously depleted crew. The ruined chapel is of uncertain date but the site it occupies is pre-Viking. A beautifully carved Celtic stone was found here, depicting a procession of four priests and a mounted warrior, and possibly Jonah being swallowed by two whales: it is now in the safekeeping of the Lerwick Museum.

In the 19th century a former Marquise of Londonderry bred Shetland ponies on Bressay to work in his coalmines, after the law concerning child labour had been tightened up.

In all Bressay is a surprisingly quiet island, very different from the rapidly expanding Lerwick opposite, for although much labour has been diverted from the crofts to the oil, the outward appearance of the landscape has not been disturbed.

Accommodation:
Maryfield House (tel Bressay 207): arranges trips to the Orkneyman's cave.
Self-catering — details from Tourist Office, Lerwick
Sea Angling:
R Hunter, Tromso (tel Bressay 270)
Bank.
Mobile unit: Wednesdays, fortnightly.
Specialities:
Unfortunately the oyster beds in Bressay Sound were over-harvested in the 19th century and now they have become a very scarce commodity.

Noss
(ON nos — a nose)

Connections:
By sea: from Bressay: hail the RSPB warden at Gungstie (summer only). 2½ hr boat trips around Bressay and Noss from Lerwick, most summer afternoons (weather permitting): booking essential at Tourist Office in Lerwick.

This green and almost uninhabited island is the archetypal bird city and as such has been designated a national nature reserve. The vast colonies of seabirds must be seen to be believed!

The horizontal beds of sandstone have been so worn away by the North Sea as to make cliffs of 600 feet (185 m) on the east side, and the elements have since continued to hollow out ledges, making convenient nesting shelves for the millions of seabirds. Segregated into rows, the kittiwake, guillemot, black guillemot, razor bills, gannets, herring gulls and fulmars send out a never ceasing chorus of gossip and demands for more food, while the black shag choose to bring up their young in the darkness of the caves. Puffin and great and Arctic skuas nest on the smooth sloping back of the island, and a colony of great black-backed gulls has rejected the general clamour of the eastern cliffs for the Cradle Holm.

Once used for pasturing the stallions of the Earl of Londonderry's stud, the grass here was considered very valuable grazing. So much so that to take advantage of the grassy top of the Holm of Noss, in the 17th century a cow was offered as a reward to any man who succeded in climbing the 160 foot (50 m) of sheer cliff, to secure stakes to hold a 'rope-railway'. Anyone who has seen the straw ropes in the Croft House Museum (see South Mainland) will understand why the reward was necessary. In the event, climbing down proved more difficult than climbing up, and the man fell tragically to his death. The railway was used every year until 1864, the grassy top feeding twelve sheep for the summer.

Accommodation:
Camping — consult the RSPB Warden at Gungstie.

Mousa
(possibly ON mose — moss isle)

Connections:
By sea: from Sandwick by arrangement; T Jamieson (tel Sandwick 367).

A small grassy island, uninhabited except by grazing Shetland ponies and sheep and seals sunbathing on its empty sands, Mousa is famed for its astonishingly intact Iron Age tower which faces Sandwick across the sound. Anyone pausing on the road from Lerwick to Sumburgh will be struck by the tower's superb position — a reminder that almost every ness (headland) in the northern isles was guarded by a similar edifice, where now only a pile of rubble remains.

Unlike the site of Clickhimin, the broch of Mousa stands alone without the normal surrounding settlement houses, making this the purest surviving example of broch architecture. Built of the local old red sandstone, it still attains a height of 43 feet (13 m) (the original height cannot be determined), swelling out at the bottom to withstand battering. Within the circular courtyard (approximately 20 ft/6 m in diameter), a later, probably 2nd or 3rd century wheel house has been built where originally there would have been timber ranges or rooms. In the hollow walls, stairs lead upwards through the galleries, the floors cunningly binding the two shells together. Six of the galleries survive, all opening into the courtyard, perhaps to gain access to the upper storeys of the wooden ranges.

The exact origin of this form of tower has become the focus of an archaeologist's debate and little is known of the people who built it. Nowhere else in Europe was such a great height achieved, although its advantages for defence against all comers is obvious. However, this broch does feature in the sagas as a refuge for eloping couples. In 1153 Erland, the son of Harald the Fair-spoken, carried off a famous and not so virtuous beauty, the mother of Earl Harald Maddadson. Harald besieged Mousa but found it 'an unhandy place to get at' and had to agree to the lovers' marriage, needing to defend his title elsewhere.

The unobtrusive inhabitants of Mousa today are a large colony of storm petrels which nest within the drystone walls. They are rarely glimpsed in daylight, but great activity can be seen and heard on summer nights — special trips can be arranged.

Fair Isle
(The origin of this place name is obscured, as there are three possible Old Norn derivations, from faerey — meaning 'the sheep isle', feoer — meaning 'far off', or fara meaning 'the far isle'.)

Connections:
By air: from Tingwall (Lerwick): Mon and Fri, two a day. Loganair (tel Gott 246). From Kirkwall: Sat, two a day. Loganair (tel Kirkwall 2494.

By sea: from Grutness: Tue and Sat, weather permitting, on the *Good Shepherd* (free); 3 hr crossing (tel Fair Isle 222). There is a connecting bus service with Lerwick.

Fair Isle is a small island, measuring only 3 miles by 1½ across (5 by 2½ km), perched in the North Sea half-way between Orkney and Shetland, both of which can be seen on a clear day. Used by the Vikings as a pausing place on their long sea journeys, Fair Isle traditionally had close trading links with Orkney, the islanders even having to go to Westray to be married, but more recently the regularization of communications has linked the island to Shetland — a journey in the *Good Shepherd* will invariably be memorable, whether in fine or foul weather!

Even today, the 20 miles (32 km) of moody sea maintain the

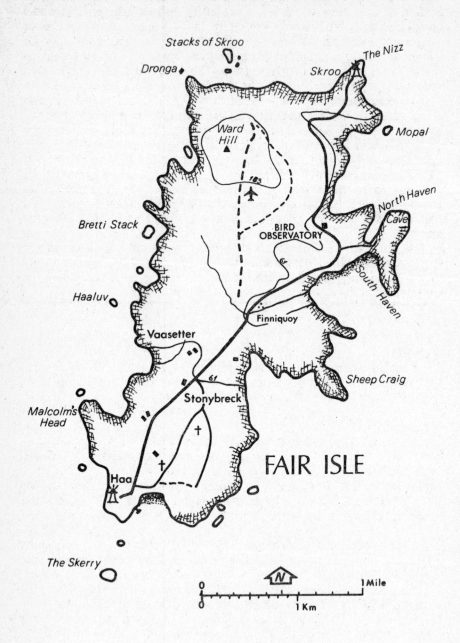

Stacks of Skroo

Dronga

Skroo

The Nizz

Mopal

Ward
Hill

185

North Haven

Bretti Stack

BIRD
OBSERVATORY

Cave

61

Haaluv

South Haven

Finniquoy

Vaasetter

Sheep Craig

61

Stonybreck

Malcolm's
Head

FAIR ISLE

Haa

The Skerry

N

0   1 Mile

1 Km

realities of isolation, particularly in winter. In one respect, however, this is the island's greatest advantage, for in its solitude it provides a welcome rest for migrant birds in the spring and autumn, and often harbours varieties distracted off course by malign weather conditions. Dr William Eagle Clarke, of the Royal Scottish Museum, Edinburgh, first recognized, early this century, the potential for finding rarieties here and enrolled the help of an islander to record the various species found. The renowned ornithologist, George Waterson, visited Fair Isle each year in the late 1930s, and subsequently, while he was a POW in Germany, concocted a plan to establish a permanent observatory. Immediately after the war he began hatching his idea, first buying the island and then in 1948 opening an observatory in a redundant naval camp. The island community was gradually dwindling to a dangerously low level, but to avert probable evacuation and desertion by the crofters, the National Trust for Scotland bought the island with a grant from the Dalverton Trust, and made extensive improvements to the pier at North Haven, and to the houses and shop. The Trust continues to be a benign benefactor supporting this now thriving community.

The Observatory, rebuilt in 1969, has a permanent staff occupied in recording and monitoring the constantly changing bird population, while also providing excellent hostel facilities for visitors in a friendly relaxed atmosphere. The hostel is open from March to October, and it is advisable to book well in advance for the spring and autumn migrations. There is a good collection of reference books. The keen (and knowledgeable) may be allowed to accompany the wardens on expeditions to count and ring the birds, or on the pre-breakfast inspections of the traps littering the stone dykes of the island.

A jagged curtain of sandstone cliffs rings the island (the only accessible beaches are at North and South Haven and South Harbour). During the summer months these resound with the choruses of seabird colonies competing with the crashing waves: every crack and ledge is the home of a young gull or auk. A boat trip around the island is the best way to appreciate the vast extent of the colonies, although peering down the gullies and cracks, or across to the stacks, is equally exciting. Grey seals can also be seen at the foot of the northern cliffs. An ever-increasing colony of great (and Arctic) skuas have taken over the moorland of Ward Hill, attacking anyone who wanders too close to their chicks, fully earning their local name of 'bonxies' with their fearless diving lunges.

Besides claiming over 320 recorded species, Fair Isle also has its own individual breed of bird, the Fair Isle wren (Troglodytes troglodytes fridarienis) which, through its isolation, has developed a different song and behavioural pattern to the mainland variety. Similarly, the field mouse has evolved into a distinctive species (Apodemus sylvaticus fridarienis), with a different skull shape and markings. The rabbit population sports a far wider than normal variety of colour markings — as there are no natural predators on the island, the mutants have an unusually high chance of survival.

When looking south from the pier, the distinctive upwards scoop of **Sheep Rock**, a huge sandstone block, reminds one of another reason for Fair Isle's fame. Although it is now deserted by everything except puffins and guillemots, Sheep Rock was once an important and valuable grazing area for sheep, which are now kept almost everywhere else on the island. The range of natural colours in the fleeces of these Shetland sheep is exploited in the all-over patterned jerseys. The special thing about these jerseys, unlike those advertised throughout Scotland, is that nowhere in the pattern is a motif repeated. They are available on order from the island shop. Traditionally the patterns were said to have been taught to the islanders by the survivors of *El Gran Grifon*, the flagship of the Spanish Armada supply fleet which was wrecked off Fair Isle in 1588. However, it seems more likely that they originated from a basic Nordic tradition, subsequently developed in isolation.

Fair Isle is surrounded by a vast number of ship wrecks, as a map in the observatory makes abundantly clear, but diving is not advised as the waters are treacherous. Frequently the victims of these wrecks caused many problems, as they proceeded to eat their way through the carefully saved winter supplies.

Of antiquities, Fair Isle has few examples, apart from the ruins of a watchtower, dating from the Napoleonic era, at **Malcolm's Head**, and the two now ruined Norse mills at **Finniquoy**, near the plantation — a pathetic weather-beaten pocket of shrub trees. Because the crofting community has evolved slowly without any rapid changes in fortune, many remnants of the rural past can still be seen on the southern half of the island, eg the round 'beehive' corn drying kilns. This island, more than most of the others, is still astonishingly self-reliant. Everything is mended by the islanders themselves — even the road.

Once a fortnight there is a dance in the new hall. This is well worth attending because, as in so many other spheres, the islanders have evolved their own routines, similar in form to the Scottish country dances, to which you will not be allowed to be a by-stander for long.

Accommodation:
The Fair Isle Bird Observatory (tel Fair Isle 258)
Work camps: organised during the summer by the National Trust for Scotland, No 5 Charlotte Square, Edinburgh (tel 031 226 5922) to restore buildings.
Sea Angling:
S Thompson, Quoy (tel Fair Isle 241)
Specialities:
Knitting, dances.

St Ninian's Isle

Connections:
By tombolo: from B9122 at Bigton.

This beautiful tiny green island is joined to the Mainland by a perfect curved tombolo or sand-bar — pebbles covered by a mat of sparkling white sand said to be the best-formed in Britain. This makes a magical picnic site, the edges being indented with caves and arches inhabited by a small cormorant colony and seals.

The history of St Ninian has been overshadowed by time. A Christian reformer, predating Columba by a century, he was described by the Venerable Bede as 'a most reverend bishop . . . regularly trained at Rome', and celebrated by a 12th century biography for converting the Picts. Whether he ever came this far north is obscured by history; more probably his followers brought his message, leaving a heritage which kept this isle as a place of pilgrimage until the 18th century.

In 1955 Professor O'Dell began excavating the isle with students of Aberdeen University and found both a 12th century church and a pre-Norse chapel. More spectacularly, under the altar they found a rotten larch box (larch was not introduced to Britain until the 18th century) inside which was a large treasure of Celtic bowls, brooches and spoons, now in the safekeeping of the National Museum of Antiquities in Edinburgh (replicas are held in Lerwick Museum). Perhaps the monks saw the Viking longboats approach their island and rushed to hide their treasure, their secret dying with them during the course of the invasions.

Burra
(ON borgar fiord — castle bay)
Trondra

Connections:
By bridge from B9074 at Scalloway.

The three islands of East and West Burra and Trondra lie in an 'H' off the south leg of the Mainland. Once they supported a comfortable fishing community, and now they have been given a new lease of life by the recently constructed bridges. Shopping expeditions are no longer made by boat to Scalloway, to the detriment of that town but to the greater convenience of these islanders.

Trondra is green and empty — not even having much peat. **Burra** is more appealing, its coast line alternating between low cliffs and sandy bottomed coves — it's always possible to find your own, even

around the southern headlands with their long views down the coas
past St Ninian's Isle to Sumbrugh Head and the open sea beyond
Here too are thatched cottages and outhouses, still inhabited despite
the recent affluence brought by the oil, yet curiously juxtaposed tc
metal caravans — these have the advantage of being dry if not sc
decorative!

Until the 19th century, the hay would be cut only when it was
wet and would then be left for two or three weeks until it had been
rained upon, due to a strange belief that it would rot unless the juices
were washed out. Even if such theories have long since been
discarded, many of the old farming techniques are still practised here.

At **Papil** there is reputed to have been a tall church similar to the
one on Egilsay, Orkney (see Egilsay). Certainly the surviving ruin of
St Lawrence's church predates the Vikings and in its graveyard were
found the two famous Celtic slabs, the **Papil stone** (now in the
National Museum of Antiquities, Edinburgh: replica in the Lerwick
Museum) and the **Monk's stone** (now in the Lerwick Museum). The
Monk's stone probably came from the front of the altar, and was
carved in the 9th century with a procession of four monks on foot
and a single rider — they had Shetland ponies even in those days! The
Papil stone is more intricately designed, with weird Pictish motifs
and creatures woven into a Christian context.

Hamnavoe is a fishing town of modern prosperity — its still blue
harbour water contrasting strongly with the crashing Atlantic breakers
spraying **Fugla Ness**.

Accommodation:
Bed & breakfast and self-catering — details from the Tourist Office,
Lerwick.
Bank:
Mobile unit on Fridays.

Vaila

Connections:
By sea: from Walls on request by Mr Anderton (tel Walls 363/213).

A small moorland island, with the usual fringe of seabird haunted
cliffs and an extraordinary wide range of plants (over 100 species of
flowers have been recorded), Vaila is significant beyond its convenient
sheltering of Walls harbour. It was from here that in 1837 Arthur
Anderson, a founder of the P & O Company, set up the Shetland
Fishery Company, which broke the stranglehold of the lairds over
their tenants. At that time, most of the population of Shetland was
dependent on the fishing industry for their livelihood, yet because

they were forced to use the laird's boats, imported from Norway, and trade at his shop, they were only too vulnerable to exploitation. Arthur Anderson introduced the skills of boat building, enabling the men to build their own in the same double-ended Norwegian form.

Slightly ironically, this century turned Vaila into a laird's isle. An owner of woollen mills in Yorkshire, Herbert Anderton, while on a visit to Shetland to buy wool and enjoy the summer pastimes of fishing and shooting, decided to buy the island and its old house, which was probably built around the turn of the 17th century by James Mitchell, a Scalloway merchant. Shipping stone across from Walls, he developed the house into a baronial mansion complete with a Jacobean hall and library. It can be visited in the summer by arrangement and a magnificent banquet is held every fortnight by the present laird and his wife (details from Mr Anderton, tel Walls 363/213). Herbert Anderton's curiosity led him to Japan, and he brought back a Buddha and temple — artefacts for which he created an adequate setting in the boat house. Unfortunately this has been vandalized in recent years.

Accommodation:
Cloudin Hostel (tel Walls 363)
Camping: permission required from Mr Anderton.
As there is no shop on the island, take food (and bedding).
Sea Angling:
Contact Mr Anderton (tel Walls 363).

Foula
(ON fuglay — fowl isle)

Connections:
By air: from Tingwall: Fri in summer, weather permitting. Loganair Ltd (tel Gott 246).
By sea: from Walls: Tue or next possible day. Mr R Holborn (tel Foula 3232).

Lying 14 miles (23 km) due west of the Shetland Mainland, Foula is for many the epitome of isolation, immortalized by the film 'Edge of the World'. Every winter it is broadcast that Foula has been cut off for four, five or six weeks at a time, and even in the summer crossings are not easy. Memories of being tossed about in a sieve are the legacy of every trip to Foula, but what a small price to pay to visit Britain's remotest inhabited island. Visible on clear days from Orkney and Shetland, this is perhaps the legendary 'Thule' that Agricola's Roman fleet saw on the horizon, but never explored.

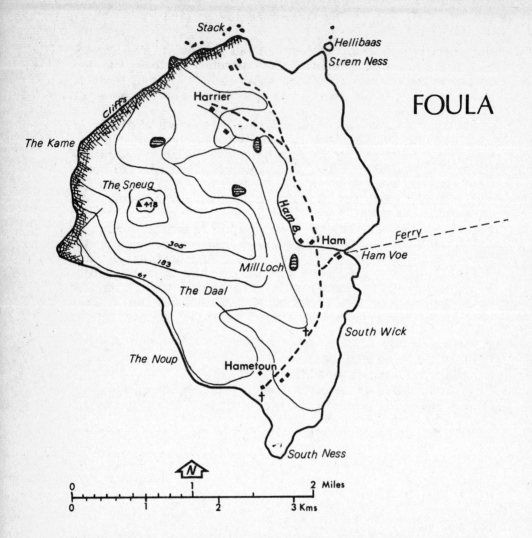

FOULA

The Atlantic has worn away the sandstone mountain of the **Sneug** (1,373 ft/419 m), making gigantic cliffs on the west side. The Kame drops a precipitous 1,220 feet (372 m), plunging steeply into the attacking ocean, the second highest cliff in Britain. Its population consists of such enormous colonies of seabirds that they are estimated to eat over a quarter of all the fish within a 25 mile (40 km) radius of the island.

This is a good place to spot storm petrels and Leach's petrels: they frequently escort the boat on the last few miles of its journey. Here, as at St Kilda (see St Kilda), the seabirds were a very important part of the island economy, the men climbing the cliffs for eggs and birds with unbelievable daring. An 18th century minister, John Brand, attributed the lack of old men to this occupation. His account of the fowlers' exploits, dangling on ropes as they scaled the cliff walls, is undoubtedly vivid, but it is more likely that the fight against the elements was lost before the onset of old age.

Today the situation has been reversed. From a figure of 222 in 1901, the population has now been reduced to 40, most of whom are pensioners, the young having left to make their fortunes elsewhere. Since Foula was almost depopulated in 1720 by the 'muckle fever' (smallpox), and recolonized from the Mainland, it is nigh on impossible to get up wind of the crofters (a game played by visiting fishermen!) so great is their fear of infection. The community is settled around the wind-washed pier at Ham Voe, farming the fertile eastern slopes while the 'hard-back' sheep wander the hill in search of food. The fleeces of these sheep are abnormally hairy, typical of primitive sheep: they may have been introduced by the Vikings, surviving as a more suitable species than the modern varieties. Like Fair Isle (see Fair Isle) evolution has given Foula its own species of field mouse (Apodermus syhaticus thuloe) which has large kind feet.

The Foula success story must be the bonxie (great skua), protected as early as the 18th century, until this rule was overturned by the Victorian egg collecting mania. At the turn of the century, they had been reduced to only a couple of pairs of birds, but then the Bird Protection Acts initiated a population explosion and now they populate every suitable moorland, viciously attacking any predators who invade their territories. The 3,000 pairs on Foula today make enjoying the view from the Sneug a risky business — a walking stick is recommended to ward off their swooping attacks.

Accommodation:
Self-catering — details from the Tourist Office, Lerwick.
Foula may appear modern, but don't expect too much. The public telephone box gives shelter to a broody hen.
Specialities:
Dancing: as on Fair Isle, the islanders have evolved their own dances and reels. The best known is the Foula Reel.

Papa Stour
(ON papey stora — big island of the priests)

Connections:
By sea: from Sandness: Mon, Wed, Fri, also by arrangement; J Jamieson (tel Papa Stour 225).

The sound between Sandness and Papa Stour, although only 1 mile (1.5 km) across, is often turbulent enough to isolate this flat-topped island for days. Much indented by voes and geos, its jagged cliffs stand ready to mince any careless craft. John Tudor, the Victorian

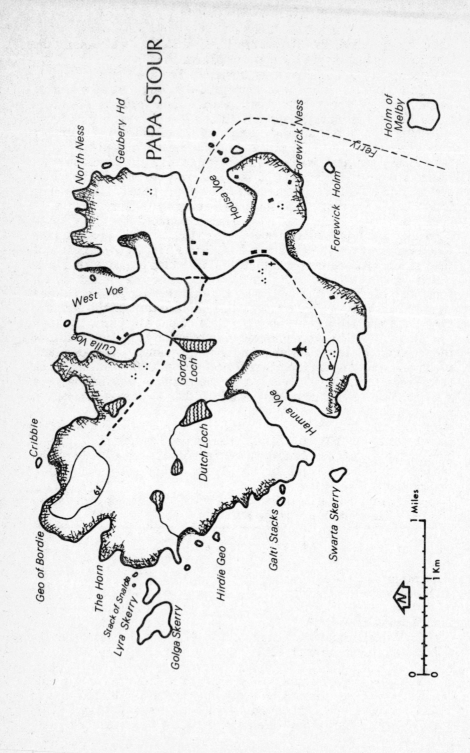

PAPA STOUR

North Ness

Geubery Hd

Holm of Melby

Ferry

Forewick Ness

Forewick Holm

Housa Voe

West Voe

Culla Voe

Gorda Loch

Viewpoint

Cribble

Dutch Loch

Hamna Voe

Geo of Bordie

The Horn

Stack of Snalda

Lyra Skerry

Golga Skerry

Hirdie Geo

Galti Stacks

Swarta Skerry

N

Miles

Km

travel writer, creates magic out of the cathedrals and dungeons of the rock formations, for although they may be dismal in bad weather, the sun brings a patchwork of colour and light to the old red sandstone cliffs, eaten and carved into stacks, arches and tunnels. In fine weather a boat trip can be arranged with the ferry man.

Lyra Sherry, hollowed by subterranean passages, is a breeding ground for common seals and just north of it is the Stack of Snalda, the old site of an eagle's nest. Seabirds abound, the cormorant and Manx shearwater colonies being of special note.

The folklore of Papa Stour has been elaborated on many a long night round the peat fire. Tales abound of the Celtic monks who gave the island its name, perhaps friends of St Ninian; of the maiden placed on Maiden's Stack by her father in an unsuccessful attempt to isolate her from men; of the friendly seal-folk, mythical magic people who saved many a sailor by carrying him home. A witch, Minna Baaba, is kindly remembered for creating a storm to drive a sinister ship out of Housa Voe, before its crew attacked the islanders; but for the equally sinister 18th century disease of leprosy, there was no such easy solution — victims were isolated from the community for the rest of their lifetimes.

There is a decided lack of turf and topsoil on the island, perhaps due to the extensive peat digging and the practice of removing turf for roofing, but today it is a haven of flowers and peace. In the last decade, it was known locally as the Hippy Isle, when its declining population was inundated with get-back-to-the-earth freaks. Now, many have moved on, leaving a settled and happy community.

Accommodation:
B & B and self-catering — details from the Tourist Office, Lerwick.

Muckle Roe
(ON — big red island)

Connections:
By bridge from A970 at Brae.

A small circular island ringed by high red cliffs of red granite, Muckle Roe supports a small crofting community on its fertile southeastern edge. The rest is a wilderness of moor and water, pleasant walking with long views across to Sandness and Eshaness, past countless tiny green holms and, on a clear day, to Foula.

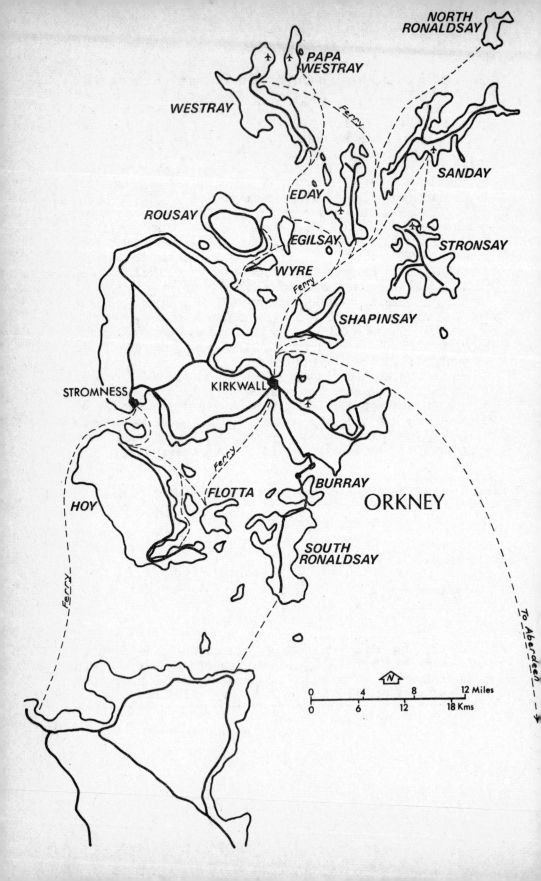

Part 2
The Orkney Islands

Connections:

By air: from Glasgow to Kirkwall (via Inverness): Mon — Sat, one a day. From Shetland to Kirkwall: Mon — Fri, one a day; Sat, two a day. From Aberdeen to Kirkwall: Mon — Fri, two a day; Sat, one a day. British Airways (Tel Kirkwall 2233).

From Inverness to Kirkwall: Mon — Sat, two a day. From Wick to Kirkwall: Mon — Sat, three a day. From Edinburgh to Kirkwall: Mon — Sat, one a day. Loganair Ltd (tel Kirkwall 3025).

By sea: from Scrabster to Stromness: Mon — Sat and summer Sun, at least one a day; cars; 2 hr crossing. P & O Ferries (tel Stromness 850-655).

From John o'Groats to South Ronaldsay (road connection to Mainland Orkney): at least two a day; 3/4 hr crossing. Thomas & Bews, Ferry Office (tel John o'Groats 353).

Orkney Life

Orkney presents a surprise, however one arrives. The boat from Scrabster edges round the monumental red cliffs of Hoy into the Scapa Flow while the aeroplane settles down amidst lush green pastures speckled with a multitude of wild flowers, neatly separated

73

into fields by well maintained drystone dykes, each confining large herds of milk and beef cattle. The landscape rolls gently over the fertile hills, rarely changing into the heather-covered slopes normally associated with the highlands and islands of Scotland. The yellow buttercups and irises gratefully reassure the June visitor that the intensive industry of farming has room enough for the wild flora and fauna and for the heritage of the past; every bog has not been drained, nor are the crops so pure that flowers are not welcome.

The geology of Orkney is its greatest asset. The old red sandstone which underlies most of the archipelago makes for highly fertile soil when combined with shell sand, and although Orkney was once similar in appearance to the other heather islands, this potential was soon discovered and exploited. On Eday, the sharp division between heather and grass can be directly correlated to the landlords' policies, one preferring sport and the other agricultural pursuits. Another advantage of the old red sandstone is that it easily separates into slabs — as any walk along the shore will reveal. Consequently the houses were simple to construct, large stone slabs being used for the roof instead of the usual island heather thatch, as well as for the walls. Many farmsteads of the last century which have since been rejected in favour of more spacious habitations stand proud and complete even now, not yet having dissolved into a heap of rubble. The drystone dykes are equally long lasting and are still preferred to modern fences which prove more expensive to maintain.

But besides the generally solid air of well-being that dominates most views of these islands, the kind geology has left for the visitor a greater bonus — the houses and edifices of earlier peoples, making Orkney the archaeologist's paradise. Skara Brae (see North Mainland) is a world-famous neolithic village, revealed in a sand-dune by a storm and now carefully excavated to show the houses as they were when swamped by a 'neolithic' storm, with even the stone dressers and benches still in place. More remarkable still, almost every island of the group claims a similar site, even if it has not yet been excavated, and even these villages are not the earliest evidence of human habitation on Orkney. On Papa Westray is the oldest house in Europe, inhabited over 5,000 years ago, yet still standing to a height of 5 ft 1 in (1.62m), with the room divisions still upright. Monumental chambered cairns delight both the novice and the expert by their size and variety. Standing stones, duns, brochs and the Viking longhouses complete the selection; on average there are three sites to every square mile. The most notable are described in the text following, but enthusiasts should refer to the three-volume report by The Royal Commission on the Ancient and Historical Monuments of Scotland (this can be found in the Orkney Room of the Public Library in Kirkwall). Anyone keen to scrape away with a toothbrush should contact North of Scotland Archaeological Services, Binscarth House, Finstown, Orkney.

Little is known about the peoples who lived on Orkney before the Vikings, beyond what archaeology has revealed, but the Vikings themselves left many traces. The *Orkneying Saga* is the story of the jarls who came from Norway and their exploits around the Scottish coast. Its complicated genealogies are typical of most oral traditions, while its evocative tales of battles and feuds, buildings and feasts can in many instances be linked to surviving places. The great cathedral in Kirkwall will come as a great shock to most visitors. Its vast scale and artistic affinities with Durham Cathedral, so untypical of any island culture, appear inexplicable until one realizes that the Viking jarls of Orkney in the 11th and 12th centuries were second only in power to the Kings of Scotland. Thus St Magnus should be compared to the ruined cathedral of St Andrew's.

The *Saga* never relates the fate of the indigenous population of the islands, but the Viking method of land holding, by which every warrior owned his own farm and only chose to offer his allegiance to a leader (hence the ceaseless quarrelling among nobles), has had a lasting effect on the social organization of Orkney. When the northern isles were ceded to Scotland by Norway as part of Princess Margaret's dowry in 1472, some of the Viking landlords retained their interests. Thus, unlike Shetland, Orkney was never dominated by the great medieval feudal landlords. Consequently, there are no crofters on Orkney, as the islanders were able to retain their farms. Although small, these are large enough to maintain one or two families comfortably even today, and although a few families rose above their neighbours, there is still essentially a one-class society.

The wealth of Orkney continued throughout the 16th and 17th centuries, as the intricately carved gravestones bear witness. In the 18th century, extra money was earned through gathering tangle, a type of seaweed blown up on the seashore by the winter gales. The tangle was spread out to dry on the grass and then burnt in a kiln — a circular stone-lined hollow, approximately 5 feet (1.5m) in diameter. The fire reduced the seaweed to a blueish-grey molten liquid which was raked to remove the impurities, and then covered with ash and left to harden, before being transported south to be used in soap and glass making. The market contracted suddenly after the Napoleonic wars, when an alternative substitute, barilla from Spain, became available once more, although the industry continued until after the First World War. More recently, seaweed was collected for an alginate factory, but that enterprise stopped in 1980 due to some complex takeover bid by its American rivals.

In the past, Orkney was famous for its egg production, the small farms providing a ready source of the intensive labour needed to look after the hens. But the double cost of transporting the foodstuff and the eggs defeated any hope of competition with the battery chickens of the 1960s, and hens are now rarely seen on farms. The women tend to spend their spare time knitting, but unlike the Shetlanders they do not work for factories. Instead, they have organized themselves into co-operatives on the basis of island or family loyalties. Using mostly Shetland wool, they are often happy to experiment with new designs and patterns.

Some of the older men continue to meet the demand for traditional Orkney chairs. The lack of trees on these islands is not immediately obvious because of their great fertility, but it has always meant that wood is extremely precious. The design of the straw-backed chair represented a compromise between the lack of timber and the need to keep out draughts. The straw is so tightly bound into backs and 'hoods' that it will last for many decades, providing it is not subjected to great variations in heat. Many originally incorporated a drawer for the family Bible and the craftsmen can be persuaded to repeat this feature. Don't expect to find them in the shops — there is too much demand and all are ordered months before they are made.

A last word of warning about the Orcadians: they are a fine, proud race, asserting their right to evaluate suggestions, fiercely maintaining their independence, and wanting little help from anyone. (The Government's plans to mine uranium in North Mainland were firmly and whole-heartedly rejected.) But their generosity to fellow-islanders and visitors alike is always overwhelming.

Mainland Orkney

Kirkwall
(ON kirkjuvagr — church-bay)
Nestling in the Bay of Firth, Kirkwall was established by Norse invaders in the 11th century and was one of the earliest Norse market towns. The name probably derived from the church erected by Jarl (Earl) Rognvald Brusason in 1040 to honour his friend King Olaf Haraldsson (1015-30), patron saint of Norway, of which only a weatherbeaten doorway arch survives in St Ola's Wynd.

Orkney originally belonged to the See of Hamburg, but by 1137 it had become a diocese under the province of Trondheim, Norway. It was then that Jarl Rognvald Kali began building St Magnus Cathedral in honour of his uncle Jarl Magnus, who was executed on Egilsay in 1116/17. Relics of both these men were built into the piers flanking the high altar. Made of red and yellow sandstone, the cathedral has no distinctive Norse features; in style its closest cousin is the Romanesque cathedral of Durham, and Durham masons probably carved the stonework, now sadly weatherbeaten on the exterior. The interior still displays a wealth of decorative detail on the capitals and arches.

Kirkwall was exceptional at this period for housing both an ecclesiastical and a secular court, its nearest contemporary parallel being St Andrew's, Fife, and the whole of the interior and possibly the exterior would have been polychromed and gilded, quite alien to the solemnity of its mood today. Completed in the transitional style (pointed arches), its bell tower being added in the early 14th century, it suffered surprisingly little from the Reformation except through lack of finance. A powerful reminder of the affluence of this trading town is to be found in the collection of carved tombstones dating from the late 16th and early 17th centuries, laid on the floor but later moved to the side isles of St Magnus. Many incorporate memento mori and other symbols, one even showing the influence of the Renaissance in the pose of Christ. Also within the cathedral is housed the original market cross with an incised date of 1621.

Beside the cathedral are the impressive ruins of the Bishops's palace (open Apr-Sep: 9.30 — 7 Mon-Sat, 2 — 7 Sun; Oct-Mar: 9.30 — 4 Mon-Sat, 2 — 4 Sun), built by Bishop William the Old (1102-68), where King Hakon of Norway died after his attempted invasion of Scotland and defeat at the battle of Largs in 1263. The round corner tower, known as the 'Moosie To'or', was added by Bishop Robert Reid (1541-58) when he also strengthened the original structure. The Earl's palace is next to the Bishop's (open same hours) and was built by Earl Patrick Stewart, the illegitimate son of the brother of Mary Queen of Scots. It is described in Sir Walter Scott's novel, *The Pirate*, with images of great northern hospitality, perhaps justified by the enormous kitchen chimney. Less fantastically, the delicately carved decoration, deriving from English and French sources, harmonizes this stronghold-palace into the most mature example of Scottish Renaissance architecture.

Behind the palace is the town's bowling green where a midnight bowling match annually celebrates the longest day of the year (21st June).

The Tankerness Museum (open 10.30 − 1, 2 − 5 Mon-Sat), founded by the town council in 1969, is housed in a 16th century merchant's house opposite the cathedral. It clearly and simply traces the 4,000 years of Orkney's history. The archaeological displays are excellen· for placing the various local monuments in time while other exhibits illuminate the more recent Orkadian way of life, eg the 'kraa-kruik', a windle used for twisting the 'sookans' (straw ropes) necessary for farming the seacliffs for birds and eggs. The famous Orkney straw chairs are shown beside a record of the curious history of straw plaiting. This was first introduced to the islands in 1805 by Mr Larking, an agent of some London bonnet firm. Up to 7,000 women were employed in plaiting local rye and imported Italian straw until the industry was killed by a change in fashion and the reduction of import duty in the early 1850s. Temporary exhibitions of topographical interest are also shown, and the quiet flower garden is a welcoming retreat for footsore sightseers

Only temporarily affected by the oilmen invasion, and relatively unscatned by the recent ban on herring fishing (because Orcadian-based ships land their catches at Aberdeen and Grimsby), this town of 5,000 inhabitants appears to have been left 30 years behind. The main street, a motley collection of harled and stone houses (notice the odd fragments of carving above doors and windows) is curiously unspoilt by the shops. Although paved and with the odd tree firmly established, it is not for pedestrians only, so expect to be mown down by hurrying cars. The spirit of the town is a curious mixture of the old, typified by the 'Pavilion', a billards saloon and sweet shop, and the current, amply illustrated by the successful campaign against test drilling for uranium.

Following the Norse custom, 'Ba' is played on Christmas and New Year's days in the narrow streets, between the 'Uppies' (Bishop's men) and the 'Downies' (Earl's men), a loose scrum of men trying to get the 'Ba' into their respective goals. Another Kirkwall custom occurs on 1st April — 'Huntie Goak' or find the fool, when the children pin a tail on whoever they please It was once played all over the island with pigs' tails saved by the butchers, but now only paper or card tails are used.

Since 1977, late June has welcomed the specifically Orcadian St Magnus Festival, held in Kirkwall and Stromness. Although centred on the local community, it attracts many foreign visitors and well known outside performers, and is much inspired by its artistic director, Peter Maxwell Davies, who lives on the island and writes many new works each year.

The excellent town library has an Orkney room covering the archaeology, history, folklore, and literature of the islands in great detail. The two local distilleries, Highland Park and Scarpa, may be visited (details locally). Night life is limited to a cinema and threatre, although evenings in the local pub can be both highly entertaining and informative. Kirkwall boasts a heated indoor swimming pool and squash courts.

Accommodation
Albert Hotel (tel Kirkwall 2021)
Ayre Hotel (tel Kirkwall 2197)
Kirkwall Hotel (tel Kirkwall 2232)
Royal Hotel (tel Kirkwall 3477)
West End Hotel (tel Kirkwall 2368)
Scapa Flow Guest House (tel Kirkwall 3339)
B & B list from Tourist Office
Youth Hostel(tel Kirkwall 2763)
Camp site
Car Hire:
Scarth Hire, Gt Western Rd (tel Kirkwall 2125)
J & M Sutherland, Junction Rd (tel Kirkwall 2158)
J D Peace, Junction Rd (tel Kirkwall 2866)

Kerr, Manse Rd (tel Kirkwall 2260)
Ritchie, Gt Western Rd (tel Kirkwall 2601)
Tulloch, Castle St (tel Kirkwall 3212)
Bicycle Hire and Repair:
Paterson, Hornersquy (tel Kirkwall 3097)
Rent-a-bike, Albert St (tel Kirkwall 2995)
Tulloch, Castle St (tel Kirkwall 3212)
Yacht charter:
Orkney Yacht Charter (tel Kirkwall 2072)
David Reed (tel Kirkwall 3730)
Harbour Master:
Mr Foulis (tel Kirkwall 2292)
Tourist Office:
(tel Kirkwall 2856); open Jul-Aug: 9.30 — 7 Mon-Fri, 9.30 — 5 Sat;
May, Jun, Sep: 9.30 — 5 Mon-Sat; Oct-Apr: 9.30 — 5 Mon-Fri.

East Mainland
The East Mainland is a rich and beautiful fertile area. It comes as
something of a surprise to those who land by plane, for this is not
how one thinks of an island landscape! Neat fields, regularly squared
out, filled with fat beef cattle, are an unusual image for an industrial
landscape, but Orkney in general claims more cows per acre than any
other part of Britain, and more tractors! Unlike most islanders, the
Orcadians have remained essentially farmers, going fishing only as a
small sideline. The underlying geology of old red sandstone makes
fertile pastures easily capable of supporting the population on the
small farms. The unpopular Stewart earls of the 16th century failed
to impose effective feudalism on these freemen of Viking ancestry
and although this delayed the enactment of the agricultural improvements of the 18th century, it has meant that essentially a one-class
society has been retained. Orcadians are very proud of their
independence, claiming their rights to accept or reject advice offered,
and firmly supporting their Liberal MP, Jo Grimmond. The intensive
farming is far from fanatical: wild flowers smother the fields in
yellow — buttercups, yellow irises, and eggs and bacon, and the grey
stone cottages — a witness to the wealth of the last century — stand
proud without the protection of hills or trees. Only this lack of trees
reminds the summer visitor that this Arcadia has bleaker moments of
winter gales.
On the road south from Kirkwall (A 961) the ground rises to the
Hillock of Garth and Nether Button, both of which give views across
the land to the east and Scapa Flow to the west, a blanket of green
on one side, of blue on the other. The Second World War brought a
jungle of sky-stretching masts and radar equipment listening to the
continent, now happily replaced by BBC transmitters, marking the
spot near the shore where the *Royal Oak* went down. An instance of
heroic adventure led a German submarine through the then shallow

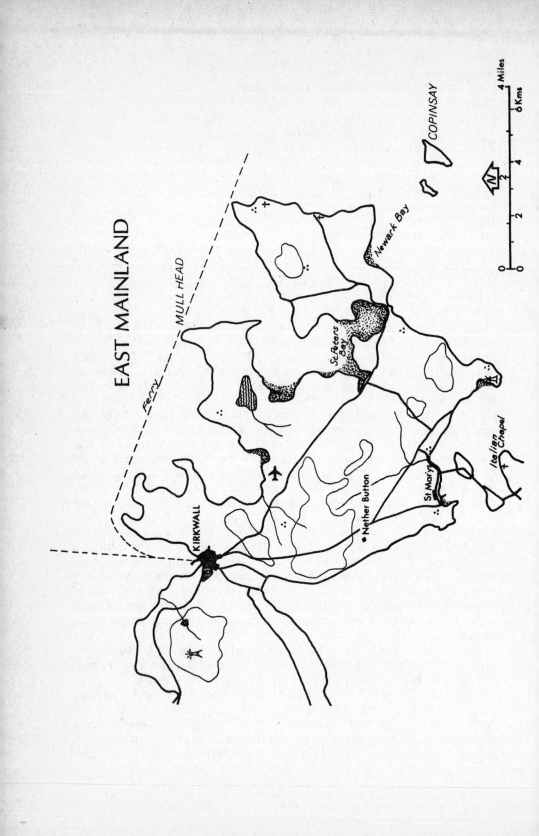

EAST MAINLAND

Ferry

MULL HEAD

KIRKWALL

St Peters Bay

Newark Bay

Nether Button

St Mary's

Italian Chapel

COPINSAY

N

0   2   4

0   2   4 Miles

0   6 Kms

straits of Holm Sound (see Burray) to torpedo the ship whilst she was at anchor in the Bay of Deepdale. A supply tug alongside was able to rescue a few of the crew but over 800 died. Suggestions that the ship should be raised for its steel met with emotional refusal, and so the wreck was made a National War Grave, and its eerie form can be seen lying on the sea floor on a calm bright day. (Diving is forbidden.)

St Mary's was a ferry point to Burray and South Ronaldsay before the Churchill Barriers were erected (see Burray). It is now a very peaceful village, its loch often graced with a family of swans nesting in the rubble remains of a broch on its shoreline. Nearby is Graemeshall, a substantial residence of one of the few large land-owners of the area, impressive amidst its extensive collection of farm buildings and now housing a spectacular collection of antiques (enquire at the Tourist Office for visiting hours).

The eastern edge of the landmass is slightly raised, enough for the sea to sculpture a comb of cliffs and geos that only rarely allows sandy beaches to disrupt the pattern. One of these beaches achieved great fame during the 1890s when a creature presumed to be a mermaid was sighted many times off Newark Bay, unromantically described in the *Fish Trades Gazette:* 'It is about six or seven feet in length, has a little black head, white neck, a snow-white body and two arms, and in swimming just appears like a human being. At times it will appear to be sitting on a sunken rock, and will wave and work its hands.' Whatever it was, it proved a great tourist attraction, partly because so many tales and legends of these islands are linked with the 'sea people' (see Eynhallow). It is easy to dismiss all folklore as superstition but recently an old Orcadian saying that metal is sharper when the tide is coming in has been scientifically proved, and so has solved many problems connected with precision instruments. Along the shores can be found the circular remains of old kelp kilns. The kelp industry caused a great shortage of domestic servants in the early 1800s as it provided much higher wages. Records surviving from Deerness parish show that a man could earn 16 shillings and four stones of meal for a month's labour and women approximately half that amount.

Near Mull Head is the ruin of an old chapel, an important place of pilgrimage until the 17th century (the Reformation did not hit so hard in Orkney as in other places). According to a 16th century writer, 'Jo Ben', male pilgrims walked barefoot around the holy building, chanting recitations and scattering stones and water behind them. No other records throw any further light on the whys and wherefores. Close by can still be seen hog-backed stones, renowned as houses of the dead, and keel-shaped triangular-sectioned stone slabs, often with incised patterns of decorations, which were probably Viking graves. Thus, this is almost certainly a very old site of worship.

The waters of Mull Head are recorded as the scenes of several Viking sea battles. The *Orkneyinga Saga* recounts in vivid detail how Earl Thorfinn, one of the most powerful of the Orkney earls who built the chapel at Birsay (see North Mainland), was chased by one Karl (possibly King Duncan of Scotland) from Caithness across the Pentland Firth, until with the aid of darkness he was able to shelter off Deerness. Morning brought a surprise attack by Karl but although his boats and men outnumbered those of Thorfinn, the Viking's stamina, cunning and seamanship routed the Scots. The *Saga* later describes the battle between Earl Paul and Olvir Rosta (Roaring Oliver) of Helmsdale, enacted in these same waters. This was decided when one of the Earl's warriors hurled a large rock at Olvir and knocked him overboard. The age of chivalry had not yet begun to dictate fighting procedures!

A monument on the coast west of the head is a sad reminder of fighting of later centuries. In 1679 the Covenanters were defeated by Government forces at Bothwell Brig because of the quarrelling between their own leaders. The captives were held for five long months at Greyfriars in Edinburgh before most of them undertook not to take up arms again if freed. The stubborn ones, numbering about 250, were placed in a ship, the *Crown*, which set sail for Jamaica or Virginia (records do not agree) in November, a hazardous time to begin such a journey. She subsequently came to grief on the rocks of Scarva Taing, nearly all the crew and captives being drowned. Ugly rumours that the ship was never meant to reach its destination, being of bad repair and having practically no food on board, were much exploited by the religious historians.

St Peter's Bay is a popular place for wintering duck and waders, as it is well protected from the blasts of the North Sea.

Accommodation:
St Nicolas Guest House, Holm (tel Holm 320)
B & B or self-catering — details from the Tourist Office
Sea Angling:
Wells, St Nicolas Manse, Holm (tel Holm 320)

South Mainland
The central area of Orkney Mainland is dominated by the three peaks of Wideford Hill (740 ft/275 m), Keelylang (770 ft/220 m), and Ward Hill (860 ft/263 m), all of which are worth climbing on a clear day for views over the archipelago. Often in Orkney the most exciting views are illuminated when the light is heavy and intense, with only patches of direct sunlight, as then the difference of shades is exaggerated, as immortalized by the canvases of Stanley Cursiter, R.A. Too much sun hazes the vistas, casting a magic over the greenness of the isles.

In **Summerdale**, the valley separating Keelylang from Ward

Hill, was fought the last battle on Orkney soil, in 1529. When Orkney had passed to Scotland in 1471, it had been agreed that the Earldom would not be alienated from the Scottish crown unless it was given to a legitimate son of the king. As with so many other medieval agreements, this clause was disregarded, never once having been given to a legitimate royal son! At first the guardians were sympathetic and generous men, but Lord Henry Sinclair, the King's Justice, was killed at the Battle of Flodden, 1513, with his master, and although his duties were transferred to his brother, Sir William Sinclair of Warsetter, his widow, Lady Sinclair, continued to collect the rents. This ambitious lady managed to get her son, William, appointed Justice depute, and with his mother's encouragement and active help he seized the Palace of Kirkwall. Sir William's sons, James and Edward, evicted him, whereupon he fled to Caithness and persuaded James V to place charges of homicide against his cousins. With the help of the Earl of Caithness, William landed an army on the Orphir coast in 1529 and met his cousins with their local supporters on the moors of Summerdale. St Magnus looked after his own people and William was severely defeated. James was soon pardoned and knighted although for some mysterious reason his brother Edward had to wait several years before he too earned royal approval. James V offered the Earldom to the Earl of Moray, who was wise enough to reject this headache. After negotiations by Denmark to redeem the islands had come to nothing, Orkney continued to be managed by the Sinclair family until the Stewart earls began their unpopular reign.

These moors are still haunted by their warriors, human no longer but birds of prey. Many can be seen at the National Nature Reserve of **Hobbister Hill**, notably merlins, kestrels, short-eared owls and the polygamous hen harriers. Waders can also be found along the shores of **Waulkmill Bay**. The images of folklore are not out of harmony with recorded history: in the 1830s a sea monster raised a long neck and head out of the water of **Swanbister Bay** and contemporary descriptions suggest that this beast was not dissimilar to that believed to inhabit Loch Ness.

The parish of **Orphir** (ON or-fjara — 'out of' low water) which envelops all this area, owes its fame to a tiny, now ruined church. Jarl Hakon Paulsson, the rival and murderer of St Magnus (see Egilsay) appeared to have been reformed by his guilt into a model ruler. As penance for his sins, he went on a pilgrimage to the Holy Land and returned to instigate the building of a 'magnificent church'. As the circular design of Orphir church can be related to the Church of the Holy Sepulchre in Jerusalem, and the surviving masonry can be dated back to the early 12th century, it seems likely that this is the Jarl's church. Only the apse remains standing as much of the stonework was reused in the later, now demolished, parish church, but its geometrical form is clearly indicated on the ground, as is the great Viking drinking hall or Bu also described in the *Orkneyinga*

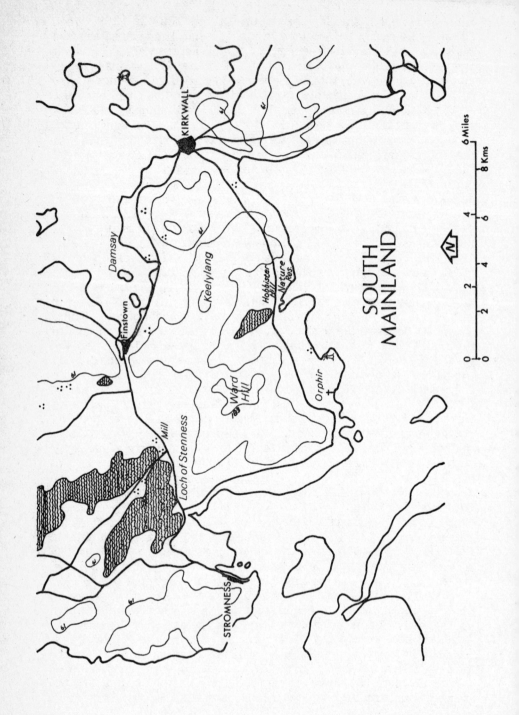

KIRKWALL

Damsay

Finstown

Keelylang

Hobbister Hill

Nature Res.

Ward Hill

783

Mill

Loch of Stenness

Orphir

STROMNESS

SOUTH
MAINLAND

N

0   2   4   6 Miles
0   2   4   6   8 Kms

Saga. The Christian Vikings frequently grounded their boats to celebrate the Christmas festivals by a mixture of prayers and drink.

The two brother earls, Harald Hakonarson (Smooth Tongue) and Paul, sons of Hakon Paulson, inherited his domain although they had been quarrelling since birth. At Orphir one Christmas, Harald spotted a fine linen shirt which his mother had made as a seasonal gift for his brother and was overcome with jealousy. Although she warned him that his life would be at risk if he wore the shirt, he insisted on trying it on and soon became ill with shivering and died. Paul was eventually forced to renounce the Earldom in favour of Rognvald, the cathedral builder (see Kirkwall), but he does not seem to have been unduly concerned by the wandering spirit of his sibling.

By the 18th century, the islanders had become more superstitious. An inhabitant of Orphir was hauled up before the Kirk Session, for his heathen practices — he had placed grains of corn between his dead spouse's toes, fingers and teeth, that her spirit might be prevented from returning to trouble her step-daughter.

The **Hill of Midland**, west of Orphir was renowned for its small quarries which yielded the red and yellow sandstone used in many of the 17th century tombstones and commemorative plaques throughout Orkney.

The **Unstan Chambered Tomb** (key from the nearest cottage) is a neolithic cairn of the stalled type. Its exterior is in the shape of an over-turned pudding basin of green turf, and its interior divided into a series of compartments by large upright slabs bound into the masonry. Not as spectacular as Midhouse (see Rousay) for its size or stonework, Unstan is notable for the quantity of pottery found within the chamber, dating from the mid-4th millenium BC. Quite why the pots were left here is an archaeologist's puzzle. The cairn gave its name to the type of pottery found here — coarse earthenware with simply decorated rims, though none can be seen inside it today. It sits beside **Loch Stenness**, one of the best trout fishing lochs in Orkney (boats from Standing Stones Hotel, tel Stromness 850 449), which boasts a record catch of a 29 lb (13 kg) trout. One wonders if the neolithic peoples enjoyed a menu of sea trout. The fishing varies considerably around the loch, as the salt water in the southern part seems to numb the brown trout, and even if it is too windy to fish from a boat, a pair of waders will usually gain positive results.

Frequently in these modern times, we hear complaints of how hard it is to maintain the fabric of a church from decreasing ecclesiastical funds, but ministers in the past had similar problems, especially as the thatch took so much upkeep. Responsibility was rotated around the parish, but the minister of **Stenness Parish Church** also demanded certain fines for those of his flock who broke the Lord's commandments. For women who violated the seventh commandment, the going rate was 'Bastard Bairns . . . a simmon clue (ball) apiece', as this straw rope was necessary for holding down the thatch.

A narrow strip of land separates Loch Stenness from Loch Harray which also provides excellent fishing (boat from Merkister Hotel, tel Harray 289, and Esslemont, Rango, Sandwick). This loch is important for wintering wild duck, especially pochard and tufted. Between the lochs stand two stone circles, the **Stones of Stenness** and the Ring of Brodgar. Silhouetted against the moors, they seem harmless on a sunny day, foreboding in less kind weather. The Ring of Brodgar is surrounded by a circular ditch cut out of the bedrock — a work of great labour but of a now unknown significance. The original 60 stones (27 are still standing) were laid out with careful precision, using the megalithic yard (2.72 ft/830 cm), round a circle with a diameter of 50 megalithic rods (1 rod equals 2.5 meg yards). The site has been dated to around 2000 BC. The Stones of Stenness are of a smaller scale and perhaps of an earlier date; the central altar is a misguided modern addition and attempt at explanation. Local folk traditions as recorded by Dr Robert Henry, an 18th century 'archaeologist', hold that the circle of Brodgar was a temple of the sun and that of Stenness a temple of the moon. Young lovers would make solemn vows and promises, she in the temple of the moon, he in the temple of the sun, and then together they would join hands through the hole in the Stone of Odin (felled in 1814) to complete their oaths. This ceremony was considered so binding that a Stromness woman followed her pirate lover to London and as he swung on the gallows, took up his hand once more and retracted her vows — the only possible way to free herself. The spring at **Bigswell** at the foot of Wardhill was considered even in this century to contain medicinal qualities.

The pudding basin of the Unstan Cairn is echoed on the shores of Loch Harray by the cairn of **Maeshowe**, the largest chambered cairn in Britain, described by Linclater as 'the masterwork of all, magnificent in construction and unique in its truly megalithic grandeur' (open Apr-Sep: 9.30 — 7.00 Mon-Sat, 2 — 7 Sun, Oct-Mar: 9.30 — 4.00 Mon-Sat, 2 — 4 Sun). Even the size of the pudding basin, 115 ft (35 m) in diameter and 24 ft (7.3 m) in height, does not prepare the visitor for the scale within. The long narrow passage, which forces all intruders to bend double, opens into a large central chamber, itself beautifully designed, the sides tapering inwards towards the roof, with three smaller chambers leading out of it. It may not be on the scale of the pyramids, but surely represents an admirable feat for people scraping a living in this hostile northern climate.

No grave goods were found by J Farrer, the 19th century archaeologist who excavated the tomb, but he was not the first intruder of recorded history. The walls bear an incredible collection of 12th century graffiti, some of it definitely coarse, some of it more poetic and artistic. Lines claim that 'The pilgrims to Jerusalem broke into Orkahow' which links this break-in to Jarl Hakon Paulsson, and other lines refer to a great treasure hidden in the north-west. If Maeshowe was used as a treasure house by the Vikings, and the lines refer to a contemporary treasure, not a neolithic one, then it is probably the treasure of Viking ornaments found at the **Bay of Skaill** in 1868, weighing 16 lb. Verses were also incised by the best runster in the west, using the axe that Gauk Thrandilsson once owned in the south of Iceland (there was nothing parochial about these men), and a warrior with an artistic eye inscribed the famous Maeshowe Dragon commemorating his visit.

The empty moor is generally unfriendly, yet one Victorian gentleman solved the problem of choosing a relatively sheltered site for his residence by erecting twelve flagstaffs one winter along the road to Finstown. The following spring he began to build Binscarth House where the least shredded flag stood, and now one of Orkney's largest woods is close by, a few acres squashed between **Cuiffe Hill** and the **Hill of Heddle** (good views north). Finstown is a pleasant village with a few old cottages still happily inhabited. For a change, it is not called after a Viking warrior or a mythological beast of the sea, but after an Irishman, Phin, who settled there in the early 19th century and established the Toddy Pub. He seems to have been a man of gentle disposition who ensured relative peace among his customers. A nice story is told of how two of his neighbours, both veterans of the American Civil War, but from opposing sides, met once a month at the Toddy Pub, to toast another Orcadian war veteran, General Cursiter, and to drink the Federal pension between them.

The **Bay of Firth** once had famous oyster beds, but a get-rich-quick plan to extend them by introducing foreign stock brought in disease and wiped out this delicacy. With the problems over fish quotas, many Orcadian fishermen have gone back to harvesting shell fish, the smaller boats gathering crabs and lobsters, the larger boats dredging for clams.

The small island of **Damsay** in the bay was a favourite refuge for quarrelsome Vikings as it was easy to defend. One of Jarl Rognvald's rivals came to an unseasonal end when he retired to his boat on the island's shore, dead drunk from celebrating the Christmas feast. The name Damsay has been linked with St Columba's biographer, Adamnan, for no very clear reason, but at one time there was a nunnery and a chapel on the island, dedicated to the Virgin. This serves as the explanation as to why no rats or mice survive there.

Chambered cairns were not always built on low-lying land. There are two on the hillsides of Wideford Hill and Cuween Hill of the Maeshowe type, but much smaller, good excuses for an easy walk across the moorland to views across the northern half of the island group. At **Rennibister** and on the outskirts of Kirkwall are two fine examples of **earth-houses** (sometimes known as souterrains), small chambers reached by sloping passages buried underground. The earth-house at Rennibister has small recesses or 'cupboards'. It has been suggested that these were used as larders or storehouses, although the method of construction does seem over-elaborate for simple food storage.

Accommodation:
Standing Stones Hotel, Stenness (tel Stromness 850 449)
Waulkmill Lodge, Waulkmill Bay (tel Kirkwall 24 27)
B & B, and Self-Catering — details from Tourist Office in Kirkwall.
Specialities:
Orkney Chairs — R Towers, St Olaf (tel St Olaf 3521)

Stromness
Best approached from the sea, Stromness's jumble of houses around the shore of the bay, piled high on the slopes of the Brinkies of Brae, comes as a surprise after the sultry heights of the cliffs of Hoy and the West Mainland. Originally Stromness was called Hamnavoe (ON — Bay of the Haven) by the Norse adventurers. They never found time enough to settle here but frequently slipped into the sheltered bay to avoid the sudden wind-whipped storms of the Atlantic, so setting the character of Stromness until this century. The twisting paved streets and narrow alley ways, revealing yet more cottages, warehouses and barns, and even the odd glimpse of boats on the shimmering water of private harbours, conjure up a scene of active merchants and trading intrigues — even before you set eyes on a retired and wizened seafarer contemplating the bustle of the piers.
   Stromness began to develop as a market town in the middle of the 17th century, mainly because Kirkwall was beyond a day's comfortable travel for the farmers' carts carrying the little extra they had managed to produce to raise a few pennies. Its position at the western edge of the Orkney group, on the excellent protected inland sea of the Scapa Flow, was soon spotted and developed by the Hudson's Bay Company whose ships used it from 1670 as their last port of call before crossing the Atlantic to Canada, pausing in June and November on their outward and return journeys to buy supplies and collect water. Login's Well on the main street bears the plaque: 'There watered here the Hudson Bay Co Ships 1670-1891; Capt Cook's vessels "Resolution" and "Discovery" 1780, Sir John Franklin's ships "Erebus" and "Terror" on Arctic exploration 1845; and also the merchant vessels of former days.' Captain Cook's vessels were returning from the Pacific after the great explorer had been murdered in Hawaii. Sir John Franklin's ships never returned from their attempt to find the North-West Passage (a sea route to Asia north of Canada). They were caught by ice west of King Williams Land and Franklin himself died in 1847, although some of his men proceeded under Captain Crozier, perhaps to discover a route through Baffin Bay. One of Orkney's sons, Dr John Rae, a medical

officer to the company, eventually established the fate of Sir John's expedition during one of his five epic voyages charting the Arctic coastlines. Many Orcadians were enlisted by the Hudson's Bay Company, and at one point the islanders comprized 75 per cent of its employees. The 5-year contracts enabled many a man to put by enough money to better himself and his family, although there were many social problems in the short term as the female population of the town tended to be thrice that of the male.

Stromness had become a town of 'younger sons' but at first its growth was limited by legislation. Until 1693 only freemen and burgesses of royal burghs were allowed to contract foreign trade and thus Kirkwall monopolized this profitable activity. In 1693 Parliament extended the right to lesser burghs on the payment of a tax, but as trade increased the Stromness merchants became increasingly reluctant to hand over a third of their profits to the Kirkwall businessmen. In 1743 they refused, under the leadership of Alexander Graham, and after 15 years of quarrelling finally affirmed their independence at great financial cost. Graham went bankrupt and died in poverty, but the solid stone-built houses of the old town tell of his peers' ensuing affluence.

Some of the more unusual exports from Stromness in the 18th century were rabbit skins — in 1792 36,000 skins were sold — and smoked and salted geese, both trades bringing money to the general population. Geese were such an important part of the Orcadian economy that many houses had goose nests built into the kitchen walls and a broody bird was often mentioned in testaments of the 19th century.

As the numbers employed by the Hudson's Bay Company declined in the 19th century, the fishing industry increased and soon Stromness became an important herring station, second only to Whitehall, (see Stronsay). Remains of the curing site can be seen at the campsite at Ness. Boats similar to those used, of the double-ended Norse type, can still be seen moored in the bay. Fishing for sillock took place around the harbour in the winter months, when the weather made herring fishing hazardous. A poke-net — a cord bag 6 — 10 ft in diameter, suspended from an iron ring and long pole — would be dropped onto the floor of the harbour, and then quickly raised as the fish fed on the bait. It must have been a curious sight, for the easiest way to raise a full net was for the man to lever the pole upright while he himself fell backwards. Today, more conventional rod fishing takes place off the numerous piers. The Victorians' love of good food encouraged the lobster trade; this is still maintained, and the lobster pool may still be visited (enquire at the Tourist Office).

The local museum (open 11 — 12.30, 1.30 — 5 Mon-Sat, 12.30 Thu), founded in 1837, is filled with intriguing if musty curios and should not be missed. Upstairs there is a spectacular collection of stuffed birds and animals — obviously Stromness once housed a fanatical taxidermist. Now most of his handicraft is sadly dusty and moth-eaten, but downstairs there is a more palatable collection of vivid seafaring exhibits — old chests and model ships, bills and mementoes brought home from far-flung places. There is a permanent exhibition of the scuttling of the German High Fleet in 1920. Captured at the end of the First World War, this fleet of over 200 vessels was held in the Scapa Flow until the War Office could decide what to do with it. As the indecision continued, the skeleton crews maintaining the ships perpetrated a final act of audacity, opening the stopcocks and sinking the fleet, thus ensuring that the vessels could never be added to the British forces. Since then, salvage teams have been trying to raise the vessels, for curios and more recently for the steel, as it is less radio-active than that made nowadays and is therefore in high demand by the makers of scientific machinery. Temporary exhibitions relate to other aspects of Stromness's history and in the archives is held a fascinating collection of photographs by the Edwardian photographer Tom Kent (ask the custodian if they are not on display).

Close by is Orkney's only antique shop, full of curios and cheap items, although sadly old Orkney chairs are difficult to obtain. There is also a friendly second-hand book shop specializing in island books. Do not forget that this is the home town of that literary lion, George Mackay Brown, whose works add colour to any visit to Orkney and provide an easy introduction to the Orcadian way of life. The library at Hellihole contains many old Orcadian books.

As on Hoy, the Second World War brought a great influx of people to Stromness, but it soon reverted to trading and fishing in its old gentle manner. The private jetties have been quiet in recent years, but the main piers still bustle with activity, centred around the large modern boats. An active participant in the St Magnus Festival (see Kirkwall), Stromness opened an ambitious art centre in 1979 — the Piers Art Centre (open 10.30 — 12.30, 1.30 — 5.00 Mon to Sat, 10.30 — 1.00 Thu) in an 18th century warehouse with its own jetty. Unexpectedly, it has a permanent modern art collection including works by Barbara Hepworth and Ben Nicolson, while also displaying temporary exhibitions in the small austere rooms — a pleasant and unpretentious centre which is impressively successful in its achievements, emphasizing the relevance of 'art' to the community. The town also has an indoor swimming pool and a golf course.

Accommodation:
Ferry Inn (tel Stromness 850 280)
Royal Hotel (tel Stromness 850 342)
Stromness Hotel (tel Stromness 850 298)
B & B and self-catering — details from the Tourist Office.
Stromness Youth Hostel, Town Hall.

Mrs Brown, 47 Victoria Street (tel Stromness 850 661) (private hostel)
Camp site
Car Hire:
Brass Self Drive (tel Stromness 850 750)
Firth Blue Garage (tel Stromness 850 403)
Wishart and Sons, The Garage (tel Stromness 850 224)
Bicycle Hire:
Groat & Leask, 65 Victoria Street
Swanson, Ferry Road
Sea Angling:
enquire: T Keldie, Bangor, Stromness.

Tourist Office:
Stromness (tel Stromness 850 716); open mid-June — mid-Sep:10-6
Mon — Sat; and to meet late ferries.
Bank:
The Royal Bank of Scotland
Early Closing:
Thursday
Specialities:
Fudge, oat cakes
Festivals:
July — Shopping Week

North Mainland
Along the west coast of Mainland Orkney is a low ridge of old red
sandstone hills, battered and beaten by the Atlantic waves into
monumental sculptures. Over the centuries, each fault and weak
point has been savagely attacked by the sea, which has eaten far into
the land. To appreciate the mammoth scale of these forms to the
full, one must walk along the edge — but not too close, as the carpet
of sea pinks is very slippery; much of the rock is rotten from the salt
spray and likely to crumble, and rescue cannot be guaranteed. The
best route is along the relatively inaccessible southern half, joining
the coast near Breck Ness and soon climbing the sharp slope of the
Black Craig, from where basking sharks can be seen circling the
waters below. All this coastline supports seabird cities, but do not get
sidetracked: better things are to come!

At Neban Point the cliffs have been carved into deep caves, arches
and stacks, and the view out to sea humbles all observers. It is a pity
that these cliffs have not attracted a Mendelssohn, for the combined
choruses of birds and waves, although not melodic, is most awe-
inspiring. Continuing along the green cliff tops, three crow-flying
miles brings the wanderer to Yesnaby, a renowned beauty spot with
extensive formations of caves and stacks in the making. Here the
carpet of spring green is speckled with the pale green leaves of
Primula Scotica, a very special small plant with rich purple flowers,
not unlike a small cowslip, which is found only in Caithness, Orkney

91

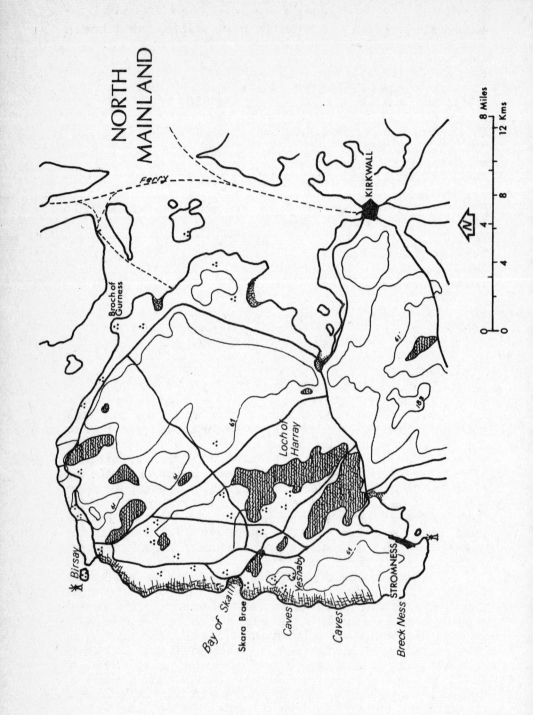

NORTH
MAINLAND

Ferry

KIRKWALL

Broch of
Gurness

Loch of
Harray

61

Birsay

Bay of Skaill

Skara Brae

Caves Yesnaby

Caves

STROMNESS

Breck Ness

N

0   4   8   12 Kms
0   4   8 Miles

and Shetland. Enjoy the flowers in May and June and again in July and August, but please do not pick them.

Along this coast you may find edible mushrooms which are much more tasty than shop bought specimens, but do not be overcome by mercenary impulses — Scottish law forbids picking wild produce beyond your own consumption. Always be careful to identify any other tempting fungi: only three species are fatally poisonous, but many more induce discomfort. Clear days bring views of Scotland beyond the sinister fringe of cliffs, but watch out for the bombing terns, who will fearlessly attack anyone who makes the mistake of venturing too near their nests. 3 more miles (5 km) north bring the walker to the point of the **Hole o'Row**, the most spectacular natural arch of this coast, and even more unexpectedly to the wide white sandy beach of Skaill, excellent for swimming as the seafloor drops away steeply.

It is said to be here that the Fin King was eventually conquered by the men of Sandwick. The Fin Folk were a people who farmed the seabeds (see Egilsay), often appearing to sailors in human form but sometimes more mischieviously chasing their boats disguised as monsters. Luckily their avarice enabled the crews to distract them easily enough, by throwing overboard a silver coin, and then slipping away unnoticed in the resulting quarrel for possession. Mermaids counted as one of their number, being able to cast off their tails and keep their beauty for life if they succeeded in wedding a human; the other option was to become increasingly uglier and bad tempered until they eventually evolved into the revolting Fin wife. Many tales are told of these folk but it was generally held to be a good thing when their fearsome King was killed in the Bay of Skaill.

It was in this sand that the Viking hoard of silver ornaments, possibly from Maeshowe (see South Mainland), was found in 1856. An even more exciting discovery was made here five years earlier, when a wild storm lifted vast quantities of sand from the surrounding dunes to reveal part of an ancient structure. Further archaeological investigation revealed the now famous neolithic village of **Scara Brae** (open Apr-Sept: 9.30-7.00 Mon-Sat, 2.00-7.00 Sun, Oct-Mar: 9.30-4.00 Mon-Sat, 2.00-4.00 Sun; admission 20p). Built about 4,500 years ago by a small community of Stone Age dwellers (probably numbering about 30), the village was inhabited for several generations, until the people were forced to move out by a sandstorm which choked their dwellings. Ten of these homes have been excavated, circular cells packed tightly together and connected by covered walk-ways meant for people smaller than us 20th century, meat-eating giants. They are in an astonishing state of preservation, most lacking only their roofs; the stone beds and dressers, cupboards and querns are exactly as they were when they were abandoned in c 2450 BC. Any woman walking through the huts will be grateful for her modern labour-saving devices, but the stone seats are surprisingly comfortable. Refuse heaps are at present being excavated in an attempt to determine the diet of these people, as they appear to have been farmers as well as fishermen and hunters.

Skaill House itself is a pleasant H-shaped building built in 1633, a witness to the early wealth of some of the lairds. Close by is the farm of **Stone**, of which a curious story is told to explain the title of The Belted Knights, handed down through the Kirkness family until the 19th century. Supposedly in the 1530s, the patriarch of the family was asked for work by a young wanderer with red hair. Like his neighbours, he tended to distrust strangers, but his hospitality overcame this dislike and he offered him breakfast. A daughter of the house begged that the young man be given the job of tending the geese and would not allow her father to drive too hard a bargain, although money was short. He proved to be a remarkably tidy goose-herd, taking a great deal of care over his appearance and the neighbours soon noticed that he used a golden comb, which aroused their curiosity. He became irritated by this unwelcome attention and decided it was time to move on. Informing his employer, he asked him to kneel, and dubbed him Sir John Kirkness, the Belted Knight of Stove. Could this have been one of James V's mysterious jaunts in disguise?

This area of the Mainland is less green and more moorlike than the rest of the island, partly because most of it has not yet been subjected to the plough. Much of Orkney was covered with the purple heather up until the Second World War. The parish of **Harray** is the only one of the archipelago which lacks a coastline, and hence there are many jokes at the expense of these landlubbers. Harray retained the old Viking system of land tenure for a long time after its neighbours and so became known as the parish of a hundred lairds, for all were freemen, unbound by the restraints of feudal obligations.

At **Corrigall** a farming museum has been opened to preserve memories of a rapidly fading way of life (open Apr-Sept: 10.30-1.00, 2.00-5.00 Mon-Sat, 2.00-7.00 Sun; admission free). These buildings date from the mid-18th century but have been restored to the mid-19th, showing the typical two rows with the living rooms in one unit and the byres, stables, barn and corn drying kiln behind. Similar to many of the ruins by the roadsides, Corrigall does not show a vast improvement on the houses of Scara Brae. The box beds, a 19th century innovation, may have been draught-free, but they were too small to stretch out in and in poorer houses a large family would pile into one, sometimes adding a shelf at the feet end for some of the children to sleep on. Note the stone flag roof carefully insulated with a lining of turf, and how similar the cow stalls are to the neolithic stalled cairns.

The story of agricultural life is completed by the **Norse Mill** off the B9057, built at a contemporary date from a design common to all Norse countries and, extraordinarily, also found in the mountains of North Pakistan. Sometimes called a 'click-mill', due to the sound made by the rotating wheel, it uses a very simple direct-drive mechanism, the water turning the paddles of the lower horizontal wheel which turns the grinding wheel — a very simple adaption of the hand quern. Cutting a pair of stones required great skill, since one had to be concave to fit the convex curve of the other. If the slope was too steep the corn was not properly ground when it reached the edge, and if the slope was too flat the precious effort of the crofting wife was wasted. Life was not without amusement in those days, and even a death brought some light moments. It was the custom to sit up with the body until it was buried, the neighbours all gathering around the bereaved before and not after the funeral, when the whiskey bottle was naturally circulated. One drunken funeral party dropped the coffin they were carrying to the grave-yard as they crossed a stream in full spate; they eventually recovered it floating down the middle of Loch Harray.

One of the tragedies of the First World War occurred off **Marwick Head** on the night of 5 June 1916, when HMS *Hampshire* hit a mine and went down with all but a handful of the crew. She was carrying Field Marshal Lord Kitchener of Khartoum, who was on his way to give some much needed advice to the Russian generals. The incident is shrouded in mystery as War Office reports do not coincide with local memories of the evening, and it seems odd that the ship should have been travelling on an unswept route. Because of a general neurosis over security, the islanders were forbidden to help in the rescue and many lives were needlessly lost. A memorial now marks the headland (good for bird watching).

At **Birsay** there are the ruins of another Stewart palace-cum-fortress, built in 1574 and described in the 17th century as having walls painted with biblical scenes. An armorial stone can be seen above the doorway. Now a mere shell hugged by the road, the palace was a masterpiece of planning, the architect making sure it could easily withstand a siege by incorporating archery butts, kail-yards and even a rabbit warren within its walls.

A low causeway leads to the small tidal islet of **Brough of Birsay**, ringed with small cliffs, and a favourite site of the early Christian and Viking settlers: (open Apr-Sept: 9.30-7.00 Mon-Sat, 2.00-7.00 Sun; Oct-Mar: 9.30-4.00 Mon-Sat, 2.00-4.00 Sun). The first community was a group of monks who built a small chapel and left several graveslabs including one (now in the National Museum of Antiquities, Edinburgh) carved with abstracted Pictish symbols and three bare-headed armed warriors in stately procession. Continuing excavations every summer by the students of Durham University have revealed a large village of Viking longhouses and it appears to be they who rebuilt the church. This is possibly the Christchurch built by Jarl Thorfinn the Mighty on his return from a pilgrimage to Jerusalem in the 11th century, which soon became the episcopal seat of Orkney.

After St Magnus was killed (see Egilsay), his mother gained permission to move his remains here and it is said that a light shone continuously over his grave. Soon this became an important pilgrimage centre, though without official approval, the poor and the ill journeying from all over the island to be cured. The then Bishop William (see Kirkwall) became increasingly antagonistic towards such shows of piety and tried to prevent them. One day, however, he was struck blind while at prayer, and his sight was restored only when he promised to treat the relics with due respect. Eventually they were transcribed to the new cathedral in Kirkwall.

Aikerness is a superb example of how the Iron Age peoples chose their fortress sites, for the Broch of Gurness commands an extensive view of Rousay across the Eynshallow Sound. Little could have passed through the Strait without escaping the notice of the occupants of Gurness or Midhouse (see Rousay) (open Apr-Sept: 9.30-7.00 Mon-Sat, 2.00-7.00 Sun: Oct-Mar — 9.30-4.00 Mon-Sat, 2.00-4.00 Sun). This is the most extensive broch site yet excavated in Orkney. It is slightly difficult to identify the dwellings which circle the sturdy fortress, but there is a good detailed guide, and a museum on the site contains many of the artefacts found there.

In the church yard of Rendall, there is a hogbacked Viking tomb stone (see East Mainland, N Ronaldsay) which has a curious association, supposedly marking the Queen of Morocco's grave. Could this be associated with some ship wreck, or did a high ranking noblewoman of the Mediterranean really visit the Orkney parliament at Tingwall, catch flu from the cold, and die there?

Accommodation:
Barony Hotel, Birsay (tel Birsay 327)
Smithfield Hotel, Dounby (tel Harray 215)
Woodwich Guest House, Furie (tel Evie 221)
B & B, and Self-Catering — details from Tourist Office, Kirkwall
Birsay Hostel, contact Mr Drewer, Education Offices, Kirkwall (tel Kirkwall 3535)
Mrs Taylor, Evie Hostel, Flaws (tel Evie 208)
Boats for Loch Fishing:
Swanney Loch — Sinclair (tel Birsay 230)
                E Sabiston (tel Birsay 256)
                F Sabiston (tel Birsay 255)
Boardhouse Loch — Barony Hotel (tel Birsay 200)
                Moar (tel Birsay 282)
                Hay (tel Birsay 270)
                Leask, Birsay
Harray Loch   Sinclair (tel Harray 289)
                Esslemont, Sandwick
Hunland Loch — Sinclair (tel Harray 257)

Specialities:
Weaving — Kerdroseed, Sandwick (tel Sandwick 628); open Mon-Fri
2.00-5.00
Sheepskins

Westray
(ON vestrey — west island)

Connections:
By air: from Kirkwall: Mon, Wed, Fri, Sat, two a day; Tue, Thu,
three a day. Loganair Ltd (tel Kirkwall 2494).
By sea: from Kirkwall: three times a week, route varies around
northern isles. Details from Orkney Islands Shipping Co Ltd (tel
Kirkwall 2044).

Westray is the largest of the northern isles, sheltered by its own ridge
of hills running down its western side, with very fertile fields which
continue to support a (relatively) large population. Other Orcadians
claim that these islanders are to be distinguished by their Spanish
blood, introduced at the time of the Armada when a storm drove
the Spanish fleet north, wrecking many boats on these northern
isles. Why this should apply to Westray in particular has never been
satisfactorily explained, but perhaps the overwhelming love of their
home island has knit the community bond tighter here than elsewhere.
Even today, the young are not keen to leave the island even for a
short while to train. As yet few southerners, or incomers as they
are called, have settled here and the harmonious community extends
an open-handed hospitality to all visitors.

The cliffs of the west coast are not especially high, rarely rising
above 200 ft (60 m) but the sea has carved out marvellous forms in
the red sandstone. Around **Noup Head** is a very large colony of
guillemots and other seabirds, breeding on the weathered shelves
of the sandstone; this whole area, including North Hill, is controlled
by the RSPB as a nature reserve. Wild-fowling was especially important in Westray, for up until the end of the 19th century, many
men depended on harvesting the cliffs for their livelihood. As early
as 1693, writing pens made from goose quills were one of Orkney's
main exports. Over the centuries the fowlers developed ingenious
methods of catching their quarry. The most efficient way was for
men in two boats to hold a net on poles across a geo or cave, while
some others frightened the birds into leaving their roosts and flying
straight into it. Often the site was not suitable for this, so many were
caught by a small triangular net suddenly raised across their flight
paths as they left or returned to their nests. To take sitting birds,
a noose of horse hair was fixed to a long pole and slipped over the

97

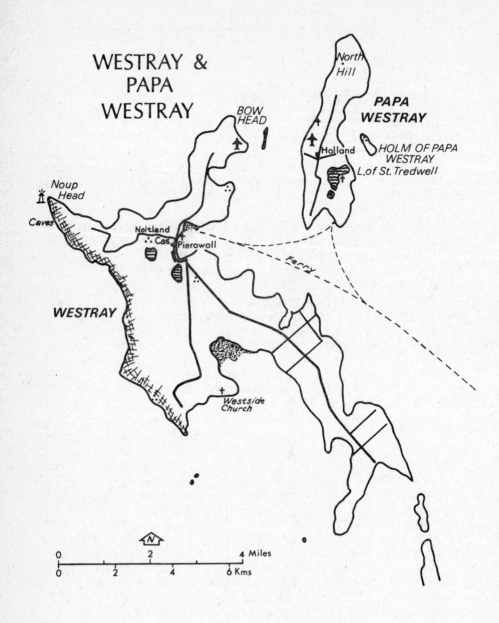

WESTRAY &
PAPA
WESTRAY

BOW
HEAD

North
Hill

PAPA
WESTRAY

Noup
Head

Holland

HOLM OF PAPA
WESTRAY
L. of St. Tredwell

Caves

Noltland
Cas.
Pierowall

Ferry

WESTRAY

Westside
Church

N

0			2		4 Miles
0	2		4	6 Kms	

poor broody bird's neck, before it realized what was happening. Here, as elsewhere, many eggs were collected from the ledges, involving an initial expedition to break those already laid and a second a few days later to collect the fresh eggs.

To watch the crashing waves and the thousands of screaming birds is mesmerizing even for the most ignorant onlooker — a pair of binoculars and a bird book makes this pastime addictive. Many caves have been carved in the foot of these cliffs. To the Gentleman's Cave, one of the Balfours of Trenabie (later of Shapinsay fame) retreated with some friends for the winter, after having supported the Young Pretender, Bonnie Prince Charlie, in his defeat at the Battle of Culloden (1746). The men of Westray are claimed to be the only Orcadians to have supported the Jacobite cause, and for many years they continued to gather in the cave to drink the health of the 'King Over the Water', so avoiding the beady eyes of the Government informers.

Noltland Castle, a rugged fortress with more gun loops than is normal for Renaissance buildings, commands the hill slope above Pierowall. The z-shaped form of a rectangular keep and two square corner towers, each protecting two sides of the centre, is a standard 16th century formula, combining the practicalities of defence with a desire for more comfort. As Dr Simpson has pointed out, 'it was built for a man with a bad conscience — for a man with fear in his heart'. This man was Gilbert Balfour from Fife who was given the lands of Westray by his brother-in-law, Adam Bothwell, Bishop of Orkney, in 1560. Gilbert and his two brothers were deeply involved in the intrigues surrounding Mary Queen of Scots and her court. Having associated themselves with the Protestant cause early, they were involved in the murder of Cardinal Beaton and the subsequent siege of St Andrew's Castle in 1566. For this crime all three of them served in a French galley with John Knox. Described by Knox as 'men without God', the brothers were not deflated for long and Gilbert soon reappeared as Master of Queen Mary's household. A friend of the Earl of Bothwell, he may have played a dominant part in the murder of Darnley, but on Bothwell's disgrace, he retired to his castle, furiously quarrelling with his brother-in-law, Adam, and refusing help to the fugitive, Earl Bothwell, when he too arrived in Orkney. Parliament found him guilty of treason in August 1571 and confiscated his lands, presumably including Noltland; however, by October, he was leading troops in support of Queen Mary, successfully capturing Blackness Castle on the Forth. Lord Robert Stewart, later Earl of Orkney, the Queen's half-brother, had meanwhile seized Noltland, but the Bishop Adam having changed his loyalties from Rome to the Reformation, put forward a rival claim, and in the end the Privy Council returned it to its legal owner, ie Gilbert Balfour. Life proved too quiet at Noltland and with the collapse of Queen Mary's cause he fled to Sweden, where his intrigues against their King led to his execution in 1576.

The 71 gunloops were obviously considered necessary by this lawless man, and make the interior of the castle very dark and foreboding. However, the rooms of the first floor are convenient and pleasantly lit (with good views across to Papa Westray). The wide and easy stairway was built by Earl Patrick Stewart, the architect son of Robert, after he had won the castle from Sir Michael Balfour. Note the large carved capital newel with the double-headed eagle of the Holy Roman Empire — sadly, some of the details of this carving have now been eroded. The castle was probably never finished, although the courtyard dates from a late period, the arched entrance forebodingly inscribed 'When I see the blood I will pass over you in the night'. The key and a guide are available from the farm opposite (Apr — Sep: 9.30 — 7.00 Mon-Sat, 2.00 — 7.00 Sun; Oct — Mar: 9.30 — 4.00 Mon — Sat, 2.00 — 4.00 Sun).

On the dunes north of the castle, an interesting excavation has been In progress for several summers, trying to determine something of the lifestyle of the peoples who inhabited neolithic villages, such as Skara Brae (see North Mainland). There is not much to look at in the winter for this settlement is not as spectacular as Skara Brae, but the archaeologists and the 30 — 40 volunteers who help them each summer will turn it into a mine of information about diet and lifestyles, all deduced from their scholarly analysis of the midden piles. As can be imagined, this minute scraping of waste heaps, all be they neolithic ones, gives rise to much local humour. This was especially true in the summer of 1980, when all the islanders were themselves digging trenches for hydro-electric cables (before this each house had its individual battery-run generator).

The Westray folk are great ones for pulling a yarn — an evening spent in the local pub at Pierowall will be remembered for a long time. One famous tale concerns the farmer who summoned two neighbours to help him make a coffin in which to bury his wife. On hearing that there were whales in the bay he slipped off to join the boats chasing them onto the beach, carefully leaving his helpers at work. When the laird, who was in charge of dividing the catch, expressed surprise at seeing him on such a day, he replied, 'I could na afford to lose baith wife and whales on the same day'. Here as elsewhere, the whale oil brought in a welcome bit of cash.

The golf course, even if grazed by cattle in winter, is a fine place to enjoy the long summer nights (enquire at W I Rendall's Shop, Pierowall).

Pierowall is a pleasant little village strung out around the bay, recorded even in Viking times as a fine harbour. Jarl Rognvald Kali Kolsson used it in 1136 at the beginning of his successful campaign to subdue Orkney, having first made a vow to build a church to St Magnus — the cathedral now standing in Kirkwall. A large number of pagan Viking graves were found in the sandy banks of the bay in the 19th century (no traces are left today), and it is probable that the church where Rognvald attended a service was on the same site as the 13th century Lady Kirk. This is a small roofless church, considerably altered around 1674 (the date on the skewput of the gable between the nave and chancel). Inside are two 17th century tomb slabs with beautifully carved lettering for 'ane vertuous gentlewoman' and 'ane worthy gentleman'.

The Westray islanders have always been renowned fishermen, and several large trawlers are based here beside many smaller lobster boats. The old mill buildings, still in good repair, are now used to store the creels. Recently the boats have started fishing for clams; with the dredging technique, there is no longer any need to leave valuable equipment out in waters whose moods change so impulsively. The local fish factory at Gill Pier provides much needed employment.

Westside church is reached by any easy walk across the flower-rich meadows. This is another ruin dating from the 12th century. Only an arch remains standing, by the seashore — a reminder of the times when people came to church by boat, with good views south of the little skerries and islets, Rousay, Egilsay and Eday.

Accommodation:
Pierowall Hotel
B & B and self-catering — details from Tourist Office, Kirkwall.
Car Hire:
J Hume, Pierowall Cottage (tel Westray 317).
T Logie (tel Westray 218).
Bank:
Sub-office, twice weekly, enquire locally.
Specialities:
Knitting: this is organized into the Westray Knitters Society Ltd, East Surriegarth (tel Westray 323). The local women make up Fair Isle and plain jerseys, experimenting with new designs and patterns. They welcome orders and encouragement.

Enquire here about the Orkney chairs still made by a few men in their homes to the old designs, with fine Japanese oak woodwork and the traditional hard straw backs to keep out the draughts. Again, orders are willingly accepted, although as elsewhere the demand outstrips supply.

There is also a good bakery at Pierowall.

Papa Westray
(ON papey) island of the monks)

Connections:
By air: from Kirkwall (via Westray) — the shortest scheduled air service in the world — a brief two-minute hop!: Tue, Thu, Sat; two a day. Loganair Ltd (tel Kirkwall 2494).

By sea: from Kirkwall: three a week; route varies around northern isles. Details from Orkney Islands Shipping Co Ltd (tel Kirkwall 2044).

A small island lying east of Westray, Papa Westray has much of interest to offer the ornithologist and archaeologist. The northern end, once the island's common grazing land, is now an RSPB reserve (a summer warden lives in the cottage opposite the gate). The cliffs of Fowl's Craig, famous as one of the last European breeding sites of the great auk (the last male bird was shot in 1813), are now covered with vast kittiwake, guillemot and shag colonies, while the moorland of North Hill is littered with the largest British colony of Arctic terns. Numbers are meaningless for the sizes of these colonies. The flurry of wings and tuneless choruses of squawks and cries give an overwhelming impression of the multitude no cold-blooded (and necessarily in-accurate) figures could impose. There are plans to lay out a path along the coastal edge of the reserve, but meantime visitors should consult the warden before they wander onto the site, needlessly disturbing the nesting birds. The Arctic tern chicks are especially vulnerable to the predatory nature of the bombing bonxies (great skuas), although their parents will also display a vicious nature to intruders. The actual vegetation of the area is of great scientific interest, being a herb-rich dwarf shrub heath, a community of plants which forms only on old red sandstone. To the layman, this means easy walking and a chance to find mushrooms and the Scottish primrose (primula scotica) — a beautiful purple flower, with a yellow eye, found only in Caithness, Orkney and Shetland. It flowers in May and June and again in July and August.

Along the east side is a series of wetlands, caused by bad drainage — ponds and marshes covered with reeds and yellow irises which attract and shelter duck and other wild fowl. Lock Tredwell takes its name from a small ruined chapel, of uncertain date, on its eastern shore. St Tredwell was a Celtic abbess sent on a mission to the Picts, who attracted the unwelcome attentions of Nechtan, King of the Picts, who admired especially her beautiful eyes. Escaping, she plucked out her eyes and sent them to Nechtan to impress upon him the folly of admiring her physical attributes and then retired to a nunnery in Midlothian. How this chapel came to be dedicated to her is forgotten, but by the 12th century it had become a place of pilgrimage for those with eye troubles. Bishop John of Caithness is said to have been cured here in 1201, after his eyes had been gouged out by Earl Harald of Serabster. For some other obscure reasons, St Tredwell also appealed to sailors requiring fair winds.

The island is probably named after another religious site, that of St Boniface, north of the air strip, where archaeologists have traced a modest settlement predating the late 12th century and now standing in a parlous state. Boniface was the missionary bishop who converted much of Germany with the help of Charlemagne's forbears. The surrounding graveyard, besides being of interest to the ornithologist as a shelter for spring and autumn migrants, has the wider attraction of a hogbacked gravestone — a long triangular-sectioned block of red sandstone, carved with a scalelike ornament (easier felt than seen under the lichen), marking a Christian Viking's tomb. Also found here, but now displayed in the Tankerness Museum, Kirkwall and the National Museum of Antiquities, Edinburgh, were several Celtic crosses carved on stone, the motifs of which have been adapted in silver jewellery sold by Ortak Jewellery, Kirkwall.

On the farmlands of Holland was discovered the oldest standing house in Western Europe, the Knap of Howar (knob of the mounds). From radiocarbon analysis of the bones found in the midden heaps, scientists have proposed a date of inhabitation of c 3500 to 3100 BC. The two adjacent houses face across the sound to Westray. The internal division of stabs and posts is still obvious in the larger cell, presumably separating the inner kitchen or working area with the hearth (a quern is still in its original position by the wall) from the outer room, perhaps used for sleeping (note the low bench against the wall). The second building, built slightly later, probably provided extra storage space, hence the stone shelves and 'dressers'. Artifacts have been found which link the inhabitants with those who built the chambered tombs; doubtless they were attracted to the unusually fertile pastures here.

On the uninhabited Holm of Papa Westray is a large chambered cairn. Essentially of the Maes Howe type (see South Mainland), the long (100 ft/30 m) cairn has been hollowed into a central chamber passage with 14 cells built into the thickness of the wall. The size and high quality of the stonework implies the importance of this site, as do the few stones decorated by the original users with eyebrow, zigzag and circular motifs. (Enquire at the Co-op about a possible boat trip, but the sound is fast flowing and even on a calm summer's day the passage may be difficult.)

Papa Westray is a good place to study the traditional Orkney buildings. Because the land is often passed on to the farmers of Westray, many houses now stand empty while the fields are still pastured. The Co-op has brought a revival of enthusiasm among the remaining islanders (around 100), providing a wide selection of goods while bolstering up their pride in the old traditions and crafts.

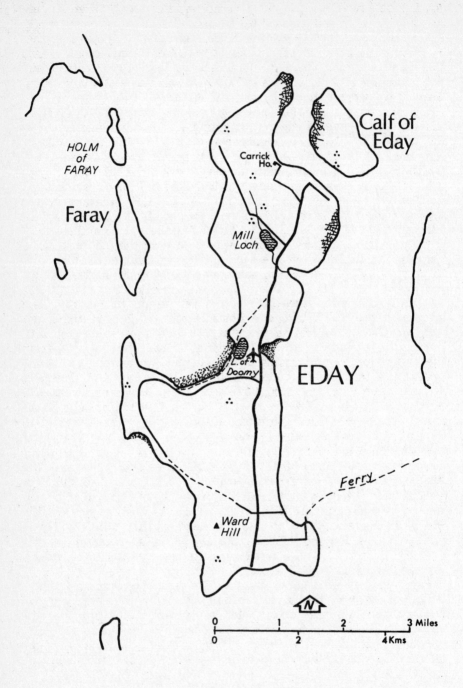

Calf of
Eday

HOLM
of
FARAY

Faray

Carrick
Ho.

Mill
Loch

L. of
Doomy

EDAY

Ferry

▲ Ward
Hill

N

0   1   2   3 Miles
0   2   4 Kms

Accommodation:
Enquiries to the Papay Community Cooperative Ltd, Baltane House (tel Papa Westray 267).

Until the guest house and hostel is completed (? 1981/2), visitors are invited to stay in the islanders' houses, joining other travellers for meals as arranged by the Co-op. The project is still in its infancy, but although there may be minor teething problems, these are more than compensated for by the openhanded welcome and general spirit of camaraderie that envelops this island.

Bank:
Monthly.

Specialities:
Traditional and modern straw work.

Eday
(ON eioay — island of the isthmus)

Connections:
By air: from Kirkwall: Mon, Wed, Fri, two a day (via Stronsay); Sat, two a day (continuing to N. Ronaldsay). Loganair Ltd (tel Kirkwall 2494).

By sea: from Kirkwall, three times a week, route varies around northern isles; details from Orkney Island Shipping Co Ltd (tel Kirkwall 2044).

Eday is the most bleak and barren of the northern isles, dominated by moorland, with only the southern end being extensively cultivated. The sharp division between cultivated and uncultivated land is due not so much to the qualities of the soil as to the difference of ownership, and thus shows what most of Orkney must have been like prior to enclosures and intensive farming. Eday is different to its neighbours in that its blanket of moorland covers extensive supplies of peat; in the 18th and 19th centuries this fuel was Eday's major export commodity. The variety of habitats to be found on the island makes it a favourite for birdwatchers. The moorland lochs attract divers and the Red Head cliffs (red sandstone) at the north end house many seabirds, mainly kittiwake and guillemot, while the small woodlands nearby give shelter to smaller species, such as the tree sparrow. On the eastern cliffs of the Calf of Eday there are large colonies of kittiwake and guillemot, while on its heather top moorland-nesting blackbacked gulls rear their young. Calf Sound is very fast flowing; even on the calmest day the currents may shoot through at 6 knots, so it is advisable to ask an islander to ferry you across.

Eday has the usual (for Orkney) selection of archaeological edifices — the setter standing stone looking like a giant's hand, and

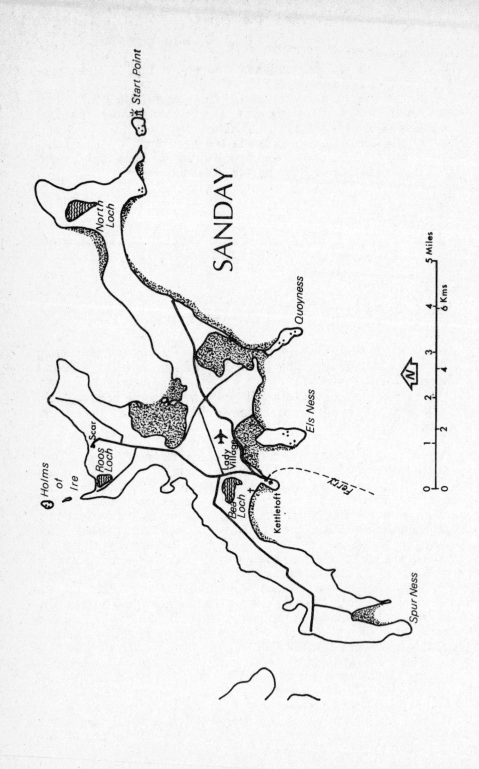

SANDAY

Start Point

North Loch

Quoyness

Scar

Holms
ot
Ire

Roos
Loch

Lady
Village

Els Ness

Bea
Loch

Kettletoft

Ferry

Spur Ness

N

0   1   2   3   4   5 Miles

0   2   4   6 Kms

the stalled cairn near Sandyhill Smith which yielded some Iron Age implements when excavated in 1937. The chambered cairn by Huntersquoy is unusual because it is composed of two contemporary cairns placed one above the other, each with separate passages. (None of these sites is in care.)

Perhaps more exciting is the history of **Carrick House.** James Stewart, the second son of Earl Robert Stewart, was created Earl of Carrick in 1628 and proceeded to build Carrick House — the dating stone of 1633 can still be seen above the door. However, he was then accused, in association with the local witch, Alysoun Balfour, of plotting to poison his brother, Earl Patrick Stewart. Need it be said that while she was tortured into confessing, he had only to survive the gossip and went scot-free. In 1725 James Fea of Whitehall, Stronsay, again brought Carrick House, by then his home, into the limelight, by capturing the notorious pirate Gow. Born in Stromness, Gow returned to Orkney with an elaborate reputation, only to run aground on the Calf of Eday, hence James Fea's success at securing him for trial in London and inevitable execution. His exploits are crystallized in Robert Louis Stevenson's story of 'The Pirate'. The bell of Gow's ship, *The Revenge*, is now kept within the house.

In the 18th and 19th centuries Eday was remarkably wealthy; besides selling peat, its quarries supplied the slate for Kirkwall while most of Orkney's salt came from the salt pans on the Calf of Eday, all of which accounts for the many largish buildings. In the 1860s the island suffered a rapid decline, due directly to the importing of coal, and it now presents a rather sad aspect with many crumbling cottages and continuing depopulation.

Accommodation:
Eday Hotel, Mr W Grey, Schoolplace (tel Eday 263).
Self-catering, details from the Tourist Office, Kirkwall.
Car Hire:
T Reid, Croyhouse (tel Eday 228).
Bank:
Sub-office open monthly. Enquire locally.
Sea Angling Boat Hire:
Mr Thompson, Heathercrow (tel Eday 256).

Sanday
(ON sandey — sand island)

Connections:
By air: from Kirkwall: at least two a day except Sun (one via Stronsay). Loganair Ltd (tel Kirkwall 2494).

By sea: from Kirkwall: Mon, Wed, Fri, via other islands. See monthly timetable for details. Orkney Island Shipping Co Ltd (tel Kirkwall 2044).

An accurate map of 1750 shows Sanday as a much smaller island, suggesting that its present size is due to sand banks joining up with smaller outcrops of rock. Its long spars are held down by a net of marram grass housing an incredible number of rabbits (rabbit skins were a major export from Orkney at the turn of the 18th century), together with the red-billed black and white oyster catchers, lapwings and curlews. The land appears less well maintained than on the other eastern isles, and room has been found for the Sanday golf course on the dunes of 'Plain of Fidge': apply at Newark Farm (golf clubs available) but be warned that it is grazed by cattle all winter!

Archaeological remains abound: at Start Point a cairn was disrespectfully used as a potato store by the lighthouse keepers while at Quoyness there is the largest chambered cairn yet excavated in Orkney (collect the key from Bridgend Cottage before you leave the road side). The irregularly shaped mound reflects the complex structure of the cairn within, formed of a large internal chamber 13 ft (4 m) high, with six irregularly shaped cells opening off it. Radiocarbon dating of bones found within the cells suggests that the tomb was in use c 2900 BC, and the few bone and stone objects are paralleled in the finds of Skara Brae. On every ness there is the trace of a broch. More recently, the history of the island centred on the attempts of a farmer Patrick Fea to improve the agricultural techniques employed in the second half of the 18th century. The ground proved very suitable for potatoes and the islanders produced one quarter of the total kelp exported from Orkney.

As on North Ronaldsay, fuel was a great problem. By the 18th century the wealthy inhabitants were importing peat, but for the poor, cutting turfs was the inevitable winter occupation of the womenfolk. The islanders came in for much derision for burning cow dung — a Pentland Firth song refers to 'The little island o' Sanday, where coos shit fire'.

Superstition on Sanday is typical of Orkney. At Scar there is a block of 20 tons of gneiss brought by the ice from Scandinavia, now called the Saville stone, which local traditions attribute to the fury of a witch on Eday, who flung it at her eloping daughter and lover. The weight made her aim inaccurate and she missed the young couple. At the parish church of Lady, now roofless, scratches on the cope stone of the external stair have been attributed to the Devil's fingers.

Today Sanday is a quiet island, and its long white beaches are always empty.

Accommodation:
Kettlestoft Hotel (tel Sanday 217).
B & B — details from Tourist Office, Kirkwall
Car Hire:
Wilson, Kettletoft Garage (tel Sanday 321).
Moodie, Leyland (tel Sanday 325).
Bicycle Hire:
Wilson, Kettletoft Garage (tel Sanday 321).
Harbour Master (tel Sanday 227).
Specialities:
Sanday knitters: a group of women from Sanday and the other northern isles produce hand and machine knitted garments, mainly for retail, although visits can be made by appointment with Mrs Sinclair of Lady Post Office.

North Ronaldsay
(Meaning obscure, but pronunciation indicates that it is unrelated to South Ronaldsay.)

Connections:
By air: from Kirkwall (via Sanday): Mon, Wed, Fri, & Sat; two a day. Loganair Ltd (tel Kirkwall 2494).
By sea: from Kirkwall: one return sailing weekly. Orkney Islands Shipping Co Ltd (tel Kirkwall 2044).

North Ronaldsay, the most northern and the most isolated island of the Orcadian group, still maintains a close-knit thriving community of about 120 people, known not by their surnames (of which there are basically five) but by the houses in which they live. The local dialect, almost unintelligible to an Orcadian from Kirkwall, is supposedly very similar to the traditional Norse dialect of these parts, Norn.

Famous for its sheep and its dyke, this island perhaps presents the ultimate achievement in the adaptation of an agricultural way of life to the small acreage available. The fertile land is surrounded by a drystone dyke standing 5 — 6 ft (1.5 — 2 m) high, outside which the small scruffy sheep are kept, forcing them to maintain a seaweed diet. This makes the mutton darker in colour and richer in flavour. As the sheep's fattest season is around the turn of the year, the inhabitants have always been assured of fresh meat in mid-winter, unlike most of Britain, where all but a few beasts were killed in the autumn to avoid the expense of winter feeding. The numbers are kept stable at around 2,000 head, each dwelling being allotted a certain number and marking according to the 1902 Regulations: this agreement is still strictly upheld in this communal system of farming.

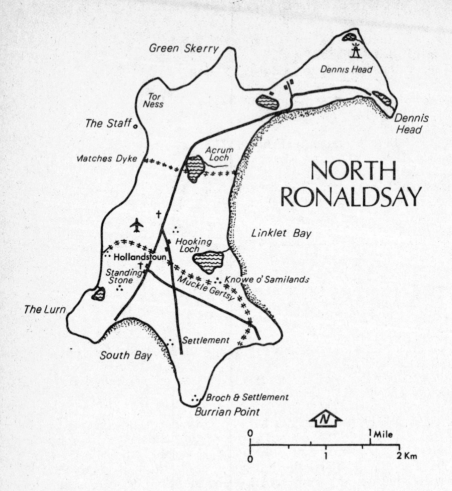

Green Skerry

Dennis Head

Tor Ness

Dennis Head

The Staff o

Matches Dyke

Acrum Loch

NORTH RONALDSAY

Linklet Bay

Hooking Loch

Hollandstoun

Standing Stone

Knowe o' Samilands

Muckle Gersty

The Lurn

Settlement

South Bay

Broch & Settlement
Burrian Point

N

0   1 Mile

0   1   2 Km

On North Ronaldsay is preserved a great deal of evidence of earlier techniques of farming now abandoned. Throughout Orkney, settlements were centred on the easily cultivated land, in 'toonships', the size of which varied with the land available, but all were separated from their neighbours or the wasteland by a boundary wall. The two dykes which, according to tradition, divided the island between the three sons of an unknown owner, called **Matches Dyke** and **Muckle Gersty**, can still be seen as distinct raised mounds, running in an east — west direction. At Dennis Ness, there are still traces of the old running system, used up until the 1880s, of long thin parallel field strips undivided by fences or walls. Until the 18th century this was the usual way of sharing out the land, so that each cultivator had an equal share of the good and the bad. It was abandoned because of its lack of efficiency. Outside the sheep dyke are 'plantiecrues', an ingenious system of bringing on the young kale plants by surrounding them with a stone wall, thus protecting them

110

from the wind. They were placed near the shoreline to protect them from the frost. These are still maintained by the lighthouse keepers for growing potatoes. Close by are shallow circular hollows, about 5 ft (1.5 m) in diameter, which were used for burning the tangle (a variety of seaweed) to produce kelp (a source of iodine and potassium salts greatly in demand in the 18th century and vital to the island's economy). More recently, tangle was collected for the alginate industry but this employment has also collapsed due to the escalating production costs. Fuel has always been a major problem, as there is no peat or wood (except driftwood) available on the island. Cattle dung and turfs, cut from the wasteland, were used, and peat was 'imported' when it could be afforded, from the Calf of Eday. Besides kelp, the other major source of income was from the fishing industry. The inhabitants of North Ronaldsay were held in great repute as fishermen from the 17th century onwards, but today this activity is essentially centred on lobsters, an industry now threatened by the Canadian catches.

Like all the Orkney islands, North Ronaldsay is littered with archaeological sites. A fine broch and surrounding settlement can be found at **Burrian Point**, now threatened by the sea, and there are many other sites along the coast, exposed by the winter gales. Little has been excavated although almost every bump and mound is man-made.

1½ miles (2.4 km) off the south of the island is a submerged rock reef called **Reef Dyke**. This has claimed many lives and ships, the most famous being the *Svecia* of Gothenburg, an armed merchant ship of the Swedish East India Company which lost its bearings and hit Reef Dyke on a return journey from Bengal in 1740. For three days the craft remained virtually intact, but no rescue was attempted, probably because the islanders knew how treacherous the area was and possessed only small boats. Of the 104 crew, only 44 survived. The cargo of spices, silks and dyewood was probably worth around £200,000 sterling — a vast sum in those days, and much of the cloth blown up over the shore was salvaged, both by the rightful owners and by the grateful islanders. The wreck was rediscovered in 1975.

The wildlife on North Ronaldsay is exceptional, partly because the island is so remote — common seals with their pups can be seen stretched out on the sandy bays and rocks, partly because of its exceptional combination of different types of habitats — notably wetlands, unusual in this modern day of land drainage, which play host to carpets of yellow irises and nesting duck, and also partly because of its latitude, which makes it a great migration centre, equal perhaps to Fair Isle. The resident doctor ornithologist keeps detailed records.

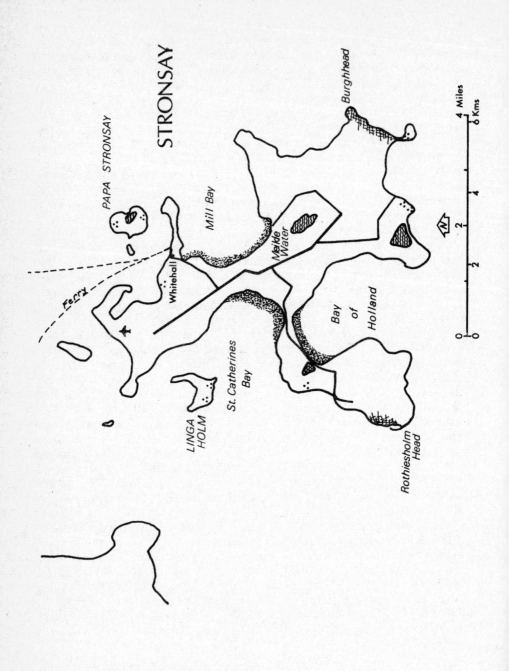

STRONSAY

PAPA STRONSAY

Ferry

Whitehall

Mill Bay

Meikle Water

Burghhead

Bay
of
Holland

St. Catherines
Bay

LINGA
HOLM

Rothiesholm
Head

N

0   2   4   6 Kms
0   2   4 Miles

Accommodation:
Problematical. There is talk of setting up a hostel, but at present only one householder does B & B: enquire at the Tourist Office in Kirkwall (advanced booking necessary).
Taxi:
Muir, Garso (tel N Ronaldsay 244).
Specialities:
North Ronaldsay sheep.

Stronsay
(ON strjonsey — island good for fishing/farming)

Connections:
By air: from Kirkwall: Mon, Wed, Fri, three a day (continuing to Eday); Tue, Thu (continuing to Sanday). Loganair Ltd (tel Kirkwall 2494).

By sea: from Kirkwall: three times a week, route varies around northern isles. Details from Orkney Islands Shipping Co Ltd (tel Kirkwall 2044).

Stronsay is another quiet agricultural island, typical of the northern isles, its flat pasture lands merging with the long sandy beaches. The regularization of the field pattern in the 18th century, from running strips to squares, is the most dominant feature of this island's landscape, which does much to endorse the meaning of its name. The main settlement is at Whitehall, around the bay sheltered by Papa Stronsay — a string of abnormally large two-storeyed houses which were occupied by fishermen, their families and their lodgers. Although only a handful of boats are based here today, supplying the local fish factory, from the 17th century until the First World War it was the most important herring station in the north of Orkney. At the height of its prosperity, the fleet of 300 boats supplied the 15 fish curing stations of Whitewell and 5 on Papa Stronsay, providing employment for 1,500 women. Whaling was a major source of light oil and revenue, and whenever the opportunity arose the islanders would chase the shoals with their boats. In November 1834, 50 small whales were driven onto the sand of Mill Bay, yielding £100-worth of oil.

In the centre of this bay is the Mermaid's Chair where, traditionally, one of Orkney's storm witches, Scota Bess, was believed to sit pronouncing her spells. Eventually, she became so feared by these people, dependent on a kind sea for their livelihoods, that she was beaten to death with flails, and her body was buried in the local cemetery. But each morning they would find it lying on the surface of the ground and so they flung it into the nearby loch —

Meikle Water. If any girl has the courage to sit in the Mermaid's Chair, it is believed that she will understand the mysteries of life and be able to foretell the future.

The boats were also used to collect young cormorants, or 'scarfs', in the winter from the caves of the two southern headlands, **Burghhead** and **Rothiesholm** (still good places to watch seabirds). Scarfs were considered to be a culinary delicacy, if buried in the ground for 24 hours or more to make the meat more tender and less fishy. They were still being collected up until the Second World War.

Around the shoreline can be seen kelp kilns, circular stone-lined hollows of approx 5 ft (1½ m) diameter and 1 ft (30 cm) depth. When James Fea of Whitehall introduced the industry at the early date of 1722, the crofters greeted it with mixed feelings. Although they could supplement their earnings by collecting 'tangle' (a type of seaweed), they were frightened of a sea monster by the name of 'Nuckelavee', who so disliked the smoke that he smit all their houses with a deadly disease which then spread to all the other kelp-producing islands. By 1762, the anti-kelp faction was still not pacified and enacted litigation against James Fea, blaming the industry for bad harvests, dying cattle and a lack of fish. They won the case but eventually financial considerations convinced the population, and Stronsay became 'like a volcano' from the smoke of the fires.

The local weaver in Whitehall village, Mr Shearer, is happy to spend hours talking about his craft and his island. He makes high quality tweed and welcomes specific orders.

Accommodation:
Stronsay Hotel (tel Stronsay 213).
Self-catering details from Tourist Office, Kirkwall.
Taxi:
Swanney, Claremont White Lake (tel Stronsay 224).
Bank:
Sub-office, open weekly — enquire locally.
Specialities:
Weaving, woodturning.

Papa Stronsay

Connections:
By sea: a matter of persuasion — try your luck around the pier at Whitehall, Stronsay.

A small islet, conveniently sheltering Whitehall harbour, Papa Stronsay was an important ecclesiastical site before and during Viking times. The *Orkeyinga Saga* recounts how in the 11th century, Jarl Rognvald, believing he had finally conquered his great rival Thorfinn, visited the Culdee monks to collect their famous brew of ale to warm the Christmas cold. This seasonal enjoyment was interrupted by a counter-attack by Thorfinn. Rognvald's forces were soundly defeated and the Jarl himself was killed.

Shapinsay
(ON Hjalpandisey — Hjalpandi's island)

Connections:
By sea: from Kirkwall: twice daily except Sun: crossing ½ hr. Orkney Island Shipping Co Ltd (tel Kirkwall 2044).

This fertile island is dominated by the history of one family, the Balfours of Trenabie (Westray). John Balfour was a typical nabob of the 18th century, making his fortune out in India and supplementing it by marrying the widow of a Colonel Mackennan. Mackennan was one of those who advanced money to the notorious Rajah of Tanjore; he subsequently defaulted and so the lenders appealed to the British Government to pay them back. John Balfour became the MP for Orkney and Shetland in 1790 and supported the lenders' claims, regaining for his wife enough money to begin accumulating estates on Shapinsay and other neighbouring islands.

Balfour castle, a magnificent Scottish baronial edifice (private) which dominates the approach to the island, was begun by John, but extensively enlarged by David Bryce, the Victorian architect employed by his heir, Colonel Balfour, a self-styled military man on account of his raising a troop of volunteers. Remembered as a petty tyrant, he imposed much needed but most unpopular agricultural improvements, organizing the farms into sizeable units and squaring the fields into 10 acre (4 h) units separated by open drains. He also built the picturesque village of Balfour to house craftsmen such as joiners and weavers, and provided the islanders with a large mill, still complete with its water course and situated ½ mile (1 km) out of the village. He was never popular, and it is said that he evicted those who would not participate in his 'harvest homes' because of their religious beliefs. Until recently, his descendants still dominated the island, even vetting the school teachers before they took up their appointments.

Although there is said to be a neolithic village of a size to rival Skara Brae, this has not yet been excavated, and today the island is essentially a quiet but thriving agricultural community, with few neglected houses, where every passing invokes a greeting.

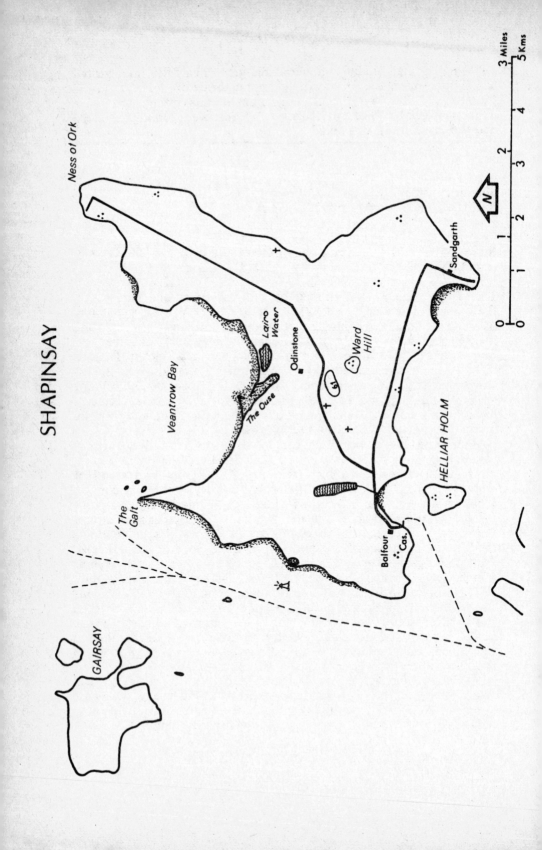

SHAPINSAY

Ness of Ork

GAIRSAY

The Galt

Veantrow Bay

Lairo Water

Odinstone

The Ouse

Ward Hill

Balfour Cas.

HELLIAR HOLM

Sandgarth

N

0   1   2   3 Miles
0   1   2   3   4   5 Kms

Accommodation:
Restaurant and B & B (tel Shapinsay 376).
Car Hire:
J Sinclair, Balfour Post Office (tel Shapinsay 200).

Rousay
(ON Hrolfsey — Hrolf's island)

Connections:
By sea: from Tingwall: Mon — Sat, twice daily; crossing ½ hr. M Flaws, Helziegatha, Wyre (tel Rousay 203). From Kirkwall: one return sailing a week, usually Thu. Orkney Island Shipping Co Ltd (tel Kirkwall 2044).

Rousay is a surprisingly mountainous island, surrounded by relatively flat islands. The three hills of Blotchnie Field, Ward Hill and Kierfea Hill, carpeted with heather, make wonderful lookout points across the surrounding seascape. If not typical in landscape, Rousay does present a relatively comprehensive potted history of the Orcadian civilizations strung out along its south coast.

The landing pier and associated cottages (and shop) were built in the 1870s by General Traill Burroughs of Trumland House. He was the principle shareholder of the first steamship company operating among these northern isles and so ensured himself and Rousay a regular service to transport livestock and produce to market. West of the village in a private woodland (a good place for small birds) is the house he had designed by David Bryce in 1873. Having made his fortune in service in India, he married the Traill heiress of Rousay but he considered her house at Westings too small and inconvenient. So, in typical Victorian manner, he built this monstrosity of the Scottish baronial style. He introduced 'improvements' which consisted of reducing the crofters to labourers, making more room for new breeds of sheep, earning for himself the censure of even the other Orkney lairds.

His wife appears to have possessed a gentler nature. Deciding that a fairy knoll outside the woodland would make an excellent site for a 'lookout' seat, she discovered Taversoe Tuick. This is an unusual neolithic cairn, for although it is of the simple chambered type, two of the chambers have been built on top of each other, each originally having its separate entrance. The lower chamber also has an associated earthhouse, normally considered to be for storage when built beside neolithic houses but here in some way associated with the rites of the dead. Skeletal remains were found on the shelves of both chambers, along with some cremated bones, but none were found in the earthhouse, only three almost complete

117

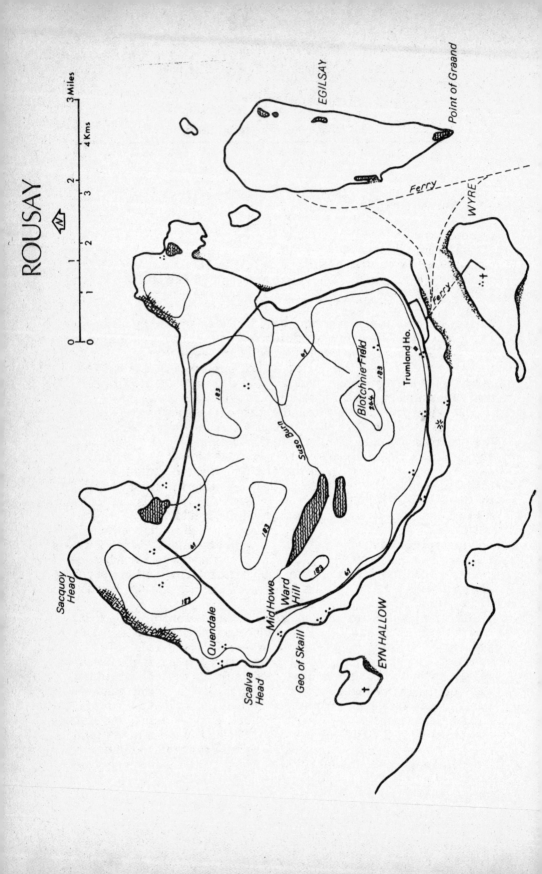

pottery bowls.

Close by is the **Blackhammer chambered tomb** of a contemporary date, c 3000 BC, but built to different traditions. The chamber is covered by an oblong mound, and within this form is a 'stalled passage', the long corridor (43 ft/13 m) being divided into compartments by upright slabs of stone built in at right angles to the wall. Only two skeletons were traced inside, along with an Unstan bowl, a stone axe and several flint objects, thus raising many questions as to why so much effort was spent in making the cairn if it was only to be used twice. Perhaps it was for chieftains, perhaps a new religion brought new burial customs. Further up the hill is a similar but smaller stalled cairn, that of the **Knowe of Yarso**. Here 29 remains of humans were found, along with flints and food vessels and animal bones, including the remains of 30 red deer, which have been dated to c 2900 BC. The construction of the stone work is slightly different from that of Taversoe, the slabs of stone being placed at an angle instead of flat so creating a herringbone pattern on the exterior.

3 miles (5 km) west along the shore is what looks like a factory building, but what is, in fact, the covering for the most significant archaeological site on Rousay, the **Midhowe chambered cairn**. It was excavated in the 1930s at the expense of W G Grant, who bought Trumland House when he brought the Highland Park Whiskey Distillery to Kirkwall. He became a great benefactor to Orkney archaeology, financing many of the best archaeologists, in this case J Callender and J Craw. What they found was a mammoth stalled cairn 76 ft (23.2 m) long, divided by upright slabs into twelve compartments. The original height of the chamber would have been approximately 8 ft (2.5 m). The east wall shows clearly the herringbone pattern of this now fragile drystone construction, inside which were buried 25 people with the remains of sheep, cattle and deer and even an Orkney vole. Traces of a neolithic village were found at Bigland, but there is little to see on the ground.

This site continued to attract settlers. On this strip of coastland there are three brochs, only one of which has been excavated. The site is protected by a ditch carved out of the rock endorsing the geo, or creek, on either side of the broch, and by a series of dykes and walls on the landward side. The actual building is rather complex, with a number of later dwelling houses around the exterior and a confusion of slab partitions inside, but it appears to have an internal gallery within the wall at ground level, a feature more characteristic of the surviving Hebridean brochs than of the other Orcadian and Shetland examples. Clearly visible are the door checks of the entrance passage and the tank with its slab-lid which is still supplied by good spring water, a necessity in times of siege, whosoever the mysterious attackers were. Numerous domestic implements were found during the excavation, many of which were of Roman origin, for example pottery and coins, but there were also indications that ironworking had been carried out in one of the later buildings.

A gentle walk back along the shore, with picturesque views of the Broch of Gurness and Mainland, leads to Westness, where a Viking site has been in the course of excavation since 1978. Recorded in the *Orkneyinga Saga* as the home of Sigurd, the noble Viking farmer and generous host, this is the place where Jarl Paul was kidnapped while hunting otters by Swein Asleifarson, a typically immoral warrior who changed allegiances as often as the wind changed direction. The site of a Norse cemetery was discovered in 1963 when a farmer dug a hole in which to bury a dead cow, and chanced upon the extraordinarily rich grave of a young woman — three silver brooches (now on display in the National Museum of Antiquities, Edinburgh), dating from the 9th and 10th centuries, were already heirlooms when placed beside this maiden who died in childbirth. Sadly the sagas for once fail us and leave no indication of her name. So far, a boat house and at least four other buildings have been discovered, comprising a farm which was probably part of the earlier Viking settlement. This site of Skaill is a strong contender for Sigurd's home. The name is normally associated with a major Norse settlement, 'Skali' meaning hall, but the present ruins are a farmhouse from which tenants were evicted in the last century to make room for the sheep. The old church of Skaill (look at the typical stone cupboard within the walls) may be pre-Reformation and an excavation of the Wirk (from Virki — meaning fortication) north of the church yard may yet reveal a structure similar to Cobbie Row's Castle on Wyre.

Westness House, the home of the Traill family, was rebuilt in the 18th century, having been burnt down when the then laird John Traill was hiding in the Gentleman's Cave (see Westray), suspected of supporting the Jacobite cause. The house, private chapel (seating all of nine people) and the beautiful gardens are open to the public by appointment only (Mrs H Firth, tel Rousay 262).

For the energetic there is curious cliff scenery at Scalva Head and Sacquoy Head, remarkably organized into squares and rectangles and topped by maritime sedge heath — don't wander too close to the edge as it is very slippery. In the valley of Quendale is the old mansion of Tofts, now in a sad state of repair. It has been claimed to be the oldest two-storeyed domestic building in Orkney, dated to before the 17th century, but one can only wonder what gentleman would have inhabited this semi-defensive structure with stone window seats and cramped rooms.

Accommodation:
Taversoe Hotel (tel Rousay 325).
Taxi:
J Mainland, 4 Frotoft (tel Rousay 270).

C Soames, Brendale Farm (tel Rousay 234).
G Gillespie, 8 Pier Houses.
Bicycle Hire:
Major R Ritchie, Trumland House (tel Rousay 263).
Bank:
Sub-office, fortnightly, enquire locally.
Specialities:
Pottery.

Egilsay
(ON Egilsay — Egil's island, or perhaps the Norse pronunciation of the Celtic eaglais — church.)

Connections:
By sea: from Tingwall, Mon-Sat, twice, on demand. M. Flaws, Helziegatha, Wyre (tel Rousay 203). From Kirkwall, one return sailing a week, usually Thu. Orkney Islands Shipping Co Ltd (tel Kirkwall 2044).

Egilsay is famous for its **round towered church**, unique in Orkney, though similar to the Irish ecclesiastic style of the late 11th century. There is no reason to doubt such affinities: small, remote islands were favoured by Celtic monks (see especially Iona), and there could well have been a religious community on the island before the Vikings arrived. The tapering circular tower still stands at a height of 49 ft (14.9 m), although originally it was higher (in the last century it was partially dismantled and stabilized for safety reasons). It probably had four or five storeys, the windows of each rotating to mark the points of the compass. The chancel was once two-storeyed, covered with a barrel vault, while the nave was roofed with the typical Orcadian stone slabs. The 'put-log' holes pockmarking the exterior were probably used during construction for holding the scaffolding timbers.

The church is dedicated to St Magnus who was murdered near this site by his peer and rival, Jarl Hakon Paulsson, in 116/17 (the place is marked by a stone pillar). Hakon's advisers encouraged him to take double the number of agreed men to what was supposedly a peace meeting, whereupon he seized Magnus and his followers. Magnus offered to make a pilgrimage to Rome, promising never to return, or to accept captivity in Scotland, or even to be deprived of his eyes and to become Hakon's prisoner, but Hakon's advisers considered that none of these measures were sufficiently secure or extreme, and insisted that he should be put to death. In his guilt, Jarl Hakon became a reformed character. He led a pilgrimage to the Holy Land and even managed to die in his bed —

a notable feat for a Viking warrior.

The little lochs and marshes down the east side of this flat island attract duck and other marsh fowl.

Accommodation:
Enquire locally, but difficult; it is easier to opt for a daytrip.

Wyre
(ON vigr — a spear head)

Connections:
From Tingwall: Mon — Sat, two a day; crossing ¾ hour. M Flaws, Helziegatha, Wyre (tel Rousay 203). From Kirkwall: one return trip a week, usually Thu. Orkney Islands Shipping Co Ltd (tel Kirkwall 2044).

A small flat pear-shaped island lying between Rousay and Mainland, Wyre is steeped in the history of the Vikings. The *Orkneyinga Saga* mentions Vigr as the home of Kolbein Hruga (the Burly), a distinguished Norwegian who built 'a really solid stronghold'. The only traces of a castle on Wyre are virtually undateable, being of simple design — essentially a stone keep encircled by earth mounds, now in the care of the Secretary of State for Scotland. The local name for the site is **Cobbie Row's Castle**, an obvious corruption of Kolbein Hruga, and as this structure appears solid enough to withstand the attacks of a large and determined force, it seems certain that this is Kolbein's castle where Snaekoll Gunnason fled after killing Jarl John, the last of the Viking earls, in 1232. Although it is recorded as a ruin by the 16th century, the excavation revealed several different periods of building, the wings and outbuildings being constructed over the earlier defensive mounds. If the earliest part of the construction, the central keep, does date from the mid-12th century, this is the earliest surviving example of the Scottish tower house. Over the centuries, Cobbie Row developed through folk-lore into a typical Norse figure. An ambling but well-intentioned giant, he endeavoured to make bridges, but every time he loaded up his kishie (straw basket for carrying peat) with stones, the straps broke and so formed another mound or skerry.

The other important monument on Wyre is a small roofless romanesque chapel dating from the late 12th century, dedicated to either St Mary or St Peter, and now partially restored. Close to Cobbie Row's castle, it is likely that this private chapel (it was never a parish church) was erected by one of his family, possibly his son Bjarni, third Bishop of Orkney, 1188 — 1223, a major figure of the sagas and possibly the poet of *Jomsvikingadrapa* — the story of the

Homsburg Vikings. This attribution would explain why such a large chapel (for those days) was built on such a small island.

Wyre was the humble birthplace of the great Orcadian poet **Edwin Muir** who records his happy childhood years on the island in his autobiography.

Accommodation:
There is still a small community on Wyre but accommodation is difficult — easier to opt for a day trip.

Eyn Hallow
(ON eyin helga — holy isle)

Connections:
By sea: from Tingwall, problematical — contact Mr Flaws, Helziegatha, Wyre (tel Rousay 203).

Eyn Hallow was once known as Hildaland because it was thought to be the summer house of the Finfolk, mythical creatures who lived in a town under the sea with beautiful gardens of seaweeds, where pearls were so plentiful that they were ground up to be painted on mermaids' tails so giving them added lustre. The summer home was renowned for its richness and fertility — white-washed houses, fat cattle and golden cornfields. This land was supposedly enticed away from its legendary owners by a man using equal measures of the magic of Odin and the virtue of the Christian faith.

Now a peaceful island sheltering only birds and seals, Eyn Hallow's Norse name pays tribute to its importance as an early ecclesiastical site. This is ratified both by evidence from the *Orkneyinga Saga* — which records that the adopted son of Kolbein Hruga (see Wyre) was kidnapped from Eyn Hallow in 1155 where presumably he was being educated by the monks; and by archaeological research which revealed an extensive early settlement. The earliest surviving building, the church itself, dates from the 12th century.

In the 16th century the church was converted into a house, and its earlier use was unsuspected until the mid-19th century when many of the islanders succumbed to a fever and were evacuated. In the cause of hygiene the roofs were removed to make the houses uninhabitable, and so the earlier fabric of the church was revealed. The church may have been the centre of a Cistercian monastery — a monk from here became the abbot of Melrose Abbey. Today, the ground is considered so sacred that neither rats nor mice are supposed to be able to live there, although the truth in this I cannot vouch for.

Eyn Hallow is now a bird sanctuary with breeding colonies of fulmar, black guillemots and greater black-backed gulls.

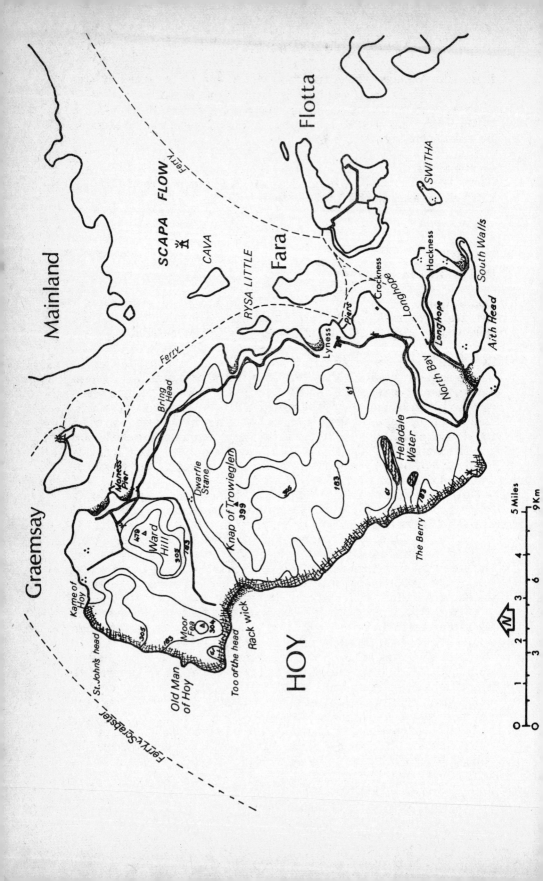

Hoy
(ON haey — high island)

Connections:
By air: from Kirkwall: Mon, Wed, Fri, Sat, one a day; Tue, Thu, two a day (via Flotta). Loganair Ltd (tel Kirkwall 2494).

By sea: from Stromness to Moaness Pier, three times daily (twice on Sundays); ½ hour crossing. Sutherland, 126 Victoria St, Stromness (tel Stromness 850 678). From Stromness to Lyness and Longhope (via Graemsay and Flotta), Tue, Wed, Sat, one a day; 1¾ hrs and 2½ hrs crossing. From Scapa (Kirkwall) to Lyness and Longhope (via Flotta); 1¾ hrs and 2½ hrs crossing. Orkney Island Shipping Co Ltd (tel Stromness 850 655).

Hoy is something of an anomaly among the islands of Orkney. The high hills and sheer cliffs first sighted on the boat north are uncharacteristic of these generally fertile isles, and it is only on the derelict, neglected eastern slopes that nature is successfully claiming her own again, although not without many scars. Most famous for its cliffs and stacks of upper old red sandstone (found nowhere else in Orkney), painted in variations of burnt red and orange by the changing light, Hoy attracts many climbers. Some aspire to master the 'Old Man of Hoy', a 450 ft (140 m) stack near Rora Head, but none but the *very* experienced should take the risk. There is no rescue equipment and the islanders should not be asked to risk their own lives in response to some child's ego trip.

A walk along the cliff tops will bring many delights to geologists, botanists and ornithologists. Geologists can easily study the exposed volcanic basalt lavae forming a floor and a pedestal to the sandstone cliffs. The botanist will find many alpine plants a mere 500 ft (150 m) above sea level, which says something about the exposed climate, and on a fine summer's day it is an easy walk from the shore meadows to see these miniature species struggling for a foothold. The cliffs at Too of the Head and The Berry are the best places to watch the seabirds; Aith Head, Bring Head, the Kame of Hoy and St John's Head (with cliffs 1,140 ft (345 m) high) also house large populations. As on other cliffs of the northern isles, in the past many birds and eggs were collected by the wildfowlers to feed their own families, and to provide some income to pay for the few purchases they made in the Stromness markets each year. Romping about these hills are the mountain hares, found nowhere else in Orkney, while red throated divers can be seen in many of the lochans. As usual, beware of the bonxies (great skuas) when walking on the cliff slopes.

The tiny village of **Rackwick**, squeezed between Moor Fea, Ward Hill and Knap of Trowieglen, has many champions claiming it to be the most picturesque in all of Orkney. Once a bustling fishing village, the boats kept on the pebbly beaches, its crofts have been

125

deserted by many in search of the bright lights, leaving only the old to continue their timeless ways — charming to the summer visitors but grim in winter and unlikely to continue for many more years.

On the hillside of Knap of Trowieglen above the road is the **Dwarfie Stane.** An isolated block of red sandstone, standing on a terrace with views down to Rackwick and across the water to Stromness, it poses many mysteries. Local tradition held that it was the home of a giant who made the second cell for his pregnant wife. Other stories suggest that a giant was imprisoned there, who tried to gnaw his way out through the roof of the cell. As we see it today, there is an entrance on the west side through a short passage into a cell 5 ft (1.5 m) wide and 3 ft (0.9 m) high. Opening out of this is a slightly smaller cell, distinctly divided by a squared doorway. Dated to c 1900 BC, it is now considered to be a carved-out chambered tomb, an adaption through local inspiration of the more usual Taversoe Tuick type (see Rousay).

The tarn of **Berrie Dale** surprisingly hosts a community of tree shrubs. Stunted rowans, birches and alders, smothered by honey-suckle, give shelter to smaller varieties of birds.

Hoy offers few rainy day haunts. The little church at Hoy has some nice but simple early 17th century carved wooden panels, donated by the then minister Master Henry Smythe in 1624 (best seen on a Sunday as the church is kept locked at other times). Among the tombstones in the churchyard at **Bu** is a fine example inscribed 'Heir Lyis ane honorable woman Ieane Stewart spous to Hew Halcro of that ilk wha deceist in December 1625'.

The road creeps along the eastern shore (with good views of the Scapa Flow) to Lyness, a very important base for the navy in the Second World War when the Scapa Flow was Great Britain's most important harbour. Approximately 30,000 men were based in Lyness and on the hillside above, most activity concentrating on supplying the war ships; note the fuel drums by the pier which were constantly being filled by incoming tankers and emptied as fast by those leaving on expeditions. Lyness has never recovered from this, its heyday, never managing to revert back to its pastoral activities. It is said that the money given to the islanders to clear up the general mess was drunk instead. The navy is reluctant to let go of the land, though the islanders won a recent struggle to turn one of the two cinemas into a house.

On the two facing points of Crock Ness and Hack Ness are mementoes of an earlier warring episode, two **Martello towers.** Commonly assumed to have been built as a defence against the Napoleonic fleet, they were in fact built against the navy of the United States of America. In 1812 the United States declared war on Britain because of her repeated harassment of US ships trading with Napoleon's allies. The US navy, in turn, posed a direct threat to Britain's trade with the Baltic, and so the sound of Longhope became an assembly point for convoys crossing the North Sea. Each tower was equipped with a 24-pounder canon — the lower storey serving as ammunition stores, and the middle storeys providing living quarters for the gunners. They were repaired and restaffed during the First World War.

The bay of Longhope is more hospitable and greener than the northern end of the island. Many of the empty stone cottages have been recently reinhabited by back-to-the-earth freaks, not always welcomed by the islanders, but it is easy to sympathize with their desire to enjoy the peace. South Walls supports an active farming community, more similar to the rest of Orkney. The sagas record that it was here that Olaf Tryggvason, King of Norway (995 — 1000), forced the warrior, Sigurd Hlodvisson the Stout, Earl of Orkney, to submit to baptism on pain of death. This did nothing to curb his fighting tendencies.

Accommodation:
The Royal Hotel (tel Longhope 276). Has seen better days, recording its royal visitors on plaques on most of the doors.
Hoy Hostel (tel Kirkwall 3535). Booking through Mr M Drever, Education Offices, Kirkwall.
There is no shop at the north end of the island.
Car Hire:
Leslie, Stroma Bank, Longhope (tel Longhope 286).
Orkney Seaport Supply Services Ltd, HM Naval Base (tel Lyness 356).
Rendall, Lyness (tel Lyness 262).
Sea Angling:
Contact T Keldie, Bangor, Stromness.

Flotta
(ON flatey — flat island).

Connections:
By air: from Kirkwall: Mon, Wed, Fri, Sat, one a day; Tue, Thu, two a day. Loganair Ltd (tel Kirkwall 2494).

By sea: from Stromness (via Graemsay and Lyness, Hoy): Tue, Wed, Sat, 2 hrs crossing; from Scapa (Kirkwall): Mon, Fri, ¼ hr crossing. Orkney Island Shipping Co Ltd (tel Stromness 850 655).

Before the Second World War, Flotta was a charming but backward island; oxen were still being used in the fields and the islanders caught lobsters to supplement their living. However that war turned Flotta into a miniature garrison protecting the southern entrance to the Scapa Flow, and covered it with barrage balloons and anti-

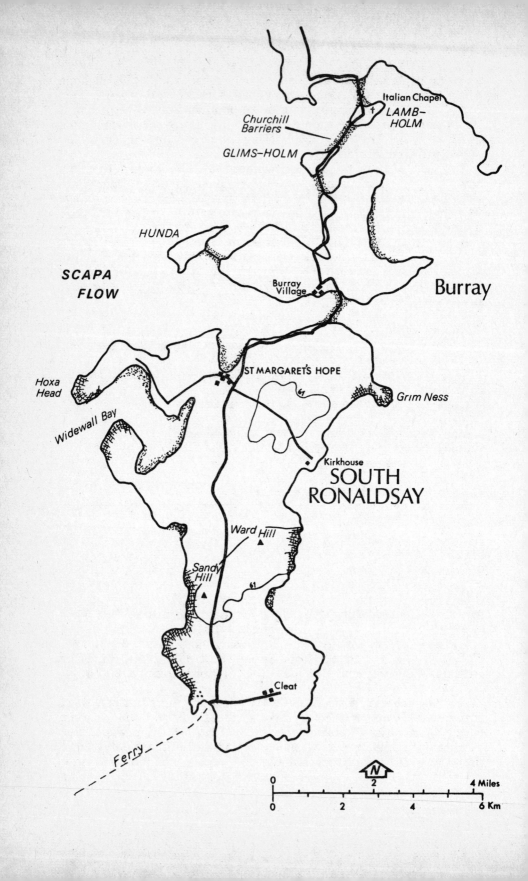

Italian Chapel
LAMB-
HOLM

Churchill
Barriers

GLIMS-HOLM

HUNDA

SCAPA
FLOW

Burray
Village

Burray

Hoxa
Head

ST MARGARET'S HOPE

Grim Ness

Widewall Bay

61

Kirkhouse

SOUTH
RONALDSAY

Ward Hill

Sandy
Hill

61

Cleat

Ferry

N
2

0   4 Miles

0   2   4   6 Km

aircraft guns. The island then seemed to recover its rural ways, extraordinarily in 1970 having a pipeline laid to bring water from Hoy, at the cost of a mere £13,000. But Flotta has the misfortune to possess the deepest and best protected anchorage of the southern isles, and so was chosen to be the centre of the oil industry around Orkney. A pause at the pier is all that is necessary now that the vast drum storage containers and associated buildings have irrevocably altered the character of this once peaceful island.

***

Burray
(ON borgavey — broch island)
Glims-holm
Lamb-holm
South Ronaldsay
(ON Rognvaldsey — Rognvald's island)

Connections:
By road along the causeway from St. Marys, Mainland.
  By sea: from John o'Groats to Burwick: Mon — Fri, two a day; Sat, Sun, one a day; crossing ¾ hr.
Thomas & Bews, Ferry Office, John o'Groats (tel John o'Groats 353).

This string of south-eastern isles once marked the eastern approaches to the Scapa Flow, but the sounds are no longer navigable. On 14 October 1939, a German submarine slipped in and sank HMS *Royal Oak* while it sheltered in these quiet waters, drowning over 800 men. The sounds were blockaded, firstly by the sunk ships, which can still be seen emerging from the shallow waters, and then more permanently by the four Churchill causeways constructed by Italian prisoners of war, captured during General Wavell's offensive in North Africa and held on the islands.

  On **Lamb-holm** these Italian prisoners transformed two Nissen huts into an Italian chapel, using any scrap of material they could obtain (the sidelight fittings are made from bully beef tins). The plasterboard interior is painted with simulated tiles and stonework restored in 1960 by the original aritst, Signor Chiocchetti, and the altar painting is his interpretation of a copy (given to him by his mother on his departure for the war) of Nicolo Barabino's 'As a fair olive tree in the plains', a moving reminder of the humanity of the victims of war.

  On the deceptively green **Glims-holm**, peat cuttings are still maintained, one couple in a hard-working summer weekend being able to prepare enough fuel for three months.

  Burray is a charming little island, rich in bird life. Many traditional stone-roofed houses are kept as barns, and the drystone dykes often protect a hedge of fuschia. **Hunda** is the local beauty spot and unofficial nature reserve. Light earthenware bowls are made at Burray Pottery and a visit is recommended. In **Burray Village** there is a boat builders yard where small wooden craft are made.

An ugly moralistic tale is attached to the once laird of Burray. When the dashing young brother of Sir James Stewart was caught in compromising circumstances by an irate retired naval officer, his pride led to a bitter quarrel supported by Sir James, which ended in the captain's death in Broad Street, Kirkwall. Both fled the country, but while his brother died in exile, Sir James returned home pardoned before many years were out. James joined the Young Pretender's standard at Culloden, but managed to escape alive from that dreadful defeat. He returned home again, only to be captured by the son of the same murdered captain and to die a miserable death in a London prison.

The little hamlets of this part of Orkney originated as herring stations, in the 19th century, but at the beginning of this century the herring moved inexplicably westwards. On **South Ronaldsay**, the old houses at St Margaret's Hope were built with their gable-ends to the shore, the traditional way of gaining some shelter from the wind. Originally called Ronaldsvoe, the hamlet's name may have been changed to St Margaret's Hope in memory of the Maid of Norway, Edward II's child bride who died on her way to Scotland in 1290 and whose ships paused here to receive Bishop Dolgfimir before returning to Norway. Less plausibly, the name has also been claimed for Malcome Canmore's wife, the saintly queen who did much to civilize the Scots. Mid-August each year sees the Festival of the Horse, when young children dress up and the boys under 15 compete in a ploughing match, using miniature ploughs to make furrows on the sandy beach.

At **Hoxa Head**, another extraordinary ratification of the Orkneyinga Saga occurred when a Viking burial was found at the exact spot mentioned for the tomb of Thorfinn Skull-splitter — a redoubtable warrior who had the privilege to die in his bed. There are good views across Scapa Flow.

At **St Mary's Kirk** there is a curious boat-shaped block of whinstone, bearing the hollowed impression of a pair of feet, traditionally explained by the story of one Gallus. Caught in a storm, Gallus prayed to the Virgin for help, promising to build her a chapel if he survived. She summoned a sea creature, perhaps a porpoise, to carry him home, and there the faithful creature turned to stone, still carrying the impression of Gallus' feet to remind all of the miracle and his promise. Shipwrecks have especially sad memories for South Ronaldsay, for the Longhope lifeboat from Hoy went down here in 1969, drowning all the men on board while they were attempting to rescue the wreck of HMS *Irene* of Cirims Ness. All her crew struggled to the rocks and survived. The road sides are littered with orchids and from Sandy Hill and Ward Hill there are spectacular views south to Caithness. South Ronaldsay is not without its ghosts: at the isolated Kirkhouse, a 'dey' (dairymaid) who declared that she had seen ghosts in the graveyard, was condemned to the fate of losing her feet; now she is reputed to walk through the passage carrying her feet under her arms!

Accommodation:
Sands Hotel, Burray.
Hikers Hostel, Herston, South Ronaldsay (tel St Margarets Hope 208).
B & B and self-catering details from the Tourist Office, Kirkwall

Copinsay
(ON Kolbensey — Kolbein's Island)

Connections:
By sea: tel David Foubister, Deerness 245, to arrange trip from Newark Bay.

Bought in 1972 by nature lovers for £7,500, as a memorial to James Fisher, the ornithologist and broadcaster killed in 1970, the island is now uninhabited except for a lighthouse keeper and the thousands of nesting seabirds (guillemots, kittiwakes, razorbills and puffins), carefully observed by the RSPB owners. In the 19th century the eggs, as on most cliffs, were collected by men dangling down the cliffs on straw ropes, but the land also provided a reasonable living to a farmer (in his house there is now an exhibition of what to see on the island, and where).

Legend has it that while this farm was in the lone hands of a bachelor, a hideous monster appeared one night at the door. The frightened man remembered that prayers and holding steel could ward off most unnatural creatures and endeavoured to get rid of it by these means, but the monster refused to move and begged to be allowed to work in return for a bowl of milk each evening. In desperation, the man agreed and gained for himself a perfect servant — so perfect that he took great care when introducing his sweetheart to it. When they married, she too extended kindness to the weird being, making it a cloak against the winter cold, for it had no clothes. As it tried on the garment it burst into tears, and fled, never to be seen again. The farm, however, continued to flourish, sheep even being grazed on the Horse of Copinsay — a sheer grassy topped stack. The remains of a chapel have been found on Corn Holm.

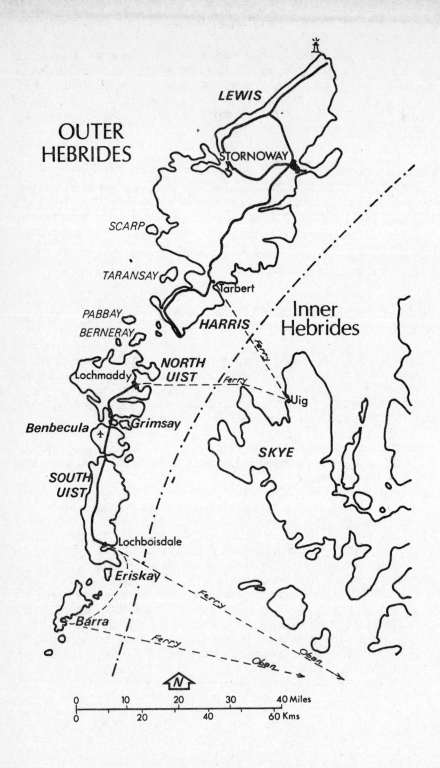

OUTER HEBRIDES

LEWIS

STORNOWAY

SCARP

TARANSAY

Tarbert

PABBAY
BERNERAY

HARRIS

Inner Hebrides

Lochmaddy

NORTH UIST

Ferry

Uig

Benbecula

Grimsay

SKYE

SOUTH UIST

Lochboisdale

Eriskay

Ferry

Barra

Ferry

Oban

Oban

N

0	10	20	30	40 Miles
0	20	40		60 Kms

Part 3
The Outer Hebrides

Outer Hebridean Life

The Outer Hebrides comprise a long string of islands stretching along the western side of Scotland, a reef protecting the indented coastline and inner islands from the full force of the Atlantic gales. The force of these winds dominates the landscape, the beautifully long white sandy beaches of the west rising smoothly to a ridge of mountains and cliffs on the east. The wind lifts the shell sand onto the lower levels where it combines with the peaty base to make the machair a very rich and fertile pastoral ground, covered more by flowers than grass and best seen from June to August.

On several occasions in recorded history, this fragile coastline has been extensively altered by storms (see North Uist), but it is the crofters' greatest asset, for much of the interior is covered by uncultivable peat bog, extremely useful for fuel, but little else. Until the Viking period, much of the interior was covered by forest, but a slight change in climate together with the Vikings' scorched-earth policy, aimed at routing out traitors, has prevented trees from regaining a foothold, except in a few sheltered corners. The spine of Lewisian gneiss protruding through the bog provides fine views west to the ocean and east to a patchwork of land and water. The eastern coast is much fragmented as the sea has worried faults in the rock structure to carve out creeks and harbours.

Although the Vikings explored and exploited the whole of the west coast of Scotland, the Outer Hebrides show little sign of any lasting Norse influence. Gaelic, the language of their predecessors, survived their invasion unscathed and is strongly championed today. Have no fears: almost everyone except the very old is bi-lingual, if not speaking English as his mother-tongue, although some islanders do betray a disconcerting habit of switching into Gaelic should a stranger come into earshot. The local radio broadcasts early evening programmes in Gaelic especially for the islanders, but a more pleasurable way of listening to it is by attending a ceilidhs (G — social evening) where you will hear many of the beautiful songs to which the language is so superbly adapted.

Some of the songs commemorate the decimation of the clan systems after the '45 (1745), when those chiefs who had supported the Jacobite cause had their lands confiscated. The old method of holding land was based on family ties, each laird having his 'tacksmen', usually relations who extracted rents from the farmers and cottars who worked the land. The new landlords soon realized that more money could be extracted from the tenants if the land was farmed more economically and so rejected any claims of rights of inheritance. By raising rents, they forced the people to move to less hospitable land, replacing them with larger farms or sheep. Much bitterness was caused all over the Highlands by this brutal expulsion, especially as the new land often had not even enough soil to bury the dead (eg the east coast of Harris).

By the second half of the 19th century, these bare patches had become hopelessly over-populated, and people were herded into boats to be transported to the new territories; hence the strong clan links all over the world. By the end of the century, the people's plight began to get a sympathetic press and a crofting commission was set up to examine their grievances. Much land was redistributed, but there were too many people to enable economical units to be established. The men were expected to fish for a living while their few acres of crofting land provided only the bare necessities of life; and soon the landlords developed a stranglehold on the fishing industry as well.

Enlightened landlords, such as Sir James Matheson and Lord Leverhulme, helped the crofters' interests by developing industry; not always successfully. In Harris in 1895, there were only eight trained weavers supplying the needs of the gentry; however, Sir Samuel Scott then recognized the potential for selling tweed in fashionable London and developed the industry. Weaving is well suited to the crofting way of life as it can be done in the croft itself, and at one time it was popular throughout the Outer Hebrides. Today, the problems of transporting the wool and the finished clothes restrict most of the production to Harris and Lewis. Even here, the unreliability of the market and the heavy costs involved in setting up the looms have steadily eroded its popularity, so that most of the tweed is now produced in the Stornoway mills.

A visitor should be prepared for the dominance of religion in the Outer Hebrides. There is a sharp division between the Catholic Isles, south of Benbecula, and the 'wee Frees', north. The Catholic islanders bear a striking resemblance to the people of southern Ireland in their relaxed attitudes and carefree way of life. On the other hand, islanders belonging to the Free Church (an off-shoot from the Presbyterian Church of Scotland) are fanatical in their observation of the Sabbath: so don't expect anything to be open on a Sunday, when even a walk along the beach will be frowned upon!

Lewis
(G — a place abounding in pools)

Connections:
By air: from Inverness and Glasgow: one a day. British Airways, Stornoway Airport (tel Stornoway 3240). From Barra and Benbecula: three a week. Loganair Ltd, Stornoway Airport (tel Stornoway 3067).

By sea: from Ullapool: summer, two a day except Sunday; winter, eight a week; cars; bus connections with Inverness. Caledonian MacBrayne Ltd (tel Stornoway 2361).

By road: from Tarbert, Harris, A859 (38 miles/61 km).

Stornoway is the major town of the Long Isle, with a population of 5,000. It is the administrative centre of the Western Isles and the main shopping centre. Fishing is the major industry, with markets on Tuesday and Thursday evenings at 9 pm. The fishing was exploited by the Dutch in the mid-16th century, but in 1598 James VI of Scotland, in an attempt to get his authority recognized on the island, encouraged the Fife Adventurers to investigate this supposed El Dorado of herring. They built the South Beach Quay but after three attempts failed to establish a settlement against the unruly natives. Today the fleet concentrates on white fish and prawns. Stornoway is now also the centre of the Harris tweed industry, and there are three mills that can be visited in the town.

The customs house, built c 1830, is a fine harled building with a Doric porch, now housing the harbour master — Captain Mackay, who should be consulted about yacht moorings in Stornoway and the rest of Lewis. Charts of the west coast of Scotland are essential and are available from this harbour office (4 South Beach; tel Stornoway 2688). Sea angling can be arranged through the Stornoway sea angling club or by asking around at the harbour.

Across the harbour is Lewis Castle, the stronghold of the MacLeods of Lewis from the 13th century until the island was granted to the Seaforths by James V. This family also rebelled

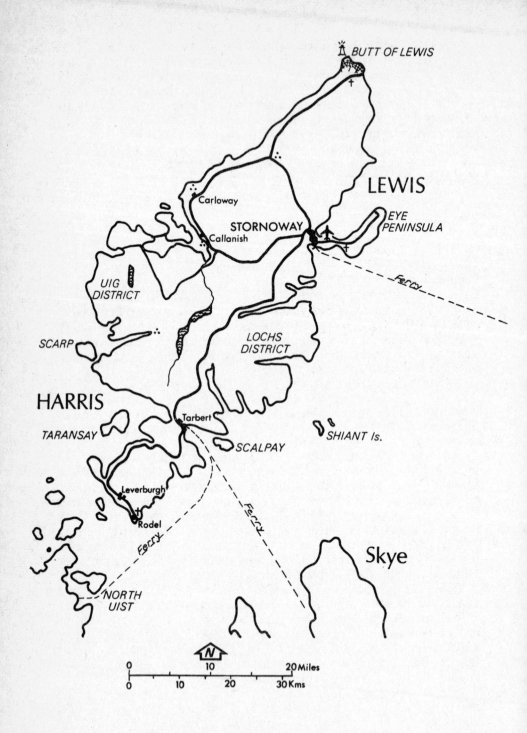

BUTT OF LEWIS

LEWIS

Carloway

STORNOWAY

EYE
PENINSULA

Callanish

UIG
DISTRICT

SCARP

LOCHS
DISTRICT

HARRIS

TARANSAY

Tarbert

SHIANT Is.

SCALPAY

Leverburgh

Rodel

Skye

Ferry

NORTH
UIST

Ferry

Ferry

N

| 0 | 10 | | 20 Miles |
| 0 | 10 | 20 | 30 Kms |

against British authority during the war with the Dutch in 1853, and again in support of the Stuarts. (The Lewis Museum, 11 Scotland Street, open May-Sep, illustrates the history of the town and the island, and has genealogical records of the local families.) In 1923, Lord Leverhulme of Sunlight soap gave the castle and the whole parish to its inhabitants, and it is now managed by the Stornoway Trust, the castle being used as a technical college specializing in practical skills such as navigation and weaving. The grounds, planted with many trees and rhododendrons by Lady Matheson, have been opened up as a large public park with a golf course.

Lewis has been noted for supplying vast numbers of army recruits ever since the first battalion of the Seaforths was raised in 1777. In 1914, the boys of the Nicholson Institute, the main secondary school of the island, attended their prize giving in uniform before joining the annual training camp. Exactly four years later, the evening Hogmanay celebrations were marred by a singular tragedy, when over 200 men returning from the war were drowned within sight of the shore, when their ship HMS *Lodiare* was wrecked on the Beasts of Holm, a rocky outcrop to the left of the harbour.

The discovery of North Sea oil has greatly affected Stornoway (making cheap accommodation hard to find). Across the bay at Arnish Point (ON — eagle's nest), beside the lighthouse and a charming row of cottages built c 1852 by Alan Stevenson (the uncle of the novelist Robert Louis), is an oil rig construction yard; often the rigs are clearly visible from the harbour.

On the Eye Peninsula, about 6 miles (10 km) from Stornoway, is St Columba's Chapel. Made of purple plumstone, it was traditionally founded by a Macleod of Lewis for the Augustinian Canons, and remained their family burial place. The tomb of Roderick Macleod 7th of Lewis is inside the building, a deep cut slab of a warrior figure. Facing it is a Celtic stone in memory of Margaret Macleod, mother of of the last abbot of Iona. Among the many other interesting tombstones is one of the first Surveyor General of India, Colonel Colin MacKenzie. The whole peninsula is densely populated with crofts, with nice beaches at Bayble (ON — priest's dwelling). At Garrabost can be seen the remains of open-cast clay workings.

The year of 1882 was marked by particularly harsh weather and a general crop failure. To alleviate their suffering, the crofters were employed in constructing the Pentland Road, from Stornoway to Carloway (an easy 20 mile (32 km) walk across the black moor). The A858 (single track) follows this route for 8 miles (13 km) before turning south to Achmore. Intensely bleak at first sight, the rolling moor catches a fascinating play of light. In the summer, the inhabitants of the Eye Peninsula and Stornoway traditionally brought their cattle to graze on the moor. Now the painted shielings are used solely for preparing fuel. Peat began forming about 7,000 years ago through organic decomposition and retains a high percentage of water: when cut, it is carefully stacked in small piles to be wind-dried before being heaped by the roadsides for transportation to the crofts. If there has been a wet summer, it is often left out all winter — the darker the peat, the hotter it burns.

At **Achmore**, it is still possible to see signs of the attempts initiated by Sir James Matheson to reclaim the moor for fertile land, by adding seaweed as manure to combat the acidity of peat. The project was abandoned as it involved too much work. This whole area was once heavily wooded and tree roots can be seen in the peat cuttings: glaciers and the scorched-earth policy of Magnus Barelegs, a Norse raider of the 11th century, finally reduced it to a barren waste. Interesting plants such as bog asphodel can be found by the patient. Beyond Achmore, Lady Matheson planted an area of larch trees, which a gale devastated in 1921. However, the Forestry Commission is now endeavouring to recultivate this area. The lochs of the black moor provide brown trout fishing. (Details of all fishing permits may be obtained from the hotels and the Tourist Organization. For salmon and sea trout, it is advisable to book well in advance.)

At **Garynahine**, there is a turn off to the Uig district — the locals are less hospitable here than elsewhere. Golden eagles are often seen circling over the hills, but those spotted perched on telegraph poles tend to be buzzards. The **Isle of Great Bernera**, now connected by a bridge (note the standing stones on the right) is famous for its lobster fishing. At **Kinlochresort** are the remains of beehive houses, and on the beach at **Valtos**, Loch Road, traces of an Iron Age stone factory have been found. The famous Uig chessmen, now in the National Museum of Antiquities, Edinburgh and the British Museum, London, were found at Ardroil. Dating from c 1150, they were carved from walrus ivory, probably by monastics for the Norse invaders. Many of the place names provide evidence of the Norse occupation of the island as a raiding base. Not until 1266 were the Western Isles finally ceded to Scotland by Norway.

Above the village of **Callanish**, standing against the horizon, are three megalithic stone circles. In 1857, Sir James Matheson excavated the major circle out of the peat. Originally there were probably 75 stones, of which 48 have remained standing, in the overall shape of a Celtic cross. The exact function of the circles is not obvious, although the remains of chambered cairns within attest to their builders' belief in life after death. In the 5th century BC, Herodotus referred to a visit to Greece by Abaros, from a winged temple of the northern isles, of which Callanish — with the Gaelic name Teampull na Greine (temple of the sun) is the only known example. Sun worship lingered on in superstitious form on these islands until the 19th century, but it is also possible that the circles were related in some way to the complex astronomical theories developed by the Druids. All along the west coast are the remains of duns, brochs, forts and defensive walls, built during the period 200 BC to 200 AD as defensive watchpoints (and therefore commanding superb views), although often seeming too small to be capable of withstanding a major attack.

At **Carloway** there is a magnificent broch, standing 30 feet (9m) high, with well preserved galleries within its double oval walls. It is possible that this sophisticated fort was built against the Roman invaders. Carloway is an interesting crofting township, nestling around the safe anchorage of the loch, although since the war little fishing has been done. A collection of blackhouses, until recently inhabited, imparts the flavour of island life in the last century. Each year sheepdog trials are held here in mid-July.

Shawbost is the second centre for tweed on the island. There are 600 weavers on Lewis, so the clank-clank of the crofters' looms can be heard in every township. On weekday mornings the completed cloths are put out at the roadside to be collected by the mill lorries. Harris wool, which does not shrink and so is excellent for knitting, can be bought cheaply at the mill shops. The school has renovated a Norse mill by Loch Raoinabhat — a small stone hut with a single mill wheel, driven directly by a horizontal wooden wheel propelled by water from a sluice channel, for milling flour. In the village there is an excellent folk museum, again set up by the school (keys from the janitor, or the weaver across the road; open 10-6 daily except Sun). At **Bragar** there is a whale-bone arch, with the harpoon that killed the animal, in 1921, hanging from the centre.

In the village of **Arnol**, a blackhouse (Tigh Dubh) is preserved as a museum (open 9.30 — 4 in winter, 9.30 —7 in summer, daily except Sun). The blackhouse was the traditional habitation of these islanders, being built of thick drystone walls with the thatched roof set on the inner wall to protect it from the wind. Originally the fire was in the centre of the room, the smoke escaping through a hole in the roof, and the whole building sloped away towards the cattle end because the animals were kept inside throughout the winter. The windows, if any, were set into the thatch although during the last century they began to be placed deep in the walls. The whitehouse (Tigh Geal) differs from the blackhouse in that it had cemented and not drystone walls, and therefore appears lighter in colour.

In the township of **Ballanthrushal** there is an impressive megalithic monolith standing 19 ft (6 m) high, called the Clach an Thrushal. This area is much flatter, greener and more fertile than the moor and opens up to the **Butt of Lewis**. At **Europie** (ON — beach place) is the church of St Motuag (keys from Macleods Store), traditionally attributed to King Olaf of Norway, but more probably built in the 14th century on the site of an earlier cell. About 1 mile (1.6 km) due west is **Luchruban** (G — Pigmy Isle) where there is still the trace of a stone cell, probably inhabited by one of the monks who would not renounce Celtic customs in preference for the Roman church in the 8th century. In the summer these stones are smothered by sea pinks.

The lighthouse standing at the Butt can be visited at the discretion of the keeper, in the afternoon before sundown. The men of the district still go on annual trips to the island of Suga Sgeir to harvest the young gannets. However, anyone wishing to taste this delicacy must place an order beforehand. The beaches of the west coast are bare stretches of white sand contained by rocky outcrops; those of **Barvas** and **Europie** are popular but it is easy to find your own by exploring lanes down to the coast.

The road south from Stornoway to Harris passes through the **Lochs district**, where some delightful villages nestle on the shores of the sea lochs. At **Keose** a seaweed factory produces alginate — a potent reminder of the vast kelp industry of the 18th century when kelp was collected from the shores to produce iodine, thus bringing great but temporary wealth to the island. **Loch Sealg** (G — Lake of the Chase) is evidence of the ancient sport of hunting and there is still a deer park forest near **Loch Erisart** containing red deer.

Accommodation:
Stornaway:
The Acres Hotel, James Street (tel Stornoway 2740)
Caberfeidh Hotel, Manor (tel Stornoway 2604)
Caledonian Hotel, South Beach Street (tel Stornoway 2411)
Crown Hotel, Castle Street (tel Stornoway 3181)
Lewis Hotel, North Beach Street (tel Stornoway 4567)
Royal Hotel, Cromwell Street (tel Stornoway 2109)
Seaforth Hotel, James Street (tel Stornoway 2470)
Hebridean Guest House, Bayhead (tel Stornoway 2268)
Isles Guest House, Lewis Street (tel Stornoway 2475)
Park Guest House, James Street (tel Stornoway 2485)
Outside Stornoway:
Borve House Hotel, Borve (tel Borve 223)
Doune Braes Hotel, Carloway (tel Carloway 252)
Cross Inn, Cross, Ness (tel Port of Ness 378)
Vig Hotel, Vig (tel Timsgarry 286)
Ceol Na Mara Guest House, Garrabost (tel Garrabost 372)
Car Hire:
Alexander Lewis Motor Garage, Bells Road (tel Stornoway 2303)
Lewis Car Rentals, Bells Road (tel Stornoway 3760)
Loch's Motor Transport, Cameron Terrace, Lochs (tel Crossbost 288)
John Mitchell (Stornoway) Ltd, Bayhead Street (tel Stornoway 2888)
Bicycle Hire:
The Cycle Shop, Cromwell Street Pier (tel Stornoway 2202)
Western Isles Tourist Organisation:
Information Centre, South Beach Street (tel Stornoway 3088): open summer 9 am — 10 pm; winter 9 am — 6 pm.
Early closing:
Stornoway — Wednesday

Specialities:
Stornoway kippers, Harris tweed

Harris
(ON har-ay — high island)

Connections:
By sea: from Uig (Skye), Mon, Wed, Fri, one a day; Tue, Thu, Sat, two a day; cars; 2 hour crossing.

From Lochmaddy, N. Uist, Tue & Fri; cars; 1¾ hr crossing; Caledonian MacBrayne Ltd. (tel Harris 2444). From Newton Ferry, N. Uist and Berneray, at least one crossing daily; 1 hour crossing. D A MacAskill, G Borve, Berneray (tel Berneray 230; if no reply, try Berneray 233).

By road: from Lewis, A859.

Harris is not an independent island in its own right, being joined to but separated from Lewis by a high ridge of mountains. Since this made communications difficult, two distinct island communities evolved. Most notable is the difference in accent, the Harris one being softer and gentler. Harris itself divides into three distinct areas, North Harris, South Harris and the Bays District.

North Harris
The four mountain peaks of Clisham (2,670 ft/799 m), Uisgnaval More (2,390 ft/729 m), Oreval (2,170 ft/662 m) and Tirga More (1,970 ft/600 m) are each divided by steep water-ridden passes channelling the endless rain off the rocky outcrops of glacier-scraped hills into the lochs and sea of fishing fame. These steep and spectacular slopes of foliated granite make for challenging walking (always be prepared for bad weather) and within a few hours of exploration one may chance upon a herd of red deer (smaller than those on the mainland but still holding proud fine heads of antlers) or a few of the wild goats that scamper over the boulders. Blue hares were introduced in 1859 and have multiplied ever since. Golden eagles and buzzards can be sighted circling overhead and one is continually impressed by the size and wildness of these hills even when a vista opens upon a hamlet of white cottages on the shoreline.

The shore-hugging road to Husinish in an exciting drive round tiny inlets, lochs and islets. Bunaveneader is a pleasant little village perched on the rocks above the whaling piers built by the Norwegians before the First World War and later sold to Lord Leverhulme (see Lewis), but closed in 1930 due to the rising costs involved. The road twists and turns (drive very carefully), every corner revealing more islands in West Loch Tarbert, until it suddenly goes through a gate

141

past a private garden of fuchsias and other flowering shrubs and down to Amhuinnsuidhe Castle, built by the Earl of Dunmore in 1868 in the Scottish baronial style. Although the imported stone gives it a warm colour, the actual design is hollow and unimpressive although there are charming cottages and a fine gate beyond. One of its guests was Sir James Barry who began his novel *Mary Rose* here, inspired, it is said, by the tiny island on Loch Loshimid.

The old type of short-haired Highland cattle can be seen grazing these rough roadside moors, benign under their long horns and more photogenic than their scruffy cousins who often steal their name. The road twists on to the township of **Hushinish**, a settlement with all the charm of an end-of-the-road atmosphere — hens wandering everywhere and cars scattered around, meadows of wild flowers and sandy coves with pebbly head walls. This is the ferry point for Scarp (see Scarp).

Tarbert is a little west coast town, useful for vital supplies and last minute Harris tweed shopping. The gardens sadly grow more litter than flowers, but the summer brings a throng of tourists (ice cream supplies run low even on rainy days), many sensibly buying thick walking socks for ridiculously low prices. The Harris of the past can be found along the road to **Kyles Scalpay**. Small thatched cottages are still the homes of old bachelors, with hay and clothes out over the fences to dry and mad collie dogs chasing every car and bicycle that passes. The progress of all strangers is followed with active curiosity, as they gaze in surprise at the palm trees, or shake their heads in disbelief at the efficiency and hygiene of the local shop.

Bays District

The east coast is totally barren. Lumps of rock are only rarely smothered with heather and the water lies in a multitude of peat-lined lochs, much favoured by the trout, yet remarkably inhospitable to everything else except perhaps waterweed. The gaunt awkward hillside offers no welcome and yet it was to this desert that the crofters were moved when the avaricious landlords could no longer resist taking the fertile western meadows. The houses are scattered wherever there is a surface flat enough to hold them, and are best seen from the sea where the boats of the crofters give them a raison d'etre, for from the land they have none. Everything grown has to be carefully nurtured on the lazybeds made from peat cut on the hill and seaweed gathered on the shore.

After journeying through this obvious poverty — furniture is often offered for sale at the roadside — it is an enlightening experience to reach **Rodel** and the beautiful cruciform church of St Clement's sitting comfortably on its grassy knoll at the southern tip of the island. This small neat 16th century building was constructed by one of the Macleods of Dunvegan (see Skye). He bought stone from Mull so that his church would be of the same material as the cathedral of

Iona, but also dressed some of the details with black schist whose surface glitters in the light. In the north transept several sword-on-the stone tombstones are displayed, but the most magnificent tomb is in the nave. Above a black schist effigy of Alistair Crotach are some lively scenes of hunting, the weighing of souls, a ship and a castle, all with very animated gestures and lively expressions. There are good views from the narrow windows of the tower over the hills. In the graveyard, there is a tombstone commemorating Donald Macleod of Berneray who fought at Falkirk for Bonnie Prince Charlie and survived to father nine children, after his third marriage at the age of 75! Below the church is a very pleasant 19th century **harbour** with oval arms designed by the Dutch — an ideal anchorage for wandering yachtsmen.

South Harris
The west coast is serene and safe, even tame in comparison with its neighbour, the tidal currents making beautiful shapes of the sand banks and dunes. At dusk the summer light often turns the sand, sea and islands into a symphony of pinks and blues — apricot sands reflecting the sky's promise of a good tomorrow and blue conical hills reflected in the mirror of calm water.

Leverburgh is the village to which Lord Leverhulme turned all his hopes and finance after the surly rejection by the inhabitants of Stornoway (see Lewis). The rocky harbour and inland loch were transformed into a busy fishing port. Its original prosperity was so great that men had to be brought in to cope with the catches but the soap magnate's death in 1925 brought an early end to a project that his trustees did not have the conviction to continue. Now the village has a sad air of having seen better times, being hollow and quiet.

Norton is a happier township flanked by extensive sands. There is an easy walk across the dunes to **Toe Head**, a ruined chapel, and an important neolithic site excavated in 1964 where many bone and pottery artefacts were found. Many waders can be seen pacing the shore for food and rabbits romp on the grass regardless of humans. **Borve** is a civilized valley with green fields and mature trees, the home of Lord Leverhulme while he lived in Harris.

Accommodation:
Harris Hotel, Tarbert (tel Harris 2154)
Macleods Hotel, Tarbert (tel Harris 2364)
Scarista House, Scarista (tel Scarista 238)
Rodel Hotel, Rodel (tel Leverburgh 210)
B & B and self-catering — details from the Tourist Office, Tarbert.
Scottish Youth Hostel, Stockinish
Gatliff Hostel, Rhenigidale (in the back of beyond)
Laig House Caravan and Camping Site, Drinishader (tel Drinishader 207)

Car Hire:
Harris Garage Ltd., Tarbert (tel Harris 2441)
Bank:
Bank of Scotland
Fishing:
Fresh water permits:
Harris Hotel (tel Harris 2154)
Rodel Hotel (tel Leverburgh 210)
Harris Angling Club, Invercarse, Kendebig (tel Harris 2087)
Sea Angling:
Harris Sea Angling Club, Tarbert
Festival:
August — Agricultural and Handicraft Show
Tourist Office:
Tarbet — open May — Sep: 9.30 — 5.30 Mon-Sat and for late ferry
(tel Harris 2011)
Specialities:
Tweed and fishing.

Scarp

Connections:
By bus from Tarbert to Husinish, Wed and Fri; then swim or persuade
a local to ferry you across.

Depopulated of its last 50 inhabitants only in the last decade, Scarp is
now used only by a few families as a holiday retreat. However, in
1938, it was the site of an important if unsuccessful experiment to
send the post by rocket. A special stamp was produced and on 28th
July, the inventor, Herr Zucker, fired the rocket across the water; it
exploded on impact, damaging most of the mail, and the experiment
was not repeated, to the delight of all stamp collectors.

Accommodation:
Try contacting the Tourist Office, Harris, but the best hope is
camping.

Scalpay

Connections:
By sea: from Kyles Scalpay: frequent service, Mon-Sat; cars; 10 min
crossing. Caledonian MacBrayne Ltd, ferryman (tel Scalpay 220).

Scalpay is a restful island with a population of 500, most of whom are supported by the fishing industry. There is an excellent harbour on the lee side of the island, surrounded by crisp whitewashed houses.

Scalpay claims to be another refuge of Bonnie Prince Charlie during his wanderings after the Battle of Culloden: he is said to have been sheltered by one Donald Campbell, in a farmhouse where the Free Church Manse now stands.

Accommodation:
B & B and self-catering — details from the Tourist Office, Harris.

Berneray (North Uist)
(ON bjarnar-ey — bear's island)

Connections:
By sea from Newton Ferry, North Uist and from Leverburgh, Harris; frequent service Mon-Sat; D A MacAskell, 6 Borve, Berneray (tel Berneray 230: if no reply, try 233).

This is a small fertile island with a relatively large population (c 300) of lobster fishermen and sheep farmers, nestling round **Bays Loch**. **Borve Hill** (625 ft/190 m) is an easy climb for views of the Sound of Harris. To the north-west is the now uninhabited island of **Pabbay** whose islanders, according to tradition, were evacuated for illicit distilling of whiskey. Many seals and birds can be seen in the Sound of Harris and the dusk panorama can be magical, land, sand and water picking up the pink hues of the sky.

This island has little to offer the tourist except a pleasant rural atmosphere and friendly locals with time enough to spare. Some of the women have begun to weave Harris tweed and welcome visitors who trace the click-clicking of their looms through the township.

Accommodation:
B & B — details from Tourist Office, North Uist (tel Lochmaddy 321)
Gatliff Hostel
Specialities:
Weaving, tranquillity.

North Uist

Connections:
By Sea: from Uig, Skye, Mon, Wed, Fri, two a day; Tue, Thu, Sat, one a day; cars. From Tarbert, Harris, Tue, Fri; 2 hours — shortest

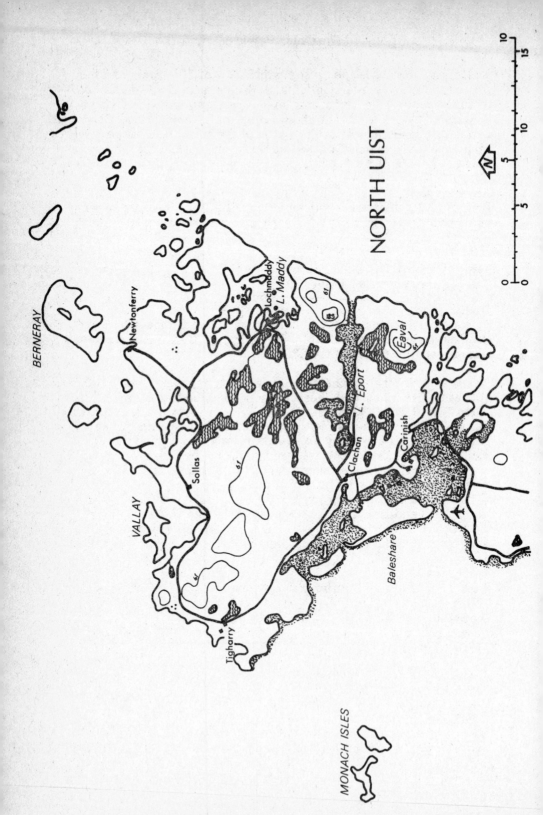

NORTH UIST

crossing. Caledonian MacBrayne Ltd (tel Lochmaddy 337).

By bridge: from Benbecula.

North Uist is an incredibly wet place and could be called the lagoon of the north. Interlocking lochs sprawl over the sunken peat moor, winding their way around small bumps and promontories. Loch Scadavay , although only 3 square miles (8 sq km) in area, is reputed to have a shoreline of over 50 miles (80 km). A fisherman's paradise, brown trout thrive in its slightly brackish sullen brown peaty water. Sheltered corners play host to white water lilies and the summer months welcome swans breeding on the tiny islets, undisturbed except by the odd fisherman.

Lochmaddy is the proud capital of this bogland, boasting a stern and solid court house, a tiny cottage hospital, a bank, garage and hotel. The hotel confronts its visitors with a huge set of scales hanging below a mammoth stuffed fish, for this indeed is the bastion of those slightly fanatical gentlemen who spend all their time and daylight hours wading thigh-deep in water. Once the hotel boasted 29 gillies to row their 29 boats on the 29 lochs, managed by the hotel. Today the number has declined, but this still remains a comfortable sporting hotel (with lots of hot water for visiting yachtsmen), specializing in Scottish cooking. This does not mean just porridge, but peat-smoked kippers and succulent North Uist lamb as well. Lochmaddy was reputed to be a favourite rendezvous for pirates of the 17th century, being named after either the rocks at the harbour mouth evocative of mad dogs, or from the oysters once found there but sadly no longer.

The road northwards has beautiful views across the islands of the Sound of Harris, their white beaches catching glints of sunlight, favourite havens of grey and common seals. On the Newton Ferry Road (boat to Berneray) is a large white house where W S Morrison was brought up. After serving as Speaker of the House of Commons, he was made Governor General of Australia, and in memory of his homeland took his title, Lord Dunrossil, from the old hillfort of his childhood playground.

The township of Sollas (G — alight) was the setting of one of the ugliest scenes of the Highland Clearances. In 1849, Lord MacDonald of Sleat proposed to move the crofters to a less fertile area, replacing them with more profitable sheep. Not surprisingly, they objected to being thrown out of their inheritance and refused to move. MacDonald brought policemen across from Skye and there ensued one of the bloodiest evictions, as the people fought to keep their homes. Many of the islanders eventually emigrated to America.

On the small island of Vallay is a house built by Erskine Beveridge, a man remembered locally for his book *Archaeology and Topography of North Uist*. Now happily occupied by a benign landlord, Earl Granville, a cousin of the Queen, who is encouraging experiments into how to use the land more profitably. Where the shell sand has blown over the peat, very rich and sweet, machair meadows are created, encouraging vivid blankets of flowers during the summer months.

In the middle of **Loch Scolpaig** is a curious 'dun'. Here there is none of the usual rubble of some Iron Age fort, but a Victorian octagonal folly complete with battlements, similar to the one at Uig (see Skye) and erected by An Dolair Ban (Dr Alex MacLeod), a chamberlain of the MacDonald estates. He took great interest in the heritage of the islands in his care. Above the road, 1 mile (1.6 km) south of his 'dun', he erected a remarkably beautiful Latin cross found in an old cemetery. It looks like a war memorial from a distance, but walking up to it reveals the happy proportions of its shape and a spectacular view out to sea, to the Haskier Islands and often as far as St Kilda.

One of the nicest rural townships of the island is at **Tigharry** (G — house on the rock), where the old crofting ways are maintained with an air of prosperity, the fields being well cared for and the houses whitewashed. This area has been included in a Nature Reserve as the use of old harvesting techniques have meant that birds such as corncrakes and corn buntings can still inhabit their traditional environments. The **Balranold Reserve** also includes moorland where the rare white tailed sea eagle may be spotted hunting; Loch Nam Feithean which is a favourite breeding ground of marsh birds such as the red-necked phalarope; the island of Causamul, a well-known haul-out for seals; and the Atlantic shoreline populated by waders. You should consult the resident summer warden at **Goular** before venturing onto the reserve; the old crofting house exhibition area is a useful source of information and identification of the birds you see. From the reserve, you can wander around the coast past the natural arches of **Tigharry**, along the beach (tempting to swimmers in the sunshine) to the promontory of **Kilmuir** and its graveyard, the traditional resting place of the Uist nobility, some of whose graves have the MacDonald coat of arms engraved on the flat slabs.

Paible was the site of an interesting experiment to rival the Dutch in their tulip production. The rich soil of the machair and the warm currents of the Atlantic provided a suitable site, but finance proved difficult and the Highlands and Islands Development Board was forced to abandon the attempt, though not through lack of support. Employment is difficult as the crofts need maintaining but will not support a family (they were never intended to do so), and few islanders are now weaving due to problems over supply from the mills of Lewis. Beyond the usual scattering of jobs, the islanders fish for lobster (most are exported).

Near **Clachan** is an excellent warehouse, Mermaid Fish Supplies, offering a wide range of fresh and cooked fish — an easy solution for those unsuccessful gentlemen in waders. They also peat-smoke mackerel, kippers, trout and salmon, permeating the flesh with a special taste, and sell at very reasonable prices. They will send fish all over the world. This is Bonnie Prince Charlie country and the locals will never let you forget it! Clachan Shop is the reputed birthplace of the unfortunate Prince's faithful servant, Edward Burke, who served him on his flight through the Outer Hebrides.

Ben Langlass, while being no great mountain, rising to only 300 ft (92 m), is worth climbing for the view. A favourite occupation for idling away an afternoon is to count the number of lochs or islets you can see — the numbers will be well into three figures before you lose track and settle for enjoying the view. On the north side of Ben Langlass is a deep megalithic cairn, set into the hillside but still well enough preserved to allow access to one of the chambers.

The road to Loch Eport passes through a crofting township left behind during the War. Many of the white houses are still thatched and inhabited, most families still milking their own cows, keeping hens and ducks off the scraps, and fishing from the boats in the sea-bays. One of these crofters, Mr MacDonald has shown much initiative and set up a tweed shop, encouraging his neighbours to weave for it. Here top quality handwoven Harris tweed is as cheap as you will ever find it.

Baleshare (G — east township) is an enchanting green machair island, with beautiful sites for swimming and camping out. Once there was a 'west township' but a ferocious gale blew it away (or at least the soil). Carnish is a site of medieval importance. Sometimes it is difficult to remember that these islands have not always been political and cultural backwaters.

At the now sadly decrepit site of Teampull na Trionard (G — Trinity Church), there was an ecclesiastical establishment founded by Beathag, daughter of Somerled, the high-powered Irish mercenary who fathered the MacDonald clan. She was the first prioress of Iona. It was later enlarged by Aimie MacRury, the wife of John, the first Lord of the Isles, and became an important educational centre for sons of chieftains, only to be destroyed in the Reformation. Probably its most famous student was Duns Scotus (c 1265 — 1308) who taught at Oxford, Paris and Cologne and argued against the philosophy of his contemporary Aquinas, maintaining that religion and theology were beyond reason and rested on faith. The term 'dunce' was one of the side products of this argument. Today the site is rather neglected but the small scale of the ruins is a potent reminder of the poverty of the islands at a time when the great cathedrals of Europe were being built. There is a good local pub.

The mountain of Eaval (1,140 ft/347 m) is a rewarding climb for those with a day to spare.

Accommodation:
Lochmaddy Hotel (tel Lochmaddy 331)
Langass Lodge Hotel (tel Loch Eport 285)

Morrison's Guest House, Lochmaddy
B & B and Self-Catering — enquire at Tourist Office, Lochmaddy
(also ask about Gaelic-speaking households).
Campsites — none. Camping Gaz from E Macaskill, Newton Ferry
Car Hire:
See Benbecula
Bicycle Hire:
A Johnson, The Old Court House (tel Lochmaddy 358)
Fishing
Freshwater fishing permits:
From Lochmaddy Hotel and North Uist Fishing Association
(Mr Cockburn, Dunrossil, Lochmaddy)
Sea Angling:
A matter of persuading a local to take you out.
Bank:
Bank of Scotland
Specialities:
Fish, weaving
Tourist Office:
Lochmaddy (tel Lochmaddy 321); open May-Sep 9.00-1.00, 2.00-5.30
and for late ferry Mon-Sat.
Early closing:
Thursday

The Monach Islands

Connections:
Enquire locally. Permission to land must be obtained from the North
Uist Estate Office (tel Lochmaddy 329) and the Nature Conservancy
Council must also be consulted.

The Monach Islands are a group of five islands and associated islets
lying 5 miles (8 km) south-west of the Hougharry Township, North
Uist. Set low-bellied in the water, their gentle shapes emerge from
the waterline, never achieving a height of 50 ft or any cliffs to be
proud of. They are now a National Nature Reserve, their grassy backs
supporting a wealth of flowers and their sandy shores many waders.
   The three largest islands, Ceann Ear (G — East Head), Skivinish
and Ceann Lar (G — West Head) are linked at low tide by sandy
causeways, and were the site of the first recorded settlement, for in
the 13th century a daughter of Iona set up a small nunnery on these
remote outliers. A monastery was built on Skillay whose monks had
a duty to keep a light burning, to warn travellers of the surrounding
rocks. Both ecclesiastical settlements failed to survive the Reformation
but the islands continued to support a small population until the

tyrannical elements succeeded in blowing and washing away the fertile top soil. However, no islander gives in easily, and the islands were very soon repopulated after marram grass had been planted to create a sandholding net above the tidelines. An active community survived with a post office and shop, wrecks often providing much needed supplies, until 1942 when the last lighthouse keeper was recalled, the monks' light finally being extinguished.

The ghost town often provides a night's resting place for local lobster fishermen and the grass is still grazed by summer sheep.

Grimsay
(ON — Grim's Island)

Connections:
By road: from N Uist and Benbecula. Since only half a mile (.8 km) of the main Long Isle road runs across Grimsay, one might be forgiven for assuming that this was an island backwater, a sandbank raised above the waterline with pastures of flowers and not a lot else. Perhaps the fact that it is by-passed by so many has helped it retain its charm. The narrow road switchbacks over the bumps and round the corners past thatched cottages and sheltered coves — a road begun by the Destitution Committee in an attempt to create work to relieve the crippling poverty caused by the potato famine of 1846. Although the potato was only introduced to the islands from North America a century earlier, it soon became part of the staple diet of the crofters, varying the otherwise endless oats, oatcakes and porridge. Even today, few other vegetables are grown. Most of the islanders take to the double-pointed lobster boats (still made on the island), as Grimsay is the centre of the lobster industry south of Harris. The Highlands and Islands Development Board have financed a processing plant which provided much needed employment (visitors are welcome to look and buy) and sells shellfish all over the world.

The harbour of **Baymore** is a scenic site with the grey gneiss rocks of Ronay towering in front, and the green grass-topped islets competing in colour with the vividly painted boats at their moorings.

The local weaver, Lachlan MacDonald, is a fine son of this shore, proud, skilful and friendly, and welcoming appreciation of his art. He has an imaginative eye for colour which make his tweeds particularly desirable

Accommodation:
B & B — enquire at Tourist Office, North Uist (tel Lochmaddy 321)
Specialities:
Lobsters

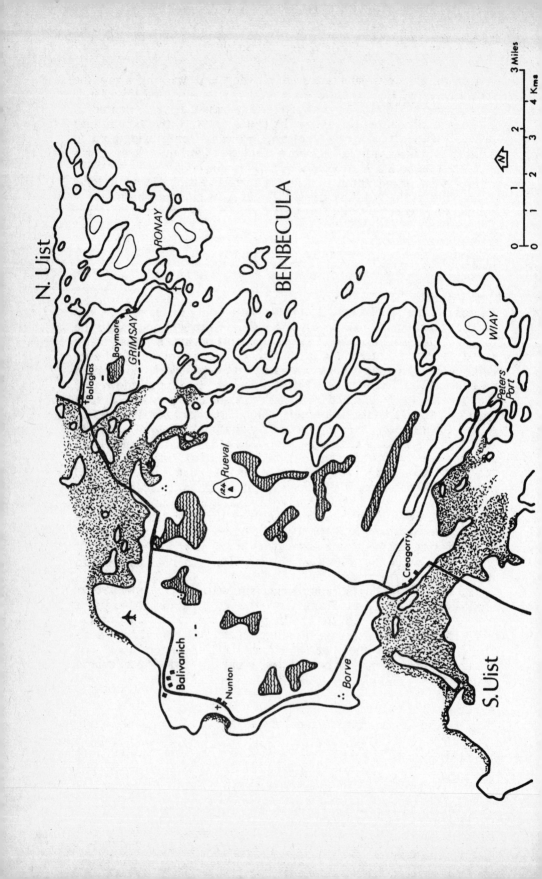

Benbecula
(G — hill of the fords)

Connections:
By air: from Glasgow: Mon-Sat, one a day. British Airways (tel Benbecula 2310). From Stornoway; Mon-Fri, three a day; Sat, one a day. From Barra: Tue, Wed, Fri, one a day. Loganair Ltd (tel Benbecula 2310) — connecting bus with Lochboisdale.
By road: from North Uist, Grimsay and South Uist.

Earlier this century, reaching Benbecula was a matter of fording the sand banks exposed at low tide which divide this flat plain of lochs from North and South Uist. This crossing was always hazardous as strong tides continuously sculpt new shapes in the sand, confusing travellers. Happily, modern causeways and bridges now link Benbecula to its neighbours, and sand wandering is now confined to shell collectors and paddlers (it's rarely deep enough to swim satisfactorily). The only feature rising above the flat bog is the hill of Rueval (410 ft/124 m), another retreat of Bonnie Prince Charlie just prior to his crossing to Skye with Flora Macdonald. His crossing of Benbecula was not without difficulties: he kept on losing his shoes in the bog, making his poor servants retrieve them, and thus slowing the pace of their retreat considerably. More recently, Hercules the bear made his last bid for freedom on these moors. One can only hope that they all enjoyed Rueval's views across to the mountains of St Kilda in the west and to the Cuillins of Skye in the east, and the patchwork of water and land below them.

The only area of dry land, the dunes of the west coast, houses the aerodrome, an important lifeline to these islands supported by the local military base. The old site of a medieval monastry at Balivanich has been redeveloped since the outbreak of the Second World War as a military camp for the troops servicing the rocket range on South Uist (see South Uist). The large condensed population of 'outsiders' deprives Benbecula of its 'Gaelic' atmosphere, since only the old folk keep up the traditions, yet it does give the island a wealth of services, which would otherwise be impossible to maintain with only a small indigenous community. The only chemist of the Outer Hebrides outside Stornoway is to be found here. Far less beautiful than the surrounding rural townships, the military housing provides much needed local work. The beach at Culla is ideal for picnics and swimming, though it is relatively crowded in comparison to the rest of Long Isle.

The ruined chapel at Nunton was the centre of a pre-Reformation nunnery and the large house close by was built by the Macdonald chieftains of Clanranald after their castle at Ormaclete (see South Uist) had been burnt down in a moment of festivity in 1715. The 18th century part of the house is easily distinguishable from later additions. Beside the road at Borve are the lichen-covered ruins of an earlier Clanranald residence, Borve Castle, stubborn and dignified in its dereliction.

Creagorry was once the central community of the island and has the only hotel, whose rooms are filled by commercial travellers and not happy families; it is definitely not a holiday hotel. However, it does maintain fishing rights on some of the hill lochs, although these are in need of much love and attention — obviously salesmen don't have time to enjoy one of the traditional pleasures of Benbecula. Loch fishing is generally neglected, but some of the lochs will respond to patience.

The pier of Peter's Port is the folly of a planner who dreamed that a pier between Lochmaddy, North Uist, and Lochboisdale, South Uist, would stimulate island life. Benbecula was chosen as the approximate halfway point and the pier was built at great expense, without any proper assessment of the need for it, or any consultation of local knowledge as to its site. Once built in the back of beyond, it had to be serviced by a road, and only when this had been constructed did anyone realize that the loch mouth was practically unnavigable. Since then, the pier has never been used, except by the locals.

The rocky island of Wiay is a bird sanctuary, attracting birds of prey as well as the marsh and shoreline birds. For access, enquire locally.

Accommodation:
Creagorry Hotel (tel Benbecula 2024)
B & B and self-catering — details from Tourist Office, South Uist (tel Lochboisdale 286) or Tourist Office, North Uist (tel Lochmaddy 321)
Freshwater fishing permits:
Creagorry Hotel (tel Benbecula 2024)
Benbecula Angling Club, Creagorry Post Office
Car Hire:
Maclennan Bros (Motors) Ltd, Balivanich (tel Balivanich 2191)
Bank:
Bank of Scotland, Creagorry
Early Closing:
All day Wednesday

South Uist

Connections:
By sea: from Oban: summer, one a day except Sun; winter, Mon, Wed, Fri, one a day; cars; shortest crossing 6 hours. From Castlebay (Barra): Mon, Wed, Fri and summer Sat, one a day; cars; 2 hours

crossing. Caledonian MacBrayne Ltd (tel Lochboisdale 288).

By bridge: from Benbecula.

South Uist is an astonishingly beautiful island, strongly Irish in flavour, with the western coastal machair strip blossoming forth in a great variety of colours and scents, and small thatched cottages, still kept crisply whitewashed. It is lined inland by a barely inhabited sultry bogland, and backed by the harsh awkward ridge of mountains rising from the eastern sea. The pace of life slows as the road gets narrower and twists round the indentations of lochs, calmly offering their white and yellow water lilies to wandering glances.

The township of Eochar (G iochdar — bottom, ie a low place) is typical with its scattering of old cottages and council houses. Not many have taken advantage of the Highlands and Islands Development Board's grants for home improvements, unlike the rest of the Highlands where houses seem to grow better than potatoes, coming in all shapes and sizes with a uniform lack of design. One of the old houses has a superb collection of junk covered with shells, and its next door neighbour, uninhabited for many a year, is a charming unhygienic crofting museum, (curator Mrs MacNeill, 8 Bualadubh (dark town), opposite the school; entrance 20p, open 10 — 5). Remarkably musty and dingy inside, it houses a splendid collection of crofting implements gathered by a local priest before he retired to Skye and subsequently left to rot. Ignore the scrap of Bonnie Prince Charlie's kilt and try out the boxbeds and the cumbersome farm tools. Imagine twisting straw ropes to hold down the thatch in winter gales and be grateful you no longer have to grind your flour with the handquern. Hanging on the wall is an interesting old school map of Scotland in 1802 (it was only this century that Scottish education went beyond the pale) and a glass cabinet holds all manner of treasures — apothecaries' scales, leather bottles and a vast collection of pipes. Further along the road is the **Hebridean Jewellery Workshop** (visitors welcome), where a small team of craftsmen produce tasteful silver to Celtic designs, many clan brooches and pins, and a wide selection of lucken booths.

Loch Bee is each summer chosen by mute swans as a suitable nesting site. By August they flock to the open water for their autumn migration, their graceful white sails echoed by the snow of bog cotton and the stars of water lilies, justifying the loch's protection and preservation as a nature reserve.

Facing all visitors to the island is **Our Lady of the Isles**, a monumental sculpture carved by Hew Lorimer and erected in 1957 to commemorate Marion Year. From the road it looks remarkably like a nondescript column, mysteriously the centre of a network of fences, but on closer inspection the cleverness of the design is apparent. Although dispelling any doubt that this island is claimed by the Catholics, its close association with the mammoth radar

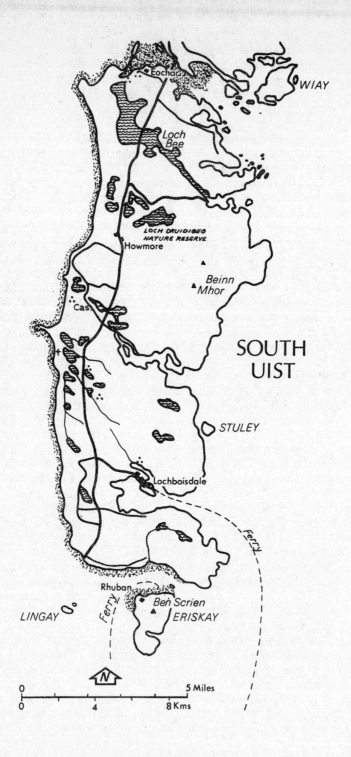

WIAY

Eochar

Loch
Bee

LOCH DRUIDIBEG
NATURE RESERVE

Howmore

Beinn
Mhor

Cas

SOUTH
UIST

STULEY

Lochboisdale

Ferry

Rhuban

Ferry

LINGAY

Ben Scrien

ERISKAY

N

| 0 | | | 5 Miles |
| 0 | 4 | | 8 Kms |

station on the hill above raises other connotations. Many of the gneiss hills are capped with radar stations, for South Uist is the controversial base of the army's guided missile rocket range. (Yachtsmen should enquire at Lochboisdale, South Uist and Lochmaddy, North Uist before sailing this stretch of coastline, as firing times vary from day to day and month to month. It is better to avoid it completely if possible.) Although the range provides some jobs for locals, it also makes checking the inshore lobster pots complicated and some of the rich farmland unusable in this relatively poor community, and so a great deal of hot air is created in non-productive discussion.

The road through the **Loch Druidibeg Nature Reserve** (warden at Stilligarry) is a delightful drive to the indented rocky shoreline of the east coast, past the odd clumps of 'relic' shrubs and rhododendron bushes. The Reserve is a favourite place for nesting herons and greylag geese, whose numbers are seasonally swelled during migration with whitefronted geese. Sheltered gorges in the hills are populated by many different types of ferns, especially the royal fern, not inappropriate because Loch Skipport is an anchorage favoured by the British royal family on their summer cruises. The redundant pier makes a happy picnic spot and fish respond well to a line dabbled from it.

Howmore (G — burial mound) boasts two very interesting but disassociated ecclesiastical centres. Overgrown by nettles and much neglected are the chapels and buildings of a pre-Reformation monastery and college, covered by yellow lichen. Notice how small some of the chapels were. In one is propped up a beautiful carved stone associated with the Macdonald family, with crisp renderings of a sailing ship, castle, horse and their armorial bearings, which would once have graced the tombstone of a Renaissance chieftain. Close by is the post-Reformation Presbyterian church, interesting for its surviving communion table. These are found only rarely, as normally temporary tables would be erected for the occasion (and subsequently entered as debits on church bill records). Here, the built-in table runs the length of the building, dividing the pews.

The roads through the machair are disappointing because they rarely intrude on the privacy of the whiteshell sand beaches and so offer no glimpses of the Atlantic waves. At **Ormaclete** there is a fine ruin of the unfortified castle built by a French architect for Allan Macdonald at the beginning of the 18th century. Taking seven years to construct, it was only inhabited for a further seven when a side of venison caught fire in the kitchen and burnt the house to a shell, traditionally on the eve of the Battle of Sheriffmuir in 1715 where its master was fatally injured.

Locheynort is another fine safe anchorage where old tree roots from the lost forests can be found around the waterline. It is a good place from which to penetrate the eastern mountain ranges, lumpy and scarcely clad, bringing delight both to walkers for the views and to climbers for the challenges offered. Many alpine flowers can be seen in the summer months. On the south side of **Stulaval** (1,230 ft/ 374 m) are the remains of a Stone Age earthhouse in an evocative state of preservation, with circles of stones close by.

Milton's (mill-village) claim to fame is as the birthplace of Bonnie Prince Charlie's reluctant helper, Flora Macdonald. Whatever webs of romance future generations spun over this couple, history reveals that the worthy lady was none too keen to take on her task, and although she became a popular heroine she and her husband became firm supporters of the government, and many years later entertained Johnson and Boswell at their house in Skye. The rubble ruins of her birthplace are marked by a cairn. The lochs of Milton are now being used for a new project of fishfarming.

Lochboisdale is the sprawling centre of South Uist with not a lot to recommend it except its safe anchorages and comfortable sporting hotel. This, the Lochboisdale Hotel (tel Lochboisdale 332), was built in 1882 in conjunction with the then new pier and exudes plenty of goodwill towards yachtsmen, though it has no special facilities. It is highly recommended, if only for a meal or a game of darts in the bar. It offers rough snipe shooting on South Uist's boggy hillsides (booking a year in advance is advisable) and also caters for fishermen. The hill lochs are well maintained, and many boats are available.

There are no camping facilities here, but those aiming to catch the early ferry can pitch a tent in front of the bank or by the Tourist Office. Caledonian McBrayne Pier Offices can be persuaded to leave their toilets and waiting room open in the event of bad weather, or alternatively an overnight berth can be obtained on the ferry.

The picturesque ruins of the castle on **Calvay** island were yet another of Prince Charlie's temporary hiding places during his flight.

At **Kilpheder** on the dunes is a Pictish wheelhouse, so called because of its circular shape, divided into chambers by radial piers. Probably built in the 2nd century AD, it is typical of the sort of house that was still inhabited by many of the native population on the eve of the Viking invasion.

The Catholic community of **Garynamonie** have a modern church of which they are justifiably proud. A mosaic of 'Our Lady of Sorrows' by David Harding welcomes passers-by, and once inside one can truly appreciate the subtleties of the exterior sculptured design, for the accoustics are brilliant. (The services are in Gaelic, but the routine is the same.) The lighting is particularly effective, as it falls directly only on the main altar. On the side walls are the Stations of the Cross, the work of a local priest, Father Callum MacNeill, simply evoked by incised and painted lines carved on greenish slates from the island of Stuley. Other examples of his artistic genius can be seen at St Peter's, **Daliburgh** — where a traditional Victorian crucifix has been brought to life by a painted backdrop of light on waves and clouds, and on the islands of Eriskay and Barra. South Uist has not always been Catholic: one of its lairds, Alexander Macdonald of Boisdale, rejected Rome in 1770 and with true reforming zeal tried to drive his tenants to his new religion with a yellow cane. Islanders don't reject their heritage easily and many preferred to emigrate to Prince Edward's Island, Canada; however, some did remain and convert to the religion of 'the yellow stick', the majority returning to the beliefs of their fathers on the laird's death.

The Inn at **Pollachar** is exactly what you would expect to find at the end of a road and in the back of beyond. Rather decrepit and neglected, it is very much a locals' pub, taking on a smuggling air as the dusk shrouds the view across the sound to Eriskay and Barra.

Accommodation:
Lochboisdale Hotel (tel Lochboisdale 332)
Borrodale Hotel (tel Lochboisdale 444)
Ben More Guest House (tel Grogarry 283)
B & B and self-catering details from Tourist Office, Lochboisdale, (also for Gaelic-speaking houses)
Gatcliff Hostel, Howmore
Loch druidibeg Caravan Site, Grogarry (tel Grogarry 210)
Fishing:
Freshwater permits from:
Lochboisdale Hotel (tel Lochboisdale 332)
South Uist Fishings, Mr Cockburn, 23 Tarlum, Benbecula
Shooting:
Lochboisdale Hotel (tel Lochboisdale 332)
Car Hire:
James Ling (tel Lochboisdale 319)
Angus John Campbell (tel Lochboisdale 267)
Mrs Reynolds (tel Lochboisdale 462)
Bicycle Hire:
James Young, Lochboisdale
Golf Course:
Details from Tourist Office
Bank:
Royal Bank of Scotland, Lochboisdale
Tourist Office:
Lochboisdale (tel Lochboisdale 286): open May-Sept, 9.30-5.30 Mon-Sat and for late ferry
Festival:
Uist Games in July

Eriskay
(G — uruisg + ON ay — goblin island)

Connections:
By sea: from Luday: weekdays frequently, depending on tides;
crossing 15-30 mins. From Eoligarry: on request (on route to Ludag).
Angus and Donald Campbell, Ludag (tel Lochboisdale 216).

Eriskay is formed by two bare and knobbly hill peaks, **Ben Scrien**
(610 ft/185 m) and **Ben Stack** (400 ft/122 m) which rise firmly out
of the Sound, catching the changing play of light as the clouds romp
overhead. Not immediately welcoming to the traveller, Eriskay is a
haven of tradition and individuality, an islander's island relatively
unharmed by the uniformity of modern Britain. The hills, a steep
scramble rewarded by a healthy view, are the grazing 'pastures' of the
Eriskay ponies, a small breed (12-15 hands) that still works on the
land. Born black, they mature to a grey or white colour. The species
is now threatened with extinction unless more interest is taken in it.

As there is little level ground or good soil, the lairds of the time of
the Clearances felt that they could afford to give this under-populated
land to their evicted tenants, and so the community expanded in the
19th century. However, Eriskay has one important bonus, a good
harbour at **Haun**, and so the men took to fishing — still the main
source of employment — while the women earned extra pennies by
travelling to the herring curing stations of the east coast for the
summer season.

Here, as elsewhere on the Outer Hebrides, summer is greeted by an
ecstasy of wild flowers, but Eriskay claims one unique to itself, the
sea bindweed (Calystegia Soldanella), known locally as the **Prince's
flower**. This was supposed to have been brought by Prince Charlie
when he landed on Eriskay, and the islanders claim that it will not
grow elsewhere in Scotland (please do not try to disprove this theory
by taking away a plant, but enjoy the pink flowers in situ). Eriskay
was the first Scottish land the Prince stepped on in his disastrous
attempt to claim the crown from his Protestant cousins. He anchored
his ship off the **Prince's Strand** on 23rd May 1674, and when a
golden eagle was seen hovering overhead, he took it to be a good
omen and landed with some companions, disguised as a young priest.
Eriskay did not have much hospitality to offer and the dashing
young man had to catch flounders on the sand for his supper,
sleeping that night in a hovel before moving on to gather support. He
left behind him the recipe for Drambuie, but it is for another alcoholic
association that Eriskay springs to mind. In 1941 the SS *Politician*
ran aground, having mistaken the Sound of Eriskay for the Sound of
Barra, on her way to America carrying 24,000 cases of whiskey. The
events that followed are fossilized in Sir Compton MacKenzie's
masterpiece, *Whiskey Galore*!

Eriskay has attracted its fair share of wrecks and some of these have contributed to the local Catholic church. St Michael's at Rhuban was built in 1903 under the impetus of Father Allen Macdonald who raised the money (persuading the fishermen to contribute one day's catch, which so happened to be the best of that particular year) and also designed the church. Visitors would not be mistaken in noticing a Spanish influence, for Father Allen worked for some years in Valladolid. The church bell comes from a German battleship, *Der Lingir*, sunk in the Scapa Flow (see Stromness, Orkney), but the altar was created out of a local wreck by Father Callum MacNeil (see also South Uist and Barra). The lifeboat of the aircraft carrier *Hermes* is painted a crisp white and is supported by golden anchors and coils of ropes, an appropriate reminder of the all important sea.

Father Allen also spent much energy collecting local folklore and his work was expanded by Marjory Kennedy Frazer who collected the songs and tunes still sung by these people. The Eriskay love lilt is famous in all Scots communities throughout the world. Island craftsmen are now producing the traditional Eriskay fisherman's jerseys, self-coloured garments lighter than the more common Arran, which are also patterned with story-telling designs.

Accommodation:
Difficult, enquire at Tourist Office, South Uist (tel Lochboisdale 286)
Specialities:
Jerseys from the island co-op (tel Eriskay 247).

Barra
(St Finbarr's Island)

Connections:
By air: from Glasgow: one a day. From Stornoway (Lewis) via Benbecula: Tue, Wed, Fri — all plane schedules affected by tide variations at Barra. Loganair Ltd (tel Northbay 283).

By Sea: to Castlebay from Oban: Mon, Wed, Fri and summer Sat; cars; 5½ hour crossing. From Lochboisdale (South Uist): Mon, Tue, Thu and summer Sat; cars; 1½ hour crossing. Caledonian MacBrayne Ltd (tel Castlebay 275). To Eoligarry from Ludag (South Uist): daily; crossing 40 mins. Angus & Donald Campbell, Ludag (tel Lochboisdale 216).

The harbour of **Castlebay** is the first safe anchorage of the Outer Hebrides north of Ireland, and was therefore of great strategic importance to anyone wishing to inflict his authority on the Northern Islands. Both warrior Celts and Norsemen settled on Barra, but there

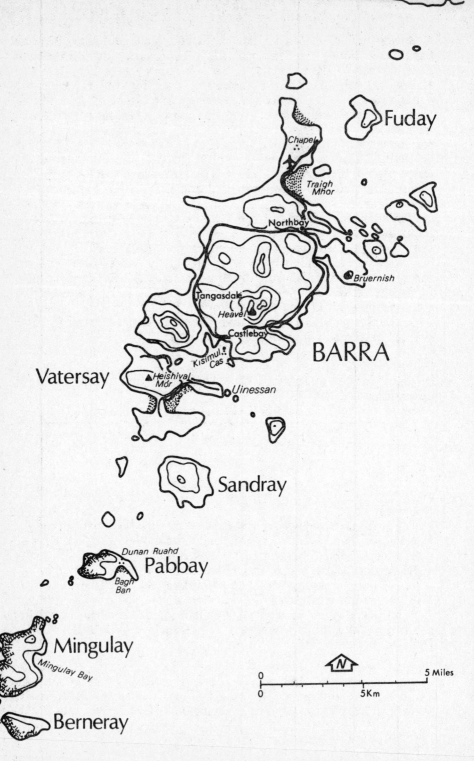

Fuday

Chapel

*Traigh
Mhor*

Northbay

Bruernish

Tangasdale

Heavel

Castlebay

*Kisimul
Cas*

BARRA

Vatersay

*Heishival
Mór*

Uinessan

Sandray

Dunan Ruahd

Pabbay

*Bagh
Ban*

Mingulay

Mingulay Bay

Berneray

N

0   5 Miles

0   5 Km

was always a problem of defence when another ambitious figure emerged, intent on carving out a kingdom for himself. Luckily for the settlers, a rocky islet in the bay was found to have a supply of freshwater (through a geological pipe) and so Kisimul Castle was built to defend the anchorage, as the stronghold of the MacNeil family. Dating from the 12th century (the MacNeils claim earlier), Kisimul stands a sturdy square around a tower keep (if the flag is flying the chief is in residence). Impressively solid, it is a worthy stronghold for the piratical family who did not hesitate to attack even the ships of Queen Elizabeth I of England. When summoned to Edinburgh, that particular chief saved his life by explaining to James VI (and I of England) that he thought he was serving his sovereign lord by annoying the 'woman who had killed his mother'.

The family traces its ancestry back to Niall of the Nine Hostages, High King of Ireland in the 4th century, but even with this inheritance the warlike instincts were gradually bred out of them and they deserted Kisimul for a more comfortable house on Barra in the 18th century. The fortress later suffered a fire and became a hollow ruin — the playground of sea otters, birds and children. The main family line died out in 1863 and succession passed to the cadet branch which had emigrated to Canada, like so many of Barra's inhabitants.

In 1937 Robert Lister MacNeil, the 45th chief, rebought the old home and slowly began to restore it, using Barra men. (There are boat trips to the castle each summer, Wed and Sat from Castlebay pier, 2-3.30 pm; £1.) Old photographs on display show the extent of the dereliction, and while the reconstruction of the barrack blocks and keep is not as authentic as it could be, the effect is impressive. Within the walls is an open courtyard surrounded by buildings, giving an astonishing and unexpected feeling of space. The all important well can be seen by the Chief's private quarters and an ingenious rock pool, used for catching fish as the tide lowered, is by the pier. Robert Lister is buried in the castle chapel and a second morbid vault is waiting for his widow. His son, the 46th chief, and the MacNeil clan are gathering family mementoes for the museum in the Great Hall.

Castlebay is a small compact town ringing the way around Kisimul, a good shopping centre. In the late 19th century it was a very active herring port, harbouring over 400 boats at the height of the summer, and bringing much employment to the islanders. This trade fell off by the First World War and now most of the fishing is concentrated on lobsters and crabs. Yachts should report to Caledonian MacBrayne's Pier Office and moor on the right of the bay (ie *not* in front of the castle as there are many hidden rocks). The Catholic church with the town clock above the bay produces the excellent weekly *Barra Bulletin* on local events — if you miss the service, copies are left in the porch. Although it is not aimed at visitors, outsiders will always be welcomed to island events, and you may even have the privilege to hear a daughter of Barra playing the clarsach — a Scottish harp, made on the island. Above the town rises the mountain of Heavel (1,255 ft/383 m) whose grassy slopes host a multitude of blossoms — Barra is a garden of wild flowers with over 400 recorded species. On a clear day there are spectacular views through a full circle of islands and water, sand and surf, cloud and sunlight. On its slopes is a statue of the Madonna and Child carved from white Carrara marble, often hidden by mist, and further to the west is Father Dugan's Pass. Father Dugan was a missionary sent by St Vincent de Paul to the islands to counter the rot of heretic and heathen practices in 1651. The site of his open air altar above Brevig Bay can still be identified.

Barra witnessed many ugly scenes at the time of the Clearances, one clergyman laird even herding his flock into immigration ships bound for Canada, others forcing their crofters onto the rocky slopes at Bruernish where there was not even enough soil to bury their dead. One owner offered the island to the government as a penal colony but was turned down. The people turned to the sea for a living but still needed to grow their basic food supplies, so here as elsewhere in the Highlands they developed a system of lazybeds — table-sized strips of earth built from beds of peat, fertilized each year with seaweed dragged up from the shore. These are still maintained for growing potatoes and other vegetables. The houses perch uncomfortably on the rocks seeking what shelter they can, making travel by sea easier than on the gnarled slopes of the land. The community spirit thrived to combat these hardships and even today fishermen will place a box of their catch on the shore to be distributed among their neighbours, remembering to put in a cod for the old lady, before taking the rest of the fish to the mainland markets.

Northbay is the second harbour of the island, sheltered and rocky, with a comfortable village feel, the pier sitting close by the road watched by the church. A small plantation of pine trees is alive with bird song, and I am assured that the roadside here is favoured by a great range of snails and slugs. Barra's flowers attract many brightly coloured butterflies, difficult to identify without a good handbook, but very beautiful as they flutter by.

The great cockle sand of Traigh Mhor (G great sand) was commented on by the earliest tourists to the islands in the 17th century. The shallow bay is the happy breeding ground for these shell fish, living below the surface of old discarded shells. They are still eaten locally as a delicacy. Due to the lack of another suitable site and the excellent firmness and drainage caused by the shells, this beach has served the island as an airstrip since 1935, and a flight to or from Barra must be one of the most memorable offered in Europe, for often the aircraft has barely left the cockles before the sea is washing them. There is a bus connection with Castlebay to meet the planes. In recent years a factory has been removing the cockleshells to make harling grit (the rough coating seen on many Scottish houses).

This has caused controversy and many problems, for although the factory provides much needed employment, it indiscriminately takes dead and alive cockles and so wastes a precious food supply and harms the self-renewing cycle of the beach. It also provides problems for the aircraft pilots, as the removal of the shells leaves a soft water-clogged sand, unsuitable as an alternative runway. Barra may yet lose one of her major tourist attractions if the airstrip is moved to the sand dunes on the other side of the road.

Eoligarry is a pleasant township isolated from the relative humdrum of the main circuit of the island. A small cemetery at **Cille-Bharra** is the traditional burial place of the MacNeil chieftains, where several nice 14th and 15th century sword-on-the-stone tombstones of warriors can be seen. Also buried here is the famous novelist Sir Compton MacKenzie, who made Barra his home (see Eriskay). Father Callum MacNeil (see also South Uist and Eriskay) restored the original 12th century chapel dedicated to St Finbarr with much local support. Tradition recounts that when St Finbarr, an Irish disciple of St Columba, came to Barra, he discovered that the people were cannibals as well as heathens, having just polished off his missionary predecessor. Whatever means he used seem to have been effective, for his reputation and fame spread and Barra continues to honour his achievement in bringing Catholicism to this island.

From **Cleat**, folklore maintains that there is an underground passage to **Uaimh an Oir** (G cave of gold) on the east coast. Two men and their dogs tried to prove the theory, and playing their pipes moved slowly into the darkness. For a while their neighbours standing at Cleat cave mouth could hear the tunes distinctly but then they suddenly ceased. Days later the dogs emerged from Uaimh an Oir, hairless and mad. There are many odd tales of disappearance on Barra, all making for spooky late night story telling, of men vanishing when they cross the mountains and of girls spirited away while washing clothes on the loch side. Whatever the truth behind these stories, remember that the mood of the hills changes suddenly and do not set off for a summer walk unprepared for storms which quickly blow over.

The west side of Barra has many white beaches suitable for swimming and camping. At **Halaman Bay**, a luxury hotel has been built on the machair by the Highlands and Islands Development Board, whose design won a Europe Nostra Diploma of Merit in 1977. A homely family hotel, with an emphasis on informality, it welcomes children, yachtsmen and even dogs. It has an excellent cuisine making good use of local produce. The Shah of Iran, sensing the Revolution, sent his children here to the safekeeping of their nurse's homeland, an ingenuous choice of hideout for no one can arrive at Barra unnoticed.

At **Tangasdale**, among the clover fields, is Barra's most famous industry, the **perfume factory**. It is disappointing that the wealth of local flowers are rejected in favour of synthetic oils from the continent. The owner will explain to visitors how he makes up the perfumes to be evocative of Scottish scents. Names like Plaid, Dark Glen and Love Lilt do much to create the illusion, and what man could resist the opportunity of acquiring Caber Aftershave!

Accommodation:
Castlebay Hotel (taste of Scotland) (tel Castlebay 223)
Craigard Hotel (tel Castlebay 200)
An Calla Guest House (tel Castlebay 270)
Dunard Guest House (tel Castlebay 271)
Heathbank Hotel, Northbay (tel Northbay 266)
Isle of Barra Hotel, Tangusdale (taste of Scotland) (tel Castlebay 383)
B & B and self-catering details from Tourist Office, Castlebay
Car Hire:
Gerald Campbell, Castlebay (tel Castlebay 328)
Bicycle Hire:
Post Office, Castlebay (tel Castlebay 286)
Isle of Barra Hotel, Tangusdale (tel Castlebay 383)
Fresh water fishing permits:
Post Office, Castlebay (tel Castlebay 286)
Sea Angling:
Castlebay Hotel (tel Castlebay 223)
Heathbank Hotel, Northbay (tel Northbay 266)
Dunard Guest House, Castlebay (tel Castlebay 271)
Bank:
Royal Bank of Scotland, Castlebay
Specialities:
Perfume, Clarsach and cockles.
Tourist Office:
Castlebay (tel Castlebay 336): open May-Sept 9.30-5.30 Mon-Sat and for late ferries.

Vatersay
(ON vatrsay — water isle)

Connections:
By sea: from Castlebay, Barra: Mon-Fri, four a day; Sat, Sun, two a day. J A MacNeil (tel Castlebay 307)

Vatersay is a solemn empty island, ponderous below the summit of Heishival Mor (625 ft/190 m), and still inhabited by a small community spread between four settlements, which exaggerates the feeling of privacy. Most families earn a living from farming, raising beef cattle which they force to swim the sound to Castlebay and the ferry which will take them to the mainland market. A few also fish for lobsters while many of the menfolk still earn a living in the Merchant Navy. Sunlight off the pier reveals beautiful patterns in the submerged sand and rocks, like a mackerel's back, and sets the mood for this dark and silver isle.

Vatersay reached the national headlines at the beginning of this century through the bravery and stubbornness of the **Vatersay Raiders**. Crofters from Mingulay and Barra, tired of the hardships imposed by their absentee landlady, Lady Cathcart Gordon, decided to move to this rocky isle. By building themselves houses within dawn and dusk of the same day (wooden thatched shacks but dwellings with a hearth, nonetheless) they subscribed to an old Scots law entitling them to own the surrounding land. Lady Gordon was not pleased, claiming that they were unsuitable tenants and that there was not enough fresh water on the island to support them, and took them to court. Their case was overruled and they were committed to the Carlton Jail, Edinburgh for six months, but national support was so strong that they were released after six weeks and allowed to return to their chosen homeland. Most cottage walls still display photographs of these determined men.

Walking round the hill shoulder to the main village, past the tragic corpse of a crashed fighter plane from the last war, one is enticed by a beautiful stretch of white sand and dunes. A granite monument by the shore records the floundering of the *Annie Jane*, on 28th September 1853, on her voyage from Liverpool to Quebec carrying a cargo of emigrants to a new life. Three-quarters of the crew and passengers never reached this shore.

On the offshore island of Uinessan are the ruins of the **Chapel of Mary of the Heads**, a curious mixture of misassociation for the Mary in question was not the mother of Jesus but the second wife of a MacNeil chieftain, who wanted her son to gain inheritance over his two elder step-brothers. Legend records that she achieved this aim by removing their heads: hence the name.

Accommodation:
None, take a tent.

Sandray
(ON — sand island)

Connections:
By Sea: no regular service. Enquire at the Tourist Office, Barra (tel Castlebay 336) for day trips.

A gaunt mountain rising out of the sea to a height of 640 ft (207 m),

Sandray was inhabited by farmers until 1934, but now it is totally deserted. Even its once-vaunted loch fishing is now neglected. The island's lower slopes often appear to be covered with snow, as the white sand is picked up from the beaches by the wind and blown onto the rocks, encouraging a multitude of wild flowers to blossom.

Pabbay
(ON papay — priest's isle)

Connections:
By sea: No regular service. Enquire at the Tourist Office, Barra (tel Castlebay 336) for day trips.

This island was also deserted earlier this century. Some traces of its original inhabitants can be seen above the sands of **Bagh Ban** (G — white bay) where three stones were found carved with pictish crosses and a fourth with a crescent, lily and cross, all beside the rubble remains of a chapel. North are the traces of a fort, **Dunan Ruahd** (G — red fort) close to the spectacular natural arch, carved so large by the sea that the herring boats of last century frequently sailed through it on calm days. An excellent picnic isle.

Mingulay
(ON — bird isle)

Connections:
By Sea: no regular service, enquire at the Tourist Office, Barra (tel Castlebay 336) for day trips.

A boat trip around the cliffs of Mingulay even on the calmest of days will take the breath away from the most inexcitable visitor, for the gradual slope climbing up from the beach of Mingulay Bay drops sheer from 820 ft (250 m) into the sea on the west, a magnificent monument to the power of the Atlantic. Swamped with seabirds — kittiwakes, guillemots, puffins and black-backed gulls to name the largest colonies — this is an excellent island for birdwatchers of all levels; binoculars are a help but not essential. The rock is moulded into exciting formations, gullies and stacks, caves and a vast natural arch, an easy lesson in 'O' level geography formations. More imaginative connections may be made with Neil Munro's romantic description of a climb up these cliffs in his book *Children of the Tempest*, but a re-enaction of this story is far from advisable.
Deserted of its last inhabitants in 1934, a ghost town remains on

the sandy shore and only harbour, but once there was a thriving community under the patronage of the MacNeils of Barra. The laird would collect his yearly rent from the crofters in the form of 'fachaich' — the fat young of shearwater caught just before they left the nest, coming himself to stay for a month to enjoy the harvest. Very much fathers of their people, the MacNeils would find wives for widowers and husbands for widows (the marriage being sanctified by a bottle of whiskey, nothing more), take a second twin into their own family to relieve the crofters of an extra mouth to feed, replace lost cows and take the old folk into the comfort of their own home.

Here, as on St Kilda, the economy was centred on the seabirds but there were also some traditions of fishing: the famous Mingulay boat song is all that survives today.

Berneray
(ON — Bjorn's isle)

Connections:
By Sea: no regular service. Enquire at the Tourist Office, Barra (tel Castlebay 336) for day trips.

Berneray takes the full force of the Atlantic gales, and it is not a rare occurrence for small fish to be blown up with the surf to land by the lighthouse (660 ft/200 m) up the cliffs! From this vantage point the western shoreline of Scotland can be watched. The deserted lighthouse keepers' cottages built from the grey granite quarries on the island have recently been offered by the National Trust for Scotland as part of their 'Little Houses Scheme', as a home for one who minds not the isolation, often enforced, or the probable lack of fresh water in the summer. After all, what difficulties are these to spoil the pleasures of living on one of the most dramatic of all Scottish islands?

St Kilda

St Kilda comprises a small group of rugged islands, lying 34 miles (55 km) north-west of North Uist, alone in the swell of the Atlantic. Its original inhabitants caught the public's imagination over a century ago, when Victorian tourists realized that they could witness an example of a 'primitive' people within the British Isles. Until then, the community had lived in virtual isolation for at least a thousand years, developing a superbly adapted economy, making full use of the large gannetry and other seabird colonies to be found on the highest cliffs and stacks in Britain — even their shoes came from the

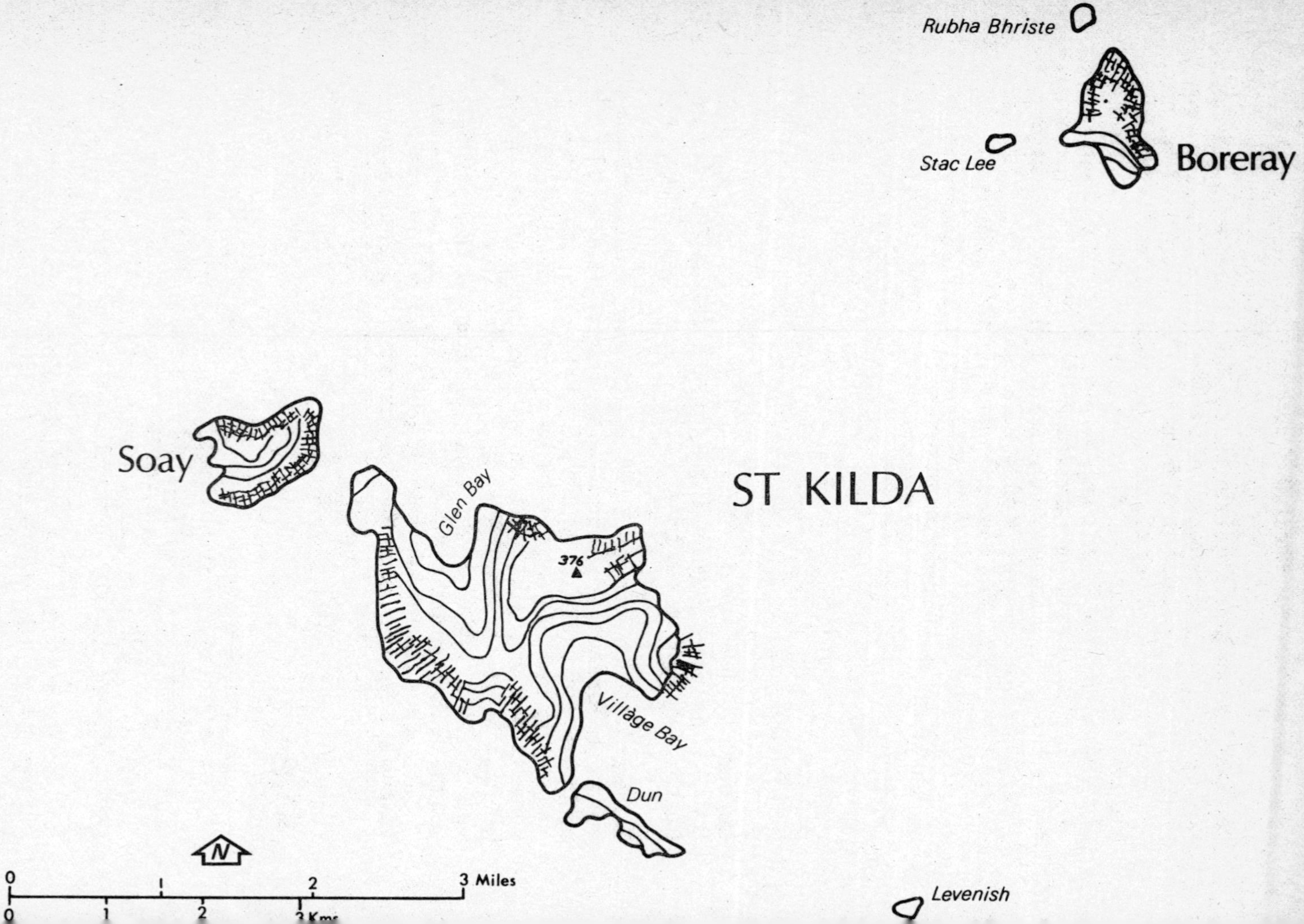

Rubha Bhriste

Boreray

Stac Lee

Levenish

ST KILDA

Soay

Glen Bay

376 ▲

Village Bay

Dun

N

0   1   2   3 Miles

0   1   2   3 Km

birds, being made from the skin covering the neck and head of the gannets. A comprehensive account of their way of life can be found in *The Life and Death of St Kilda* by Tom Steel.

In their curiosity the Victorians brought with them a disruption of the traditional way of life and much disease, and gradually the population declined. Many islanders chose to emigrate, while others were struck down by flu epidemics against which they had no immunity. By 1930 the remaining 'survivors' appealed to the government to evacuate them. The island was bought from the traditional owner, Macleod of Dunvegan, by the 5th Marquess of Bute, who turned the area into a nature reserve and bequeathed it to the National Trust for Scotland in 1957.

The Ministry of Defence has a small detachment on the island who provide a permanent population, a shop, and a pub. The Nature Conservancy manages the wildlife, monitoring the seabird colonies (St Kilda is the largest gannetry in the world with 60,000 pairs), the populations of unique soay sheep — among the most primitive in Europe, and the sub-species of wren and field mice which have evolved on the islands, while also keeping close records of all flora and fauna.

The National Trust is attempting to maintain St Kilda as it was in 1930, organizing work parties every summer to repair and restore the buildings. Applications to join the fortnightly work parties should be made to the St Kilda Secretary, The National Trust for Scotland, 5 Charlotte Square, Edinburgh (tel 031-225 9531).

Cruises are also organized to visit the island and details of other boats permitted to land can be obtained from the Secretary. *No* ambitious yachtsman should venture forth without consulting the Ministry of Defence as to the safety of his route.

An excellent handbook compiled by the National Trust, covering the geology, meteorology, archaeology and history of the archipelago, is highly recommended to any would-be visitor.

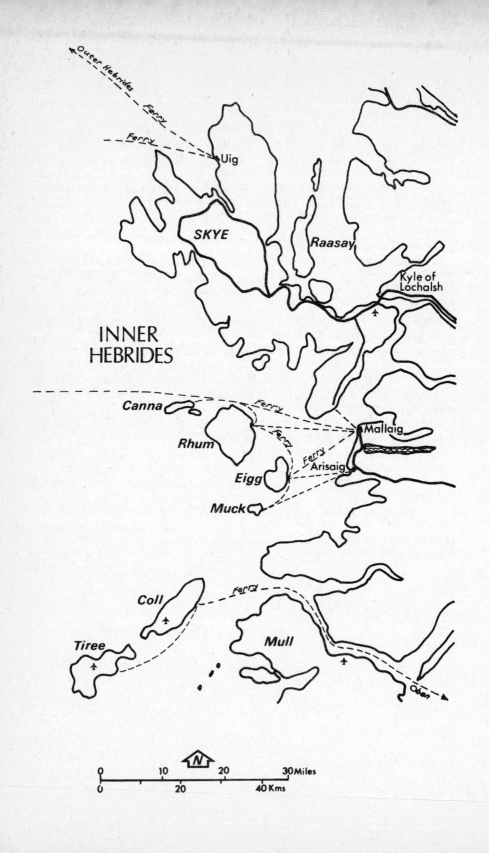

Outer Hebrides Ferry

Ferry

Uig

SKYE

Raasay

Kyle of
Lochalsh

INNER
HEBRIDES

Canna

Ferry

Rhum

Ferry

Mallaig

Ferry

Arisaig

Eigg

Muck

Coll

Ferry

Tiree

Mull

Oban

N

| 0 | 10 | 20 | 30 Miles |
| 0 | 20 | 40 Kms |

Part 4
The Inner Hebrides

The islands of the Inner Hebrides lack the unity which welds together
the other groups of Scottish islands. Tucked well into the fragmented
coastline of western Scotland by the Minch, and accessible from
several different ferry points, they share the West Highland atmosphere
of an easy-going, timeless existence, to be enjoyed and not rushed.

Some of the larger islands are well known among travellers, but
even on these there are neglected corners, harbouring otters and
sailing boats, and as a general rule tourism reaches only the towns.

Summer Isles

Connections:
By sea: excursions from Ullapool and Achiltibuie — details from
Tourist Office, Ullapool (tel Ullapool 2135).

So called because they were used for summer grazing for sheep and
cattle by the crofters of Achiltibuie and neighbouring townships, the
Summer Isles make a delightful day excursion. Any traveller with the
time to spare should make a point of visiting them before leaving
Ullapool for the Outer Hebrides. All are now uninhabited but in the
19th century Isle Martin and Ristol supported active herring curing
stations where the womenfolk gutted and cured the catches, while

Tanera More had a strong community until after the Second World War, when it was finally deserted. Dr Frazer Darling has written an account of his life alone on the island in *Island Years*, and this may have fired the imagination of Mrs Mason to buy Sgeirean Glasg for £50, to provide a *Swallows and Amazons* summer hideaway for her children.

Priest Island is reputed to have excellent fishing in its eight lochans, and many of the others are famed for their wealth of wild fowl and flowers. Oyster catchers, shag, greater black-backed gulls and ringed plovers enjoy the wide variety of habitats to be found among these isles: wild goats graze the neglected pastures, and seals haul themselves out onto the rocks and beaches. During the low spring tides, the unusual coral sands of Tanera Beg are revealed in their pinkness.

Skye

Connections:
By air: from Glasgow to Broadford: Mon-Sat, one a day. Loganair Ltd (tel Broadford 261).

By sea: from Kyle of Lochalsh to Kyleakin; approximately 40 a day, from 6 am to 11.30 pm; Sun less often; cars; crossing 20 mins. Caledonian MacBrayne Ltd (tel Kyleakin 282).

From Glenelg to Kylerhea: June — mid-Sept; frequent service; cars; crossing 4 mins. M A Mackenzie (tel Glenelg 224).

From Mallaig to Armadale: Mon-Sat, five a day; cars; crossing 30 mins. Caledonian MacBrayne Ltd (tel Mallaig 2223).

From Tarbert, Harris, to Uig: Mon, Wed, Fri, two a day; Tues, Thu, Sat, one a day; cars; crossing 2 hrs. Caledonian MacBrayne Ltd (tel Uig 219).

From Lochmaddy, North Uist, to Uig: Mon, Wed, Fri, one a day; Tue, Thu, Sat, two a day; cars; crossing 2 hrs min. Caledonian MacBrayne Ltd (tel Uig 219).

Skye, the land over the sea, is an island of contrasts more than any other. Tourists stream from Kyleakin via Broadford and Portree to Dunvegan, pausing to admire the multitude of enticing distractions put in their way, while walkers and climbers dash for the wildernesses of the Black and Red Cuillins; many valleys, ending only with the sea, continue to be havens of island life discovered only by a few picknickers.

Dr Johnson found a curious dichotomy of unexpected civilization within the gentryfolk's houses and a total lack of it in the open countryside, where the absence of any road or even tracks forced any traveller to rely on the knowledge of the islanders when choosing a route. Skye is a large 'winged' isle where each peninsula takes on its

174

own character, and so it is the corners of Skye which are the most rewarding for the explorer.

The summer ferry from Glenelg crosses the tidal rush of **Kyle Rhea** to join the traditional drove road from the Outer Hebrides and Skye, annually marched by the islanders' cattle on their way to East Anglia for refattening before reaching the London markets. **Glen Arroch**, an empty glen squeezed between two heather-clad mountains, seems to retain the spirit of those walkers, unlike today's most popular crossing at Kyle of Lochalsh where tourist traps welcome you to the homeland of Flora Macdonald.

Kyleakin (ON Haco's strait — probably named for King Hakon of Norway who was defeated at the Battle of Largs in 1263 and died in Kirkwall) was once a charming fishing village, clustered around a well protected harbour guarded by the commanding ruins of **Castle Maol**. This was the legendary home of a business-minded Viking Princess, who stretched a chain across the strait and charged every passing ship a toll. The woods of birch and rhododendrons induce a garden tameness where many exotic plants flourish in the damp mild climate, protected from the wind. Skye is wet, and there is no avoiding it, but one of the delights of this island is the continuing dance of sun and raincloud responding to the gusts and breezes, highlighting a patch of heather, then a strip of water, while numerous rainbows arc across the sky. Take rainwear and enjoy it.

Broadford (ON — broad firth) is Skye's second town and shopping centre with a hospital, police station and tourist office, a ribbon of modern development straggling along the roadside. Ugly in itself, it has great views of the **Red Cuillins**, so called because they are formed of red granite. Their screes smooth their contours and make most ascents challenging, but the walk up from **Glen Sligachan** along the summit ridge is highly recommended, both for the sense of achievement and for the spectacular views up the north-west coast of Scotland, of the placid island of Raasay, and across to the awesome Black Cuillins. The record ascent of Glamaig is 37 minutes. This was achieved by a bootless Gurkha in 1899, but it is not to be recommended as a practical yardstick. An old limekiln on the shores of **Broadford Bay** indicates a good beachcombing area for fossils, held in the limestone, while whelks can be collected off the rocks for a tasty entree. Skye's weekly newspaper, *The West Highland Free Press*, is produced in Broadford. Radical enough to provide a week's local argument, and informative if biased on local issues, it includes a useful record of local events.

Turning south, one approaches the **Sleat** district of Skye and Macdonald country. The countryside becomes gradually smoother, the woods claiming more variety, with oak and beech as well as fir and birch; stone walls are smothered with brambles and ferns, and farming takes a firmer grip of the landscape. Friendly if mischievous giants populate the legends, hurling stones to create skerries, and

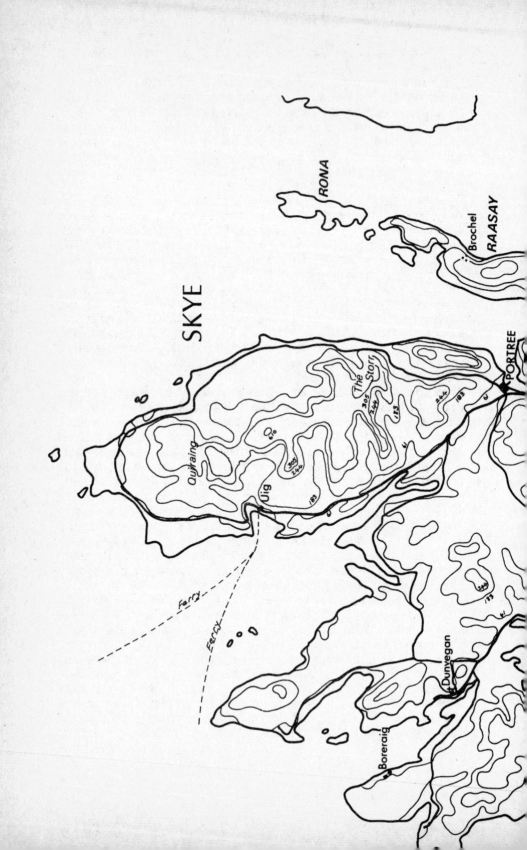

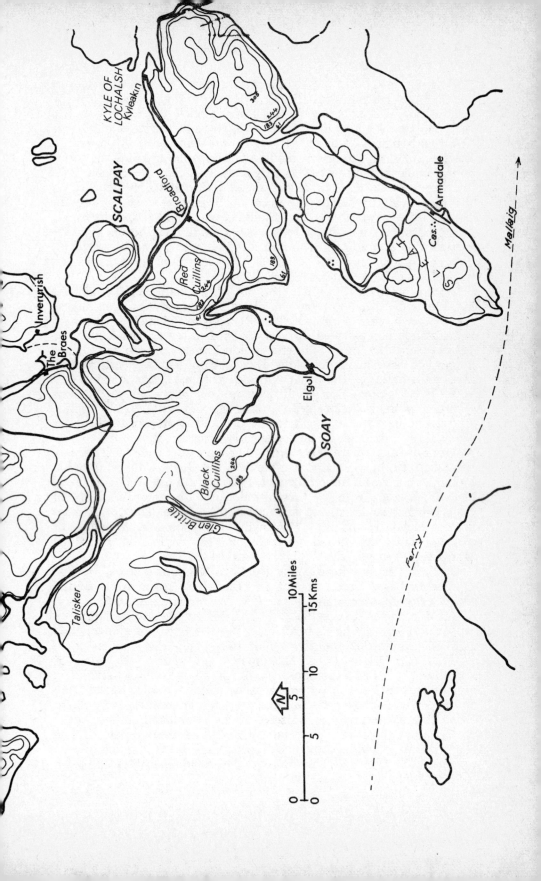

helping farmers with their toil, very unlike the wicked fairies of North Skye. Isle Ornsay (ON — St Oran's isle) was the setting of a curious tale of a monster, the Beast of the Little Horn, who terrified the inhabitants so much that a full-scale search was instigated in 1870, although it found no trace of what was probably a walrus. Castle Camus, an important medieval stronghold guarding the sound and the Sleat peninsula, was originally held by the Macleods of Dunvegan, but a careless keeper allowed himself to be surprised by the Macdonald Lords of the Isles. So began the constant feuding between these two great clans. Standing on a knoll across the Knock river, the ruins are difficult to reach — a modern endorsement of the castle's fine positioning. The village of **Knock** is a healthy crofting community; the bed and breakfast rot so often accompanied by neglected fields has not set in here.

Tradition claims **Kilmore** as the site of St Columba's first landing in Skye, and in the graveyard his stone seat can still be seen among the medieval warrior graves. The Renaissance chapel, surprisingly large, stands complete except for its roof, but was forsaken in the 18th century for a more 'modern' building. Inside this are two curious memorials, one to a Macdonald lady who lost a heartbreaking number of children, the other inscribed with extravagant claims of a youth's brilliance. This is difficult to decipher today, but was recorded by Boswell along with a deflatory comment of Dr Johnson's, who maintained that it ought to have been in Latin (not English), 'as everything intended to be universal and permanent should be'.

Ostaig House, where the literary pair were so royally entertained, is now a ruin, but in the stable block is the **Gaelic College**, founded by Ian Noble, an Edinburgh banker. He bought most of the remaining Macdonald lands from the present chief, and discovered a mission in fostering the Gaelic culture still nurtured on Skye. The College runs courses in Gaelic and piping throughout the summer, arranging for participants to stay with Gaelic-speaking families (details from Sabhal Mor Ostaig, Teanga, Isle of Skye; tel Ardvasar 239).

Death duties may have persuaded Lord Macdonald to sell out (he is now a cheery hotelier), but the Clan have rescued one of the derelict homes, **Armadale Castle**. This site had a chequered history, the first mansion house being bombarded by the Royal Navy — a repercussion of the heir's involvement in the Battle of Killiecrankie in 1689 — and subsequently rebuilt using only the original north wing. (From here, Flora Macdonald was married to Alan of Kingsburgh.) In 1815 the house was extended by Gillespie Graham, a joiner's apprentice who became a fashionable architect, but in 1858 it was partly destroyed by fire and rebuilt in an extravagant style by David Bryce. Pictures can be seen of the completed edifice, but it proved unpopular with the family and was soon deserted. The elements got in and now the unsafe wing has been dismantled into an ornamental sculpture. The rest of the building houses the Clan

Donald Centre, where an exhibition explains family links and the origins of associated tartans (many have no connection with the pre '45 highlanders but were a fashionable Victorian invention). The specialized bookstall is to be highly recommended, as are the gardens — a parkland of trees, once claiming over a hundred varieties and still having the best Wellingtonias in Britain. It is planned to move the restaurant into the stable block, a fine Victorian castellated structure with a clock tower, originally fitted with Gothic interiors.

Ardvasar (G — fatal headland), a crofting township, is still famous for breeding Skye terriers, little long-haired dogs used for hunting foxes, now popular for their pedigree. A windy road across the moor leads to the west coast with views up the indented shoreline of Skye, and to other Cuillins. On clear days, it is even possible to see across to the Outer Hebrides from the sandy Tarskavaig Bay (G — whale bay), a good place for swimming and beachcombing. On a point is Dunscaith Castle, another Macdonald stronghold, claimed to be the oldest castle of Skye, and once the home of the giant Cuchulin, a great friend and loyal supporter of Ossian. Probably originally neolithic, this site was inhabited until the mid-16th century, and the curtain walls are still in an astonishing state of repair. In the woods of Ord, botanists will be astonished to spot three mature cabbage trees, grown from seeds sent home by an emigrant to New Zealand; the only outdoor examples in Britain, they flower every seventh year. The mild climate here made flax a profitable crop for several years.

Another road south from Broadford to Elgol is well worth exploring. Less green and fertile, and less popular with tourists, it winds its way around Loch Slapin and into the back of beyond. By the sultry Loch Cil Chriosd, under the sombre Red Cuillins, is a little ivy-covered chapel set in an ancient graveyard, the traditional burial place of the MacKinnon chiefs. On their quiet peninsula, the Mackinnons appear to have been ignored by the feuding Macdonalds and Macleods — perhaps because they have fewer descendants to immortalize their victories, perhaps because the quiet solitude of their homeland had a happy effect on their nature. Loch Slapin is a very beautiful finger of water, much appreciated by herons wading in the seaweed, though slightly marred by the famous Skye Marble quarries. Said to be better in quality than the Italian, Skye marble was used in the Vatican; now it is carefully broken into the grey and white chips used to cover the exteriors of office blocks. The estate of Kilmarie has some charming workers' cottages. The gillie's by the loch side has an Indian verandah for net drying, and several others show an eastern influence, all still crisply painted and cared for.

A wild moor separates Elgol from its neighbours. Perched on the western slopes of Loch Scavaig, this is one of the most spectacular island townships, dropping down to the school on the pebbly beach. Views across the water to the Black Cuillins and Soay Island are dramatic beyond belief. The white streams of waterfalls tumbling off the vertical slopes made this niche of Skye a favourite with the 'Romantic painters'. A day's demanding walk around the coast, along the shore described by Sir Walter Scott in *Lord of the Isles*, leads to **Camasunary**, held to be the most beautiful bay in Skye, and on to the dark hidden **Loch Coruisk** (painted by Turner), lying underneath the mountain range. (A boat can be hired to make the trip. Tel Loch Scavaig 225.)

The headland south of Elgol is indented with caves, each with its own history of Bonnie Prince Charlie in hiding or of illicit stills, but the most famous is the **Spar Cave**, a tourist attraction known to Sir Walter Scott, much despoiled by his contemporaries and forgotten by later generations. The original display of stalactites dropping from the roof was as spectacular as that in the Cheddar Gorge, Somerset, but many were removed as mementoes and others were ground down to be scattered as lime on the fields. To reach the cave one must clamber down the gorge beyond, and creep along the shore as the tide falls. After penetrating the cave to a distance of about 30 ft (9 m), the explorer must then climb up onto a shelf which intrudes even further. Here the glistening stalactites can still be seen. A torch and tide-watcher are advisable!

The road north out of Broadford follows the shore past the island of Scalpay. Dr Johnson wanted to buy this island but refused to be restrained by an obligation to spend a quarter of each year in this wilderness. It is now inhabited by one family, who are carrying out some interesting experiments into the viability of red deer farming. Luib is a delightful township of fuchsia bushes and deserted thatched cottages guarded by the anti-witch rowan (mountain ash) trees at their door, juxtaposed to more modern houses. One crofter has restored his 'white house' into a cottage museum (open Easter — Oct: 10 — 7 daily) showing how Skye crofters lived 50 years ago. A curious collection of newspaper cuttings reveals much about local prejudice, while the living quarters are none too comfortable. If you are lucky you will find him shearing his sheep by hand behind the house. Loch Ainort is a sheltered corner with odd crates floating in its quiet waters — the tanks of a modern fish farm, Marine Harvest Ltd. A beautiful humpbacked bridge marks the separation of the old (scenic) and new (fast) road across the peninsula which rejoin each other at Sconser by a road-chip quarry and the ferry to Raasay.

The district of the Braes saw some of the most ferocious of the Highland Clearances, culminating in 1882 when 50 Glaswegian policemen faced the crofters in a pitched battle. Some were imprisoned but their resistance caught the attention of the Prime Minister, Gladstone, who set up the Royal Commission to look into their complaints. The small communities scattered along this beautiful if wild road facing Raasay are a living reminder of their predecessors' determination to stay.

Portree is the capital of Skye. It was originally called **Kiltaraglen**, but in 1540 James V visited the village in an attempt to affirm the royal hold on the extremities of his kingdom, and made such a happy impression that it was renamed Port na Righ (G — King's Port). Nestling at the foot of Fingal's seat, the brightly painted fishermen's houses hug the harbour joined by the gasworks (a novelty on the islands), while civic concerns are enacted above. The Tourist Office is to be found in the oldest building, the early 19th century Sheriff's court and jail. Across the harbour is the headland known fondly as the **Hump**, where the annual Skye games are held in August. Portree is a good place to stock up with supplies and to find a coffee.

The Storr dominates the Trotternish 'wing' of Skye, best seen from the east where its upper curtain of cliffs drops onto green, if neglected, crofting lands, scattered with white cottages and B & B signs. Keen walkers will want to ascend to the pinnacles of black basalt and then progress along the ridge to the **Quiraing** in the north. This walk is almost unrivalled for its views east and west, but the crumbling stone should be treated with care. Less ambitious ramblers can gain a sense of achievement by climbing up to the base of the **Old Man of Storr**, a basalt finger which carelessly lost its head in a storm at the turn of the century.

Looking across from Loch Fada (good trout fishing) is **Eilean Fladday**, supposedly the Celtic paradise of the Land of Perpetual Youth. Waterfalls drop steeply off the back of Trotternish down the cliffs into the sea, most spectacularly after a heavy shower. The most famous is the **Kilt Rock**, aptly named for its folds and creases of rock and a favourite picnic place. The old tractors littering the crofts here are a collector's delight. The **Quiraing** (G — the cup) is a similar type of rock formation to the Storr, guarded by a needle-sharp pinnacle which protected the crofters' cattle from raiders. Several rare flowers can be found sheltering in the scree behind, but the haunted air of the place has thankfully discouraged collectors from removing them.

The bleak headland of bog and moor, intensely beautiful if the sun is shining and remarkably depressing if not, soon gives way to another promontory with a spectacular fortress — **Duntulm**. Originally a Pictish fort, by the 16th century this was impressive enough to incur James V's envy. It was fought over frequently by the rival Macleods and Macdonalds and eventually deserted when the nurse let the chief's heir fall from an open window. The graveyard of **Kilmuir** has become a pilgrimage spot for Jacobite supporters, for here Flora Macdonald's grave is marked by a hideous marble Celtic cross. The **Skye Cottage Museum** (open Easter — October: 9 — 6 Mon-Fri) is a group of four cottages including a weaver's workshop and a smithy, demonstrating how life was in this area — the Granary of Skye — a hundred years ago.

Uig (G — a nook) is an odd sprawling village, its sole raison d'etre seeming to be the ferry to Harris and North Uist. An amusing

Victorian folly by the roadside was inspired by the prehistoric duns. **Kingsburgh House** (not open to the public, due to its dilapidated condition) was the pleasant refuge found for Bonnie Prince Charlie by Flora Macdonald when they crossed from Benbecula, and where she later entertained Dr Johnson and Boswell before emigrating (for a few years) to America with her husband.

Travelling west into the land of the Macleods and their fairy friends, the main road passes by the **Fairy Bridge**. This low humpbacked bridge was greatly feared by the locals and their horses for no specific reason other than its association with the little people, yet it was here that Macleod's kind fairy bride deserted him and their son, having given them the 'fairy flag' for protection (see Dunvegan). A delightful road heads north up the **Vaternish** peninsula, populated with content crofting communities. The decaying fishing village of **Stein**, a 'new town' of the 18th century, no less, claims the island's oldest inn, on the foreshore. At the end of the road is the chapel of **Trumpan**, the setting for yet another ugly episode in the Macdonald/Macleod clan warfare. A party of Macdonalds from Uist burnt the chapel whilst it was full of Macleods at prayer and only one woman escaped. She raised the alarm and clansmen from Dunvegan murdered all the raiding Macdonalds, who had become trapped by the absent tide. Also buried here is the unfortunate Lady Grange, wife of the Lord Justice Clerk of Edinburgh. Because she did not share her husband's Jacobite sympathies and could not be trusted to keep her mouth shut, she was bundled off to Uist and then to St Kilda, while a mock funeral was enacted at Greyfriars. Her ignorance of Gaelic and her refined habits isolated her from the natives, and only after 10 years did she manage to get a message to her friends, hidden in a ball of spinning wool. They sent the Royal Navy to look for her, but her mentors had already moved her to Skye, where she died on the eve of the '45 rebellion.

Dunvegan Castle (open Apr — Oct: 2 — 5 Mon-Fri; May — Sep: 10.30 — 5), the clan home of the Macleods for over 700 years, presents a rather drab early 19th century castellated exterior to visitors entering from the garden. The aspect from the sea is much more imposing, for like all Skye's castles it is sited on a rocky knoll, watching over the islands of the lochs. Inside, its various styles and treasures, spanning seven centuries, give it much charm. A piece of decorative Moorish metal work hangs in the hall, emblazoned with the bull's head of the Macleods' emblem. This is the 'fairy flag', given by the fairy wife of the fourth chief with the promise that if waved in need, it would bring help three times. As might be expected, it has twice been used successfully against the Macdonalds. Experts suggest that it was made on the island of Rhodes in the 7th century. Family portraits adorn the Victorian extensions, and a splendid family retainer reigns in the dining room, making his watchdog job a pleasure for himself and visitors by explaining who's who and acquired what, and whose wife changed the colour of her hair three times. A museum records the clan history and the woodland gardens are being restored and developed by the present chief.

Across the water can be seen Macleod's tables. Their flatness is attributed to the lack of welcome offered to Columba when he preached to the local chief: the mountains shed their caps so that that the saint might have a flat bed to lie on. Whilst dining at Edinburgh, a Macleod chief refused to be impressed by his sovereign's pomp and splendour and claimed to have far better. Wishing to discredit this boaster, the King offered to dine in Macleod grandeur a year later, while his fellow chieftans agreed to judge between the two. When the King and chiefs duly assembled at Dunvegan, they at first saw nothing but a coarse fortress and began to mock Macleod. However, as evening fell, he led them up onto the tables, to a feast served by loyal clansmen. There, even the King had to admit that the setting was much more magnificent than anything he could achieve.

The Black House Folk Museum (open Easter — Oct: daily 10 — 7) of Colbost is the most atmospheric of Skye's museums, with its peat fire on the floor waiting for a stew to cook, and a boxbed uncomfortable enough to be genuine. Originally, the house was simply divided between people and animals, but now the byre is used to store the implements. Up the hill is an illicit still, sadly neglected, in need of re-thatching and even more tragically unworkable, though it must be said that the local brews were supposed to be incredibly rough.

Boreraig is the home of the great Macleod pipers, the MacCrimmons. Legend tells how another boastful Macleod summoned eleven clan chieftans and demanded that their pipers should compete against his. On the night, his piper fell ill, yet Macleod insisted that the competition went ahead, announcing that his young son would replace him. Terrified at the prospect, fearing his chief and knowing that he must play last, the boy fled onto the battlements and burst into tears. There a fairy found him and offered him the chance to be either a bad piper but greatly acclaimed, or unknown yet a great piper. When he chose the latter, she gave him a silver chanter, asking only that when she called for him he would obey. He returned to the supper hall and astonished all with his brilliance. He set up the famous piping college at Boreraig and stayed there long enough to train his large family of sons and other talented musicians. But one day the fairy called, and obediently he stopped the lesson, put down his pipes, and walked along the shore playing the silver chanter, until he entered MacCrimmon's cave. He was never heard again, but the piping college continued to draw pupils. A new piping centre has recently been opened to record the feats of his family and propagate the art of piping, explaining the form of the instrument, organizing classes for experts, and even giving the casual visitor a chance to blow a chanter.

In Glendale, a succulent green township, is an enterprising **water mill**, now open as a museum, built on the shore under a gushing waterfall so that the crofters from Uist could bring their corn across by boat to be milled. They also had to bring peat to light the fire to dry the grain, before helping the miller feed it into the grinding stones. Neist Point lighthouse (visits possible, tel Glendale 200) commands wonderful views from the most westerly point of Skye. The surrounding slopes were once cultivated but are now neglected in favour of tourism as they are too isolated and awkward to be profitable.

Loch Bracadale is one of the most beautiful of Skye's inland seas, with spurs of land mingling with fingers of sea, and numerous little islets, all now uninhabited, adding to the confusion. This area of Skye has been under-populated since the famines of the 1830s, when many of the inhabitants appealed for an assisted passage to America. The white cottages and their protective rowans are tucked into the hill out of the wind. Following a burn down to the shore, one can visit the ruins of **Gesto House,** one of Skye's first 'gentleman's residences', once covered with roses and honeysuckle. It now stands alone beside its extensive farm buildings and boat-house, looking across to Wiay from the shelter of its protective woodland.

The famous Skye Talisker whiskey is made on the shores of Loch Harport at Carbost and south from here is the wooded **Glen Brittle**, tucked under the dark sides of the Black Cuillins, coloured by the intensely hard granite which gives them their uncompromising shape. Even marked walking routes prove tough over this range, but Scottish climbers will tell you that it is worth getting fit for. Don't venture up if you are not, but enjoy their dramatic sweep upwards from the valleys.

Accommodation:
In Portree
Caledonian Hotel (tel Portree 2641)
Coolin Hills Hotel (tel Portree 2003)
Isles Hotel (tel Portree 2129)
King's Haven Hotel (tel Portree 2290)
Portree Hotel (tel Portree 2511)
Rosedale Hotel (tel Portree 2531)
Royal Hotel (tel Portree 2525)
Tongadale Hotel (tel Portree 2115)
Viewfield House Hotel (tel Portree 2217)
Almondbank Guest House (tel Portree 2696)
Bosville Guest House (tel Portree 2846)
Craiglockhart Guest House (tel Portree 2233)

Dunalasdair Guest House (tel Portree 2893)
Springfield Guest House (tel Portree 2505)
Woodside Guest House (tel Portree 2598)
Elsewhere:
Dunringell Hotel, Kyleakin (tel Kyle 4180)
White Heather Hotel, Kyleakin (tel Kyle 4507)
Broadford Hotel, Broadford (tel Broadford 205)
Broadford House Private Hotel (tel Broadford 429)
Hebridean Motor Inn, Broadford (tel Broadford 486)
Beul-na-Mara Guest House, Broadford (tel Broadford 487)
Ceol-na-Mara, Breaknish (tel Broadford 323)
Langdale Guest House, Broadford (tel Broadford 376)
Eishort Guest House, Heaste (tel Broadford 450)
Kinloch Hotel, Kinloch (tel Isle Ornsay 214)
Duisdale Hotel, Isle Ornsay (tel Isle Ornsay 202)
Tigh-Osda Eilean Iarmain, Isle Ornsay (tel Isle Ornsay 266)
Toravaig House Hotel, Isle Ornsay (tel Isle Ornsay 231)
Post Office House, Isle Ornsay (tel Isle Ornsay 201)
Ardvasar Hotel, Ardvasar (tel Ardvasar 223)
Sligachan Hotel, Sligachan (tel Sligachan 204)
Staffin House Hotel, Staffin (tel Staffin 219)
Blarcrian Guest House, Culnacnock (tel Staffin 208)
Flodigarry Hotel, Flodigarry (tel Duntulm 203)
Duntulm Hotel, Duntulm (tel Duntulm 213)
Uig Hotel, Uig (tel Uig 205)
Ferry Inn Hotel, Uig (tel Uig 242)
Caberfeidh Guest House, Uig (tel Uig 342)
Uig Guest House, Uig (tel Uig 269)
Corriemar House Hotel, Kensaleyre (tel Skeabost Bridge 210)
Macdonald Hotel, Kensaleyre (tel Skeabost Bridge 339)
Skeabost House Hotel, Skeabost (tel Skeabost Bridge 202)
Grandview Guest House, Skeabost (tel Skeabost Bridge 234
Hillcrest Guest House, Skeabost (tel Skeabost Bridge 241)
Edinbane Hotel, Edinbane (tel Edinbane 263)
Greshornish House Hotel, Edinbane (tel Edinbane 266)
Stein Inn, Waternish (tel Waternish 208)
Atholl House Hotel, Dunvegan (tel Dunvegan 219)
Dunvegan Hotel, Dunvegan (tel Dunvegan 202)
Misty Isle Hotel, Dunvegan (tel Dunvegan 208)
Argyll Guest House, Dunvegan (tel Dunvegan 230)
Roskhill Guest House, Dunvegan (tel Dunvegan 317)
Harlosh Hotel, Harlosh (tel Dunvegan 367)
Ullinish Lodge Hotel, Ullinish (tel Struan 214)
B & B and self catering — details from Tourist Office, Portree.
Youth Hostels at Broadford, Uig and Glenbrittle.
Camping at Portree, Staffin, Edinbane, Dunvegan or wherever takes
your fancy (consult the locals first).

Car Hire:
N. Beaton Ltd., Portree (tel Portree 2002)
E. MacRae & Sons, Portree (tel Portree 2554)
A. Sutherland, Broadford (tel Broadford 225)
Clan Coach Co (Kyle) Ltd, Kyle of Lochalsh, (tel Kyle 4328)
Bicycle Hire:
Enquire locally.
Horse Hire:
Strollamas Pony Trekking, Broadford.
Boat Hire:
Strollamas Boat Centre, Broadford (tel Broadford 269
Airidh Charnach Sailing and Fishing Centre (tel Broadford 497)
Charles Barrington (tel Ardvasar 262)
Banks:
Bank of Scotland, Portree, and Broadford.
Clydesdale Bank, Portree.
Royal Bank of Scotland, Portree.
Early Closing:
Wednesday. Due to the Free Church, Sunday is a dead day: don't
expect anything to be open.
Fishing:
Fresh Water permits from Portree Angling Association, also some
hotels.
Sea Angling:
Macdonald Marine Craft (tel Duntulm 217) and details from Tourist
Office.
Swimming:
Pool at Portree for the faint-hearted; lots of empty beaches for others.
Climbing:
District Guide to the Island of Skye by the Scottish Mountaineering
Club is excellent.
Specialities:
Talisker Whiskey, Skye terriers, Run Rig — local rock group and the
West Highland Free Press.
Events:
June — Skye Mod.
August — Skye Highland Games.
Frequent ceilidhs and dances.
Tourist Office:
Meall House, Portree (tel Portree 2137); open June: 9.30 — 1,
2.30 — 7, Mon-Sat. Jul-Jul-Sep: 9.30 — 7.30, Mon-Sat. Mid-Sep-May:
9.30 — 1, 2.30 — 5.30, Mon-Fri.
Seasonal Tourist Office:
Broadford (tel Broadford 361); open April — June: 9.30 — 1,
2.30 — 5.30 Mon-Fri; July — mid-Sep: 9.30 — 7 Mon-Sat; mid-Sep —
mid-Oct: 9.30 — 1, 2.30 — 5.30 Mon-Fri.

Raasay

Connections:
By sea: from Sconser: Mon-Sat, four a day; cars; crossing 15 mins.
Caledonian MacBrayne Ltd.

Many claim that the sole purpose of Skye is to protect Raasay from the westerly storms. It is astonishing that any island could induce anyone to belittle the beauties of Skye so much, but Raasay has many charms. There are no mountain ranges, but the view from **Dun Caan** across to the Red and Black Cuillins and the Storr, and into the indented sea arms of the West Highlands, is so breathtaking that one wonders how Boswell had the energy to dance a reel in his exhilaration.

The backbone of hills descends steeply into the eastern sea and a walk north approaches **Brochel Castle**, today the home of ravens but formerly the ancient seat of the Macleods of Raasay. A cadet branch of the Dunvegan family, they were frequently too independent to acknowledge any clan allegiance, preferring to support instead the Macdonalds of Sleat. Brochel Castle watches from a rock promontory, supposedly large enough to hold the whole population at times of siege, and was only completely deserted after the Government forces' savage reprisal following the '45, when they also burned every home and boat. The Laird of Raasay had chosen to support the Jacobite cause because his Dunvegan cousins had joined the Government. He took over 100 men and 26 pipers to Culloden, and even sheltered the Prince during his escape.

Within 30 years, the island had recovered from this merciless treatment, enough to impress even Dr Johnson with its civilization. 36 gentlefolk sat down to dinner with him and the singing of Erse (Gaelic) pleased him as much as Italian songs. Orchards flourished around the house, a comfortable residence rebuilt after the '45 and later extended in a severely restrained Victorian style. Until recently, it was used as a hotel, but is now disgracefully neglected and rotting. The gardens too are now sad but curious; the wanderer will chance upon some delightful sculptures.

Macleod of Raasay ran out of money trying to support his people through the famines of the 1830s and was forced to sell his homeland in 1843 and emigrate. The new owner, George Rainy, realized that sheep would be more profitable than crofters and so forbade the young folk to marry unless they agreed to follow their old laird over the sea. Within ten years, twelve townships had been cleared, but Rainy soon died and the estate was resold. Successive buyers exported the sheep and developed the island as a typical Victorian sporting estate, much resented by those natives who had remained for they were pushed onto the most barren rocks. Verbal and physical warfare after the First World War won back some of the land for the army veterans, but the future is no longer promising as the population (about 150) is elderly and there is little employment. Probably because of their hardships, most islanders belong to a sect even stricter than the Free Church, so be careful how you behave on the Sabbath; at all other times they are charming and enterprising.

Raasay was once famous for its pipers, especially John Mackay, a foster child of the chief whose talent was discovered when he was found playing a chanter made from the stalk of a yellow iris. He was sent to study under the MacCrimmons (see Skye) and returned a master, subsequently recording many traditional tunes of the Ceol Mor.

Accommodation:
Borrowdale Hotel
Churchton House (tel Raasay 226)
Self-catering — details from Tourist Office, Portree, Isle of Skye.
Youth Hostel.
Good shop at Inverurish.

Rhum
(G i-dhruim — isle of the ridge)

Connections:
By sea: from Mallaig: Mon, Wed, Thu, Sat, one a day, (two in summer on Sat); crossing 3 hours (route varies around Small Isles). Caledonian MacBrayne Ltd (tel Mallaig 2223).

From Arisaig: Tue, Thu, via Eigg; Summer only; crossing 2½ hours. Murdo Grant, Arisaig Hotel (tel Arisaig 224).

A diamond-shaped island of mountains and glens, for a century forbidden to all except friends, Rhum offers the tourist no special facilities, no pubs or papers, tourist shops or television, and so retains the curious air of an Edwardian fantasy retreat married to modern scientific research. It is a wonderful place. Your hosts are the Nature Conservancy Council who have been conducting experiments into all aspects of the island's ecology since 1957. In order that nothing should interfere with this work, all visitors are asked to study the notice boards at the Warden's House before venturing away from Loch Scresort. Access to Kilmory is usually restricted on weekdays and to the whole island in the first weeks in May and August (telephone to check).

The departure of 350 inhabitants to America in 1826, assisted by the Macleans of Coll, left Rhum with the one family sufficient to look after the 8,000 sheep imported to resuscitate the Coll finances; but the scheme failed and the island was sold to the Marquis of

Salisbury who exported most of the sheep and imported deer, turning it into a Victorian sporting paradise. However, his financial position was none too sound either, and in 1880 he sold the island to the Cambells of Oransay, who shortly afterwards sold it to John Bullough of Lancashire, a mill machinery manufacturer and inventor. His son, Sir George, built **Kinloch Castle** (now providing the main accommodation), a fine Edwardian masterpiece designed by Leeming and Leeming of London, in which to entertain his wealthy friends. He also built Papadil Lodge on the south side of the island but this residence was so hated by Lady Bullough that it was allowed to fall into a picturesque ruin amid the trees on the lochside.

Playing the Highland laird, Sir George supervised the kilted work-force, ensuring that all mod cons were incorporated in association with the traditional fixtures of a Highland home. Ramparts combine with a colonnaded conservatory and a piper's turret to produce an imposing exterior, which mirrors the grandeur of the two-storey great hall, billiards, ball and dining rooms. Original furnishings endorse the Edwardian melodrama: a huge bronze eagle in the turret inside; an orchestrion (one of two in Britain) in pristine working condition; Waterford crystal still on the sideboard; photograph albums of Bullough's world yacht cruises; game books and many library books still unread. Upstairs the bedrooms have fine fireplaces, original wcs, and showers which gush, spray and squirt from every direction. A hospitable welcome, good cooking and reasonable prices draws the customers. The servants' quarters have been converted to hostel accommodation (bring your own sheets and food if you do not intend to eat in the dining room and be warned that the owner's dog has a penchant for Mars bars). When the island is 'closed', Rod Stenson organizes courses in upholstery, french polishing, etc. to repair this heritage properly, and he also hopes to restore the extensive gardens to their former glory of pineapples and peaches, animated by parrots and turtles.

The village is populated by NCC personnel. The wife of one worker staffs the Post Office-cum-shop (closed 12.30 − 1.30, afternoons Tue, Thu, Sat, and all day Sunday). It also sells drink, cigarettes, a few tins, basic veg and long-life milk, but no bread or plasters! It is unwise to rely on it for supplies, and visitors should bring all their own perishables, etc.

Four main glens divide the mountain mass, following the points of the compass and providing challenging walking. Good nature trail leaflets are available from the pier. (Consult the boards.)

Kinloch Glen is wide and shallow, with experimental tree planting at its foot. This, and the shore of Loch Scresort, are described in a good leaflet, available at the pier. Kilmory Glen, once densely populated by crofters, is the main area for deer research and so is usually closed. Ecologists are conducting behavioural studies and examining various different culling methods and ratios, and so some

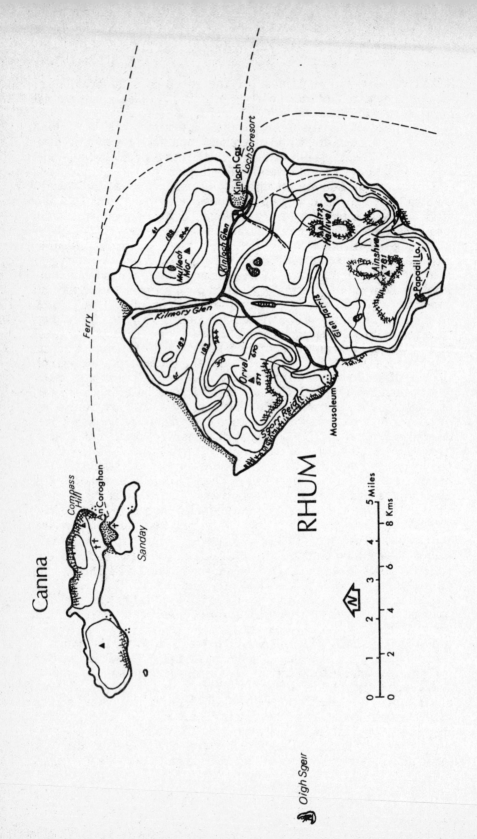

of the 1,500 deer are adorned with brightly coloured necklaces and earrings, for easy identification. At the foot of the glen is the old cemetery, the original castle laundry and a lone, inhabited cottage. Glen Harris begins in the central boggy plateau, with incredible vistas of the mountains. This was the original, desired setting for Kinloch Castle but no suitable building site could be found. Highland cattle munch their way unselectively through this grazing land (and are thus better for the vegetation than sheep or deer). The Rhum ponies, so admired by Dr Johnson and traditionally associated with the Spanish Armada and the Vikings, help in carrying the deer carcasses off the hill. On the shore is the **Bullough Mausoleum**, an extraordinary classical temple, which contains John, Sir George and his wife, Lady Monica.

The geology of Rhum is greatly varied and this is reflected in the many different shapes of the craggy hills. All are massive, rearing out of the sea and providing truly amazing views. The **Rhum Cuillins** in the south-east afford some of the best ridge walking in Britain, while the cliffs of the south-west are spectacular in their fall, the favourite haunt of the large herd (c 100) of feral goats — often hard to spot as they shelter from the wind. The climate of Rhum is extremely wet (approx 100 ins/250 cm per annum) and windy. Cloud and sunlight swap with a speed that can surprise even the most experienced hiker. Distances are longer than might be expected over this rugged terrain. Good boots are very necessary and much energy is needed for even a short walk, but don't be put off: the magnificent views will compensate for even the largest of blisters.

The sporting lairds were disappointed by Rhum's fishing potential, for although the hill lochs provide respectable trout fishing, they contain no salmon. The Marquis of Salisbury and the Bulloughs embarked on elaborate engineering schemes to improve the rivers — Salisbury's enormous dam in Glen Harris lasted for all of two days — but they failed to comprehend that it was not the lack of water but the lack of spawning beds that discouraged these elusive fish. (Fishing nowadays involves long walks, and there are no boats. It is free, but permission from the Chief Warden is required, and all catches must be reported.)

Flora and fauna are carefully recorded in the NCC *Reserve Handbook* (intensely scientific but useful). 19 species of butterfly can be seen, and the expected soaring golden eagles are joined by sea eagles, successfully introduced by the NCC, while a large colony of over 130,000 pairs of Manx shearwaters burrow into the mountain slopes. Beware of midges: summer workers used to be paid midge money to subsidize the tobacco needed to create a smoke screen. The island's vegetation has been relatively undisturbed since the retreat of the last ice cap and the range of species and their habitats are a botanist's delight.

Accommodation:
Kinloch Castle — hotel and hostel (tel Rod Stenson, Mallaig 2037)
Camping — on foreshore in front of the castle; permission needed from the Chief Warden.
Transport:
None (unless you can cadge a lift with an NCC Landrover).
Fishing:
Sea-angling from rocks and loch fishing; free; permission required from Chief Warden.
Stalking:
In season; popular, so enquire well in advance from Chief Warden.
Climbing and Walking:
Challenging but unrivalled on the Scottish Islands. Watch the boards for access information and leave details of your route in the hotel.
Chief Warden:
The White House, Kinloch, Rhum (tel Mallaig 2026).

Canna
(ON kannay — island like a pot)

Connections:
By sea: from Mallaig: Mon, Wed, Sat, via Eigg & Rhum; crossing 4 hrs.
   From Mallaig: Thu, Sat, crossing 2½ hrs. Caledonian MacBrayne Ltd (tel Mallaig 2223).

Canna rises out of the water with a green humped back, to echo the black backs of passing killer whales. It often emerges from the mist like an enchanted isle, promising peace and tranquillity after the long crossing. The rough flat island of Sanday (easily reached at low tide across the sandspit) shelters the deep water harbour of the green hilly island, popular with countless ships whose crews painted graffiti on the basalt cliffs to record their safe arrival century after century. It was used by Baltic traders even as early as the 16th century. In one sense, their gratitude seems curiously misplaced, for Compass Hill distorts the compasses of all who come too close, the iron in the black basalt attracting the metal north pointers.

   The cliffs, arches and stacks echo with the choruses of seabirds clinging to their shelves. On Stack An Coroghan is a ruined tower where an irate Macdonald chiefain imprisoned his beautiful wife to frustrate her supposed lover, a Macleod of Skye. She took an unusually long time to die of starvation and one dawn Macdonald watched from the hill. Thinking he saw an eagle move, he fired an arrow, only to kill one of his most loyal followers who was too kind-hearted to allow his chieftain's wife to starve to death.

   The promise of Canna's appearance is supported by its mild

weather (daffodils are known to flower here in January) and it is famous for its early potatoes and sheep production. The site of a 7th century chapel dedicated to St Columba was first cultivated by the monks of Iona (a cross they carved stands proudly on the knoll behind). They retained the island until the Reformation, though not without difficulties for by 1428 raiding pirates were such a menace that the Abbot of Iona appealed to the Pope to excommunicate them. The island remained Catholic despite missionary attempts by the Church of Scotland and the Free Church.

Today, most of the 24 islanders carve a living out of the sheep and lobster fishing, under the benevolent eye of their laird Sir John Lorne Campbell — a great champion of island life and Gaelic culture not only in Canna but in the rest of the Hebrides.

There is no accommodation on the island but serious naturalists wishing to record the wide varieties of bird, butterfly and plant life are welcome to camp (consult the estate office first — tel Mallaig 2473). There is no shop so supplies must be acquired on the mainland. On Saturdays the ferry gives day trippers 4 hours on the island, long enough to climb up Compass Hill and watch the variety of duck found around the shores.

To the south of Canna is the rocky outcrop of **Oigh Sgeir** (G — maiden rock), now a Nature Reserve where hexagonal columns of basalt similar to those on Staffa play host to a large grey seal colony and many seabirds.

Eigg
(G eag — notched)

Connections:
By air: island aeroplane on request, details from Eigg Estate (tel Mallaig 82413).

By sea: from Glenuig: two a day; island ferry; crossing 1 hr (tel Mallaig 82428).

From Mallaig: Mon, Wed, Sat; crossing 1½ hrs.

From Mallaig: via Canna, Rhum: Thu, Sat; crossing 5½ hrs. Caledonian MacBrayne Ltd (tel Mallaig 2223).

From Arisaig: Mon, Wed, Fri, Sat (2), Sun; crossing 1 hr. Mon, Wed, Fri also via Muck. Murdo Grant, Arisaig Hotel (tel Arisaig 224).

Eigg earns its name from its appearance, for from the sea it looks as though a legendary giant has chipped a hollow across the centre, leaving the two hills **Ben Buie** and **The Sgurr**. Most of the underlying rock is basalt lava of the tertiary age which produces the stepped effect, but the Sgurr is formed of pitchstone, making it a friend of climbers. In some places hexagonal columns can be seen above the

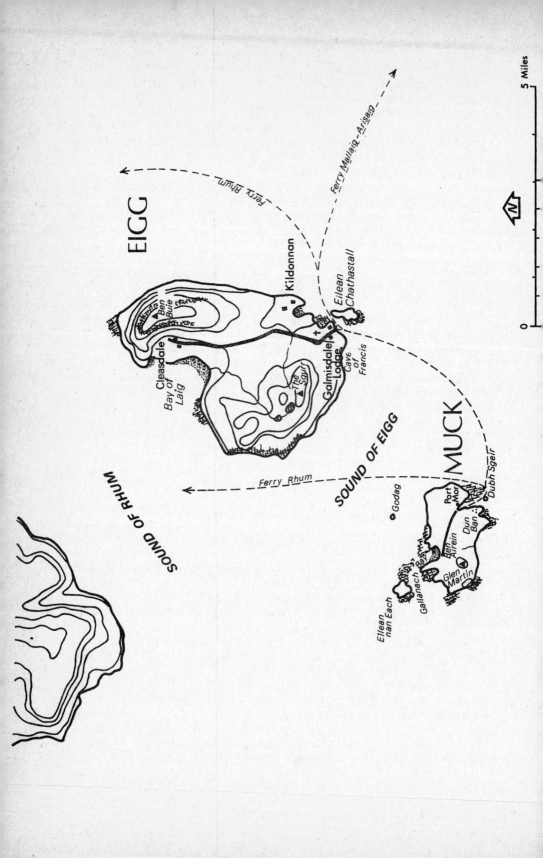

SOUND OF RHUM

EIGG

Ferry Rhum

Ben
Buie

Cleasdale

Bay of
Laig

The Sgurr

Kildonnan

Galmisdale
Lodge

Cave
of
Francis

Eilean
Chathastall

Ferry Rhum

Ferry Mallaig–Arisaig

SOUND OF EIGG

Ferry Rhum

Godag

MUCK

Port
Mor

Dun Ban

Ben
Airein

Glen
Martin

Dubh Sgeir

Gallanach Bay

Eilean
nan Each

N

0   5 Miles

fossilized traces of trees, created by the slow cooling of molten lava and similar to Fingals cave (see Staffa).

As late as the 16th century locals referred to Eigg as Eilean Ninban More (G — isle of the big women), and legend recounts how a queen and her amazons lived on the islet of one of the small lochans stringing the backside of the Sgurr. (Good fishing and nowadays used for skating if the frost is hard enough.) These amazons were responsible for the first Eigg massacre: the 7th century monk St Donan and his 52 followers antagonized the queen with their missionary zeal, and in 617 AD she had the entire community wiped out. Today the alpine slopes of the Sgurr are the favourite haunt of Manx shearwaters, although numbers have declined in the last decade. Their caterwauling by night would petrify any unsuspecting ghost.

The south side of the island is indented with caves, an obvious place of refuge in unsettled times. In 1577 some Skye Macleods arrived on a raiding escapade, raped some of the Macdonald girls of Eigg, were caught and sent home castrated. Typically 'justice' was sought and the eleventh Macleod chief launched his fleet of galleys. The Macdonalds realized that they were outnumbered and retreated unseen to the Cave of Francis. After three days they sent out a scout, but the Macleods had been unusually persistent and were still around. Spotting the scout's footprints in the snow, they found the cave but failed to force an entry. Instead, they lit a fire outside and asphyxiated all the 400 refugees inside. Now only ravens haunt these lonely caves. The bones were removed only in the last century to the ruins of the 15th century chapel. This is worth visiting for the contemporary carved cross in the graveyard and the inscribed dedication on the north wall. Other carvings have been removed for safekeeping to the lodge.

Eigg had been in the hands of the Macdonalds since the time of Robert the Bruce and was often used for the meeting of the clans, but in 1826 it was sold to the Professor of Greek at Aberdeen. In 1893 Lawrence Thompson, a ship builder who had made his fortune by selling warships to Japan, bought the island and led it to a golden age, ploughing money into the land, developing the farming and fishing, planting the woods around the harbour, and modernizing the pier to encourage the paddle steamers to stop — by the First World War ten a week were calling at the island. His lodge was burnt down but his extravaganza of a grave is visible on the highest point of Eilean Chathastall (Castle Island), from where he could see his three properties on Skye, Muck and Eigg.

Impetus was lost as the island continued to change hands and an air of neglect developed until the present laird, Keith Schellenburg, bought it in 1975. Wearing nearly all the official hats except those of minister, doctor, policeman, teacher and post mistress (Eigg is the largest isle of the Small Isles Parish and is thus the centre of these services), he has made sure that the enthusiasm which once earned him a place in the British Winter Olympic team, now vibrates through island life. The Eigg hockey team regularly plays against Muck and the island kids are dragooned into elaborate team games through the grounds of the rebuilt Lodge to the Edwardian bathing hut on the sand. Luckily his energy is also directed towards his estate and island tourism. At the north end of the island most of the islanders live independently, acting out a perfect example of traditional crofting life and rearing cattle at Cleasdale. Local ceilidhs and Scottish country dances happen nearly every week and visitors are much appreciated.

The whole island is treated as a wildlife reserve, supervised by the Scottish Wildlife Trust. The climate is astonishingly mild although wet (March to May is relatively dry), and subtropical species grow comfortably out of the wind. The most notable of these are the eucalyptus trees near the pier. Grey seals play in the harbour and off the north coast, and patient observers may spot otters sporting close to the waterline. Eigg was once an excellent place to find rare species of butterflies but the increasing use of insecticide has reduced their numbers. However, nothing has altered Eigg's greatest tourist attraction, the singing sands of the Bay of Laig. Formed by uniform grains of white quartz sand, the beach squeaks like blackboard chalk when wet, and drones when dry. Walking here is a noisy business but storms are needed to produce symphonies.

Accommodation:
B & B and self-catering — details from Tourist Office, Mallaig or Tourist Officer, Eigg Estate (tel Mallaig 82413).
Fishing:
Permits from Tea Room; also enquire here for charters.
Taxi:
Dugald MacKinnon (tel Mallaig 82431).
Eigg Estate (also bicycles) (tel Mallaig 82413).
Sailing Dinghies:
Ask at restaurant
Supplies:
Eigg PO (tel Mallaig 82432). Cottage guests and large camping parties should order in advance. (Meat from Mallaig only.)
Specialities:
Lobsters, local crafts.
Events:
August: Small Isles Games.

Muck
(G muc-mahara — sea pig)

Connections:
By sea: from Mallaig: Wed (via Eigg), Sat (via Canna and Rhum); crossing 2¼ hrs and 4¾ hrs. Caledonian MacBrayne Ltd (tel Mallaig 2223).

From Arisaig: Mon, Wed, Fri, via Eigg; crossing 2½ hrs. Murdo Grant, Arisaig Hotel (tel Arisaig 224).

Also from Eigg by arrangement, Eigg Estate (tel Mallaig 82413).

Muck earns its name not from any lack of cleanliness on the part of its inhabitants but from the porpoises (sea pigs) which frolic in Gallanach Bay. Killer whales and dolphins can be sighted cruising off-shore and grey seals rear a few pups on the islets to the north, making Muck truly an island of sea mammals. Dr Johnson met the Laird of Muck during his travels in the 18th century and was amused to find that this worthy man rebelled against the fashion of being known by his property. He claimed that the island was properly called Monk from its original owner, a hermit from Iona, but insisted that if it had to be called Muck, he should at least be given the full title of Isle of Muck.

Muck is the most fertile of the Small Isles, often likened to a well kept giant golf course, a simile endorsed by the presence of tattered flags planted in attempts to deduce the most sheltered corners possible for tree plantations. Muck has no peat and its native forest was chopped down many centuries ago. Throughout its recent history, the islanders have had to import coal from the mainland and collect driftwood from the shore, even burning seaweed collected from the rocks in times of hardship. Some trees were planted in 1922, and the enterprising MacEwan brothers who now own the island have been nurturing native and exotic species.

Muck was one of the great kelp-producing islands. In 1795, the total population of 195 was employed in gathering the tangle from the shore, but in 1826 the bottom dropped out of the market and most of the islanders were shipped to Nova Scotia, the remainder being resettled at Gallanach, to eke out a living from fishing and cultivating lazybeds. Muck has always relied on its owner's iniative, there being no crofters until 1978. The walls were made from the stones of the evicted islanders' houses. Sheep typically replaced people but the fertile slopes are well suited to cattle production (the only heather is to be found in Glen Martin). Muck cheese, which found favour with the Edwardians, is no longer produced, but a small dairy herd provides all the milk and butter required, while beef cattle are also reared.

Eilean nan Each (G — horse island) is the crowded haunt of many of the island's seabirds but was probably once used for pony rearing

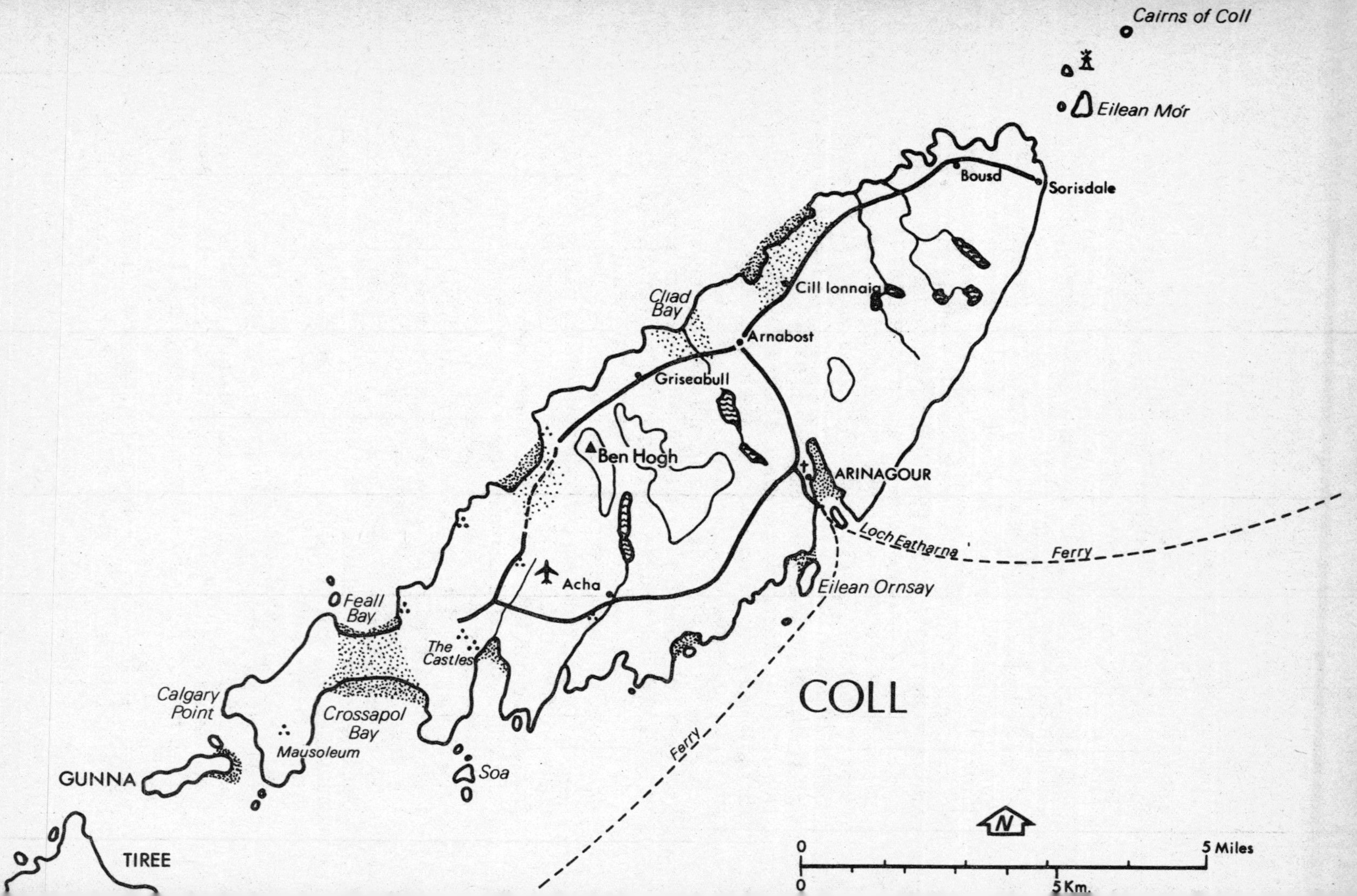

Cairns of Coll
Eilean Mór
Bousd
Sorisdale
Cill Ionnaig
Cliad Bay
Arnabost
Griseabull
Ben Hogh
ARINAGOUR
Loch Eatharna
Ferry
Eilean Ornsay
Acha
Feall Bay
The Castles
Calgary Point
Crossapol Bay
Mausoleum
Soa
GUNNA
TIREE
Ferry
COLL
N
0
5 Miles
0
5 Km.

A West Highland pony stud is well established, although since no stallion is kept the mares have to be ferried over to Rhum; these ponies are well suited to children.

Over 80 species of birds nest on Muck and many more visit it, making the island an ornithologist's delight.

Muck's only safe harbour is at Port Mor, overlooked by **Dun Ban,** a rock fortified in the Bronze Age. However, there is a welcoming shell beach at **Gallanach,** kept well stocked by the Atlantic Drift which occasionally delivers West Indian beans, carefully kept by their finders as lucky charms. Otters and a variety of rodents can be spotted on the shore but no rabbits compete with the grazing sheep.

Although there are now only 24 inhabitants, the MacEwans dream of a collective whereby crofters and incomers would each contribute their skills to make the island as close to self-sufficiency as is practical in the 1980s. They claim that this is the only way to survive the collapse of the fishing industry. As yet, the island community survives with an isolated vitality. Television cannot rival ceilidhs, dances and sportsnights, badminton is played in the barn when it is not full of hay, and all visitors are welcomed everywhere with a hearty handshake.

Accommodation:
Port Mor Guest House (tel Mallaig 2362).
Self-catering — details from L MacEwan Guest House.
Camping: permission needed from L MacEwan Guest House.
Transport:
None. The road is only 1¼ miles (2 km) long!
Supplies:
From Eigg. Meat, dairy produce and veg available locally.
Specialities:
Lobsters, wood turning.

Coll
(G — a hazel)

Connections:
By sea: from Oban: summer — Mon, Wed, Fri, Sat, one a day; winter — Tue, Thu, Sat, one a day; cars; crossing 3¾ hrs minimum.

From Tiree: summer — Mon, Wed, Fri, Sat, one a day; winter — Tue, Thu, Sat, one a day; cars; crossing 1¼ hrs. Caledonian MacBrayne Ltd (tel Coll 347).

As the ferry pulls into Coll, the island presents a bleak face of gnarled rock protruding through the scant skin of heather, similar though tamer than the east coast of Harris and equally unwelcoming.

A tiny glimpse of whitewashed cottages reassures one that people can and do live on this barren outcrop of gneiss, and the road from the pier soon leads to a charming village of whitewashed cottages, Arinagour (G Airigh na gobhar — shieling of the goats).

These smart rows represent an attempt by an enlightened laird, Maclean of Coll, to modernize the island around 1800, to encourage tradesmen to settle. Most are now holiday cottages, the collachs preferring the council houses behind. The village has remainded the centre of island life, with its two shops, cafe, craft shop, hotel, and even a laundrette (open 10 — 5, Mon-Fri, 10 — 8, Sat), built to cope with the hotel's linen and very popular with the summer yachts which moor in Loch Eatharna (G — loch of the small fishing boats). The enterprising hotelier, Alistair Oliphant, a one-time chief of conjurers, has instigated the unique island luxury of a sauna. The trim colourful gardens in front of every house bear witness both to the wind and to the sun — neighbouring Tiree has Britain's highest sunshine record! Two churches look down on the activities of the village, neither exceptional except that the Presbyterian minister of 1907 organized a huge sale of work in Inverness, lasting for three days, to pay for his.

Following the loch inland, herons can be spotted wading through the seaweed. The house of Arnabost (ON — Arne's shieling) has information on an old earthhouse discovered in 1855 when the 'new' road was laid. Nothing can now be seen of the long passage and circular chamber in which many implements and a gold brooch were found. Turning north the road clambers over the sand dunes built up by the Atlantic gales, offering enticing glimpses of empty isolated white beaches. The cemetery, Cill Ionnaig (G — St Fionnaig's cell), is traditionally said to have been begun when a team of coffin bearers felt that the night was too wild to carry their charge to the cemetery at the south end of Coll. This nice story was weakened by the discovery of a medieval chapel — a most unimpressive square of nettles — but here lies Young Coll, who so admirably entertained Dr Johnson and Boswell during their enforced storm-bound stay, and drowned the following year when crossing from Inch Kenneth to Mull.

The north end of the island was once heavily populated because the sand combines with the peat to make machair, an intensely rich soil. An experiment to grow daffodils and tulips in competition with the Dutch failed only because of the transportation costs. The townships of Bousd and Sorisdale (ON — settlement) present a pathetic sight of crumbling roofless ruins, the deserted homes of crofters. However, in Coll the saga was not as brutal as might at first be imagined. After the '45 the population increased dramatically and by the 1840s was above the capacity of the land. In the famines of that decade, the then laird impoverished himself trying to feed his people and resolved for their own benefit to transport them to the new lands of Canada and Australia. However, his financial straits forced him to sell before this could be achieved. The buyer was less sympathetic and raised the rents, but the north end of the island was under Campbell ownership and new crofts were offered to those tenants who could not pay the extortionate rents. Hence the overcrowding. The buyer soon realized the error of his ways, at least as far as his pocket was concerned, and repopulated the land with dairy farmers from Ayrshire. Until the First World War the Coll cheese they produced was one of the delicacies favoured by the House of Lords, but sadly it is no longer produced. The drift away from the northern end of the island has been caused by modern aspirations and now only one thatched cottage remains inhabited, claiming the best TV reception on the island.

The bay at the road's end is a popular picnic site, though never crowded, and a walk along the east coast will reveal many lochans ornamented with white water-lilies, a veritable wilderness of wildlife easily accessible yet rarely disturbed.

Turning south from Arnabost, the road passes the farm of **Griseabull** where an early battle for ownership took place between Iain Garbh of Coll and MacNeill of Barra in the 15th century. Iain's widowed mother married MacNeill when Iain was still a child and the unheroic stepfather chose to annex Coll. However, his garrison of MacNeills proved unpopular to the collachs, and when the boy managed to escape from Kisimul castle, Barra, his people supported his cause. Outwitting the scouts, Iain took the garrison at Griseabull by surprise and won back his inheritance. Until 1980, at least part of the island has belonged to his descendants.

Ben Hogh (338 ft/103 m) is Coll's highest hill and is worth climbing for the views south. On its shoulder is the curiosity of a 'perched' boulder, a vast rock balanced on three tiny ones, apparently stable and probably left by the Ice Age.

Coll boasts two castles. To reach them by road one must return to Arinagour, but there is a pleasant track through the sand dunes where the Coll fair was once held. Now populated by an army of rabbits, this is a good place for sighting birds of prey. It meets the road by a standing stone — Na Sgeulachan (G — the teller of tales). Sadly what tales it tells are lost in time, but active imaginations have produced a multitude of explanations for its purpose, from worship to astronomical calculations.

The 'new' castle was built for Hector Maclean in 1750 and sheltered Dr Johnson and Boswell from the gales within its honest Georgian walls. Unfortunately a Victorian owner then decided to have an extravaganza for his sporting retreat and proceeded to enlarge it, mutilating the classical proportions with turrets and battlements which are too sombre to be fun and present a grim aspect to onlookers. Subsequently found to be uninhabitable, it fell into considerable disrepair but is now being converted into holiday homes.

The old castle, Breacachadh, is a typical medieval fortress,

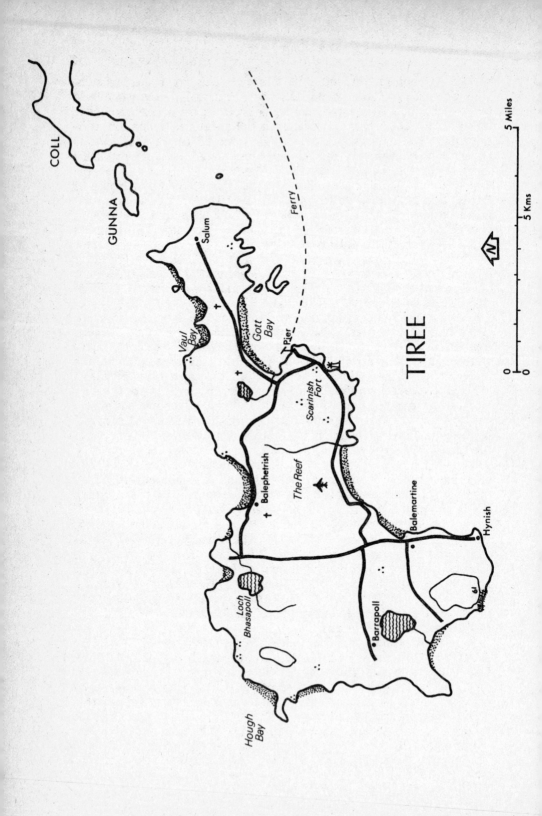

COLL

GUNNA

TIREE

5 Miles

5 Kms

N

0

0

Ferry

Salum

Vaul
Bay

Gott
Bay

Pier

Scarinish
Fort

Balephetrish

The Reef

Balemartine

Hynish

Loch
Bhasapoll

Barrapoll

Hough
Bay

watching over the southern and eastern waters. This was the 15th century stronghold of the Macleans who offered to protect any member of the MacElonich family against all comers except the king, in thanks for their protection of a young Coll widow pregnant with the Maclean heir. The solid four-storeyed tower house stands proud beside its tower, and is now the centre of an enterprising scheme to train school leavers for voluntary service in the underdeveloped countries. Locals unkindly accuse Major Bristol of concocting the Project Trust to provide cheap labour to restore the ruin into a home — an unjust allegation, as it seems an excellent and sensible method of challenging the initiative of the young adventurers. Perhaps they will proceed to restore the Mausoleum of the 13th Maclean chieftain, an isolated shell in the dunes which is collapsing from neglect.

Returning to the village one is rewarded by views of small crofts settled beside rocky creeks, crisp white in their isolation. Some of the fields rear the unusual combination of sheep and pheasants for the new owner Jan de Vries, locally referred to as the 'Dutchman'. A millionaire, he is determined to have a sporting estate and regularly flys in by helicopter to slaughter the birds which have no cover. An attempt to grow trees has succeeded only to wall height.

Accommodation:
Isle of Coll Hotel (tel Coll 334). The hotel caters for everything — information, car and bicycle hire, loch fishing and sea fishing, either directly or through connections.
Self-catering — details from Tourist Office, Oban.
Camping is permitted only behind the churches above the village.
Specialities:
Coll Herbal Products.

Tiree
(G tir-i-odh — land of corn)

Connections:
By air: from Glasgow: Mon-Fri, one a day. Loganair Ltd (tel Scarinish 309).

By sea: from Oban (via Coll): Mon, Wed, Fri, Sat, one a day; cars; crossing 4¾ hrs (and 1 hr). Caledonian MacBrayne Ltd (tel Scarinish 337).

A gentle twist of the Gaelic to Tir-fo-Thuinn gives Tiree the nickname of 'the land under the waves', and so it often seems, for Tiree has only three hillocks above 330 ft (100 m) and between them is stretched a flat fertile canopy of crofting land barely above the waterline. The rocky out-crops are of the famous Tiree marble coloured pink and flecked with green, which is made into craft jewellery locally. Long silver beaches of shell sand edge the island, strung between rocks and always deserted except for a great variety of waders and hares (there are no rabbits here). As on Orkney, because of its overall emerald green appearance, Tiree's lack of trees is not immediately obvious, but this crisp and magic land has little protection against the wind and the waves.

Tiree features in most shipping reports connected with gale warnings, and highlanders jest that you can recognize an inhabitant of this windswept platform by his 80° stance. But from May to September the weather encourages visitors, for the wind declines to a breeze and the sun has a fondness for this island, giving it more sunshine than anywhere else in Britain. The occasional showers are brief and wash the white cottages to an advertizer's brightness.

Tiree saw some of the fiercest scenes of the Clearances in 1886, when the Duke of Argyll sent 50 police and 250 marines to the island to evict his crofters. Most were kelp makers, gathering the seaweed blown onto the shore by the winter gales, to be used in soap and glass manufacture, but as the demand declined it became obvious that the people needed more land to support themselves. Many were transported and dumped without help in Canada where they were unable to escape destitution, but by the end of the 19th century, the Crofting Commission had been set up and eventually the farms were divided into crofts for the remaining population.

Today, the fertile plain is heavily populated with crofters, many of whom still use the old agricultural methods because their patch of land cannot justify modern machinery. Crofting does not bring wealth and many of the white houses (so-called because the cement between the stones gave a light appearance in comparison to the early drystone black houses) are still lived in, although many thatched roofs have been replaced by corrugated iron, well battened-down against the wind.

Few islanders bother to fish. Perhaps they have too many folk memories of sudden squalls which spread the old fleets sometimes as far as America; perhaps crofting with subsidies can now supply their wants. The volume of alcohol consumed on Tiree is considerable, for although there is a police station on the island, licensing hours are rarely observed. Possibly as a result of this, many of the crofts have an unnecessary air of decay.

The main settlement is at Scarinish around a picturesque stone harbour, no longer used except by lobster boats. Here, the wreck of the *Mary Stewart*, one of the last sailing ships to trade in these west-coast waters, lies hauled onto the sand. Above the village is the fort of Vaul, a broch dating from the 1st century BC, with galleries still visible in the 12 ft (4 m) thick walls.

Loch Bhasapoll is a small loch with vast marsh fringes, very popular with both breeding and wintering duck and geese. The charming old township of **Balephetrish**, (G — the township of the storm petrel), is imaginatively linked with St Peter for his feat of walking over the waves. Although storm petrels are rearly seen in daylight hours, they are frequently heard. The small off-shore island of **Gunna** has a small colony of grey seals.

The only land not cultivated or used for common grazing of the cattle is The Reef, an important RAF base during the last war, littered with decrepit block houses. It is still being used as an airport.

At **Hynish** is a small pier and settlement dominated by a high granite tower made from stones from the Ross of Mull. This was the workmen's base during the construction of the **Skerryvore light-house** by Alan Stevenson in 1837-43. The high tower enabled them to communicate between the two points. The cliffs here scream with seabirds, mainly kittiwakes, guillemots and razorbills, and the dense cover of meadow flowers on the rest of the island gives way to a mat of sea thrift.

Accommodation:
Scarinish Hotel (tel Scarinish 410)
The Lodge (tel Scarinish 353)
Balephetrish Guest House (tel Scarinish 549)
Self catering — details from Tourist Office, Oban.
Bank:
Royal Bank, Scarinish; open normal hours.
Car Hire:
Tiree Motor Company, Crossapol (tel 469)
Bicycle Hire:
N MacLean, Crossapol (tel 428)
Sea Angling:
Contact Tiree Motor Company
Freshwater Fishing:
Permits from Mr Gillis, Gamekeeper's House, Scarinish
Golf:
At Vaul — visitors welcomed.
Specialities:
Sheepskins, bread.

Mull
(G maol — bald)

Connections:
By sea: from Oban to Craignure: six a day, Mon-Sat; four a day Sun; cars; crossing 45 mins. Caledonian MacBrayne Ltd (tel Craignure 343).

From Oban to Tobermory, one a day, Mon, Wed, Fri, Sat; cars;

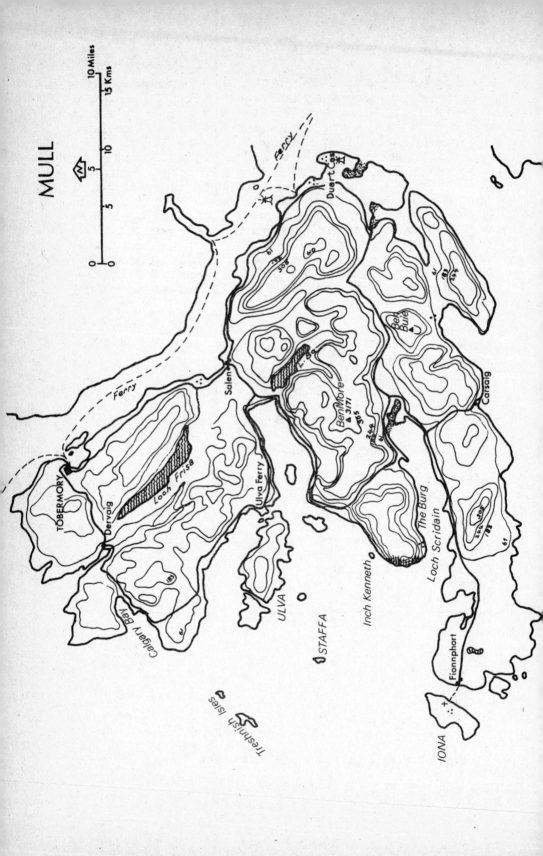

crossing 2 hrs. From Tiree (via Coll) to Tobermory: one a day, Mon, Wed, Sat; cars; crossing 2¾ hrs (and 1½ hrs). Caledonian MacBrayne Ltd (tel Tobermory 2017).

From Lochaline to Fishnish: about 17 a day, Mon-Sat; about 12 a day, Sun; cars; crossing 30 mins. Caledonian MacBrayne Ltd (tel Morvern 214).

From Oban, Fort William, Lochaline to Tobermory and Craignure: catamaran service. Details from Western Ferries Ltd.

Lying well tucked into the coastline of mainland Scotland, Mull was known even to the classical Greeks, Ptolemy referring to it as Malaeius. Today, few visitors escape the beaches and lowland woods to explore the central core of mountain peaks rising steeply from the shore, probably because of the persistent dampness. Mull is claimed to be the wettest island of the Hebrides: quite an achievement and one that should not be ignored however good the forecast.

May is the sunniest month, but the wet gradually wins the fight until the downpour in October. The everchanging weather enhances the soft beauty of emerald colours, remixing to form new patterns, a beauty quite neglected by Dr Johnson who simply got irritated by the rain but now enjoyed by artists, both amateur and professional. Most shops and hotels sell endless variations on this theme, generally easy to improve on given time. The car driver's Mull is very different to that discovered by the energetic walker, but for both there are many pleasant refuges from the rain — craftshops, museums and tea-houses. The islanders have developed an excellent line in home manufacture and many a sign will lead to an 'honesty' box containing fresh bread, jams or sweets, or sometimes even children's toys.

Tobermory (G tobar Mhoire — well of Mary), made famous by a Womble, dates from 18th century attempts to establish a fishing centre, its harbour being well sheltered by Calve Island. It is now a popular pausing place for yachts (showers available at the Suidhe Hotel, and a laundrette open Mon-Sat). The earlier settlement was at the top of the hill around St Mary's well and the ruined medieval chapel, past which the road twists sharply on its steep descent to sea level. The ring of early 19th century houses around the quay are surprisingly large, and painted in bright Mediterreanean colours in a recent attempt to cheer the town up — they succeed, and the colours are echoed in the granny seats and cast iron railings, with even a cheerful fountain creating a festive air. This is the main shopping centre with a vast (for an island) range of goods. The fish shop must be recommended for its selection of fresh and smoked fish and variety of vegetables, and even the most antiquated of touristy shops produce some pleasant surprises such as horn spoons or marble slabs.

'Old Mull' whiskey is no longer made on the island but in Oban, although the Ledaig Distillery, founded in 1823 and reopened in 1972, after a troubled history, welcomes visitors. Because of the current whiskey glut, it often proves more economical to close the plant down temporarily rather than continue production, as the liquid takes up so much storage space, but the vast copper stills are intriguing at any time. Next door is the Mull and Iona Folklore Club Museum (open 11 — 5, Mon-Sat), a chaotic collection of bits and pieces appertaining to Mull, from fossils to old chairs, set out in a large hall. A thorough browse will reveal many delights — old photograph albums and diaries or fantastical china. A display tells of the 'Tobermory Treasure' supposedly carried by the Spanish Armada galleon *Almirante di Florencia* when she took refuge in the bay in 1588 and foolishly got drawn into clan intrigues, being blown up for her folly. Divers have failed to find the hoard of gold but some lesser finds are exhibited. Many ceilidhs and dances are held in Aros Hall, popular among locals and visitors alike.

Only a small section of Mull's roads are double track. The rest cater for local carts and are a rally driver's delight as they unroll over the bumpy terrain (there is a weekend race at the beginning of every October — be warned). Driving here can be extremely dangerous: forget mainland time, pay due respect to the terrain, and enjoy the scenery. Countless waterfalls plunge off the steep slopes and the geological variations could illustrate a textbook. Most spectacular are the basalt cliffs around **Ben More**, the granite quarries of the **Ross of Mull** which provided stone for the Albert Memorial and Blackfriars Bridge in London, and the basalt columns of **Ulva** and **Carsaig** (see also Staffa). The road east clambers over ridges past **Mishnish Lochs** (good fishing and favoured by divers) to descend to the yellow and white village of **Dervaig** (G darbh and ON aig — reptile bay), set amongst the trees and planned by Maclean of Coll. A large house watches over the demure row of cottages, while many gardens are filled with fine collections of poultry (duck eggs are available from Cottage Crafts). Above the village is a typical but ancient West Highland graveyard, set around the ruins of Kilmore Chapel and bereft of any trees. Looking down from here, one sees the pencil steeple of the village church rising up in a curious Victorian attempt to imitate the medieval Irish form (see Egilsay). Camping is permitted behind the church.

Close by is a sign 'Theatre' which heralds Britain's smallest theatre — the **Mull Little Theatre**. Housed in an old barn, this seats 38 plus 2 on the window sill, and was founded by Marianne and Barrie Hesketh in 1966. A winter of touring brings good publicity to their 16 week summer season at home — very much at home, with the Heskeths acting three plays twice each week and resting on the Sabbath with a poetry reading. Children's and lunchtime programmes are also concocted and every performance has a spark of vitality breaking through the pure professionalism. A visit is essential (tel Dervaig 267). Not only do the Heskeths change all the props and lighting themselves between scenes, without disturbing the tension, but during the intervals you will find them serving coffee and chocolate cakes (the speciality of the house), and happily chatting to their guests.

The Old Byre (open Easter — Oct, 10.30 — 5 Mon-Sat, 1.30 — 5 Sun) explains what life was like for crofters 150 years ago, by means of tableaux depicting the 'black house' and the 'white house', animated by an audio dramatization recorded by locals. Slightly sterile, it lacks the smells that would make it truly evocative. Shooting matches are held by Loch Cuan (details from the Tourist Office, Tobermory), beside the beautiful treelined rocky sea loch (camping discouraged).

The road follows the old drove route through the hazel and alder woods past Penmore Hill to Croig, a tiny stone harbour where cattle were landed from Tiree and Coll to be walked across Mull to the markets at Oban (boat trips for sea angling and Staffa, tel Dervaig 242). The white sands of Calgary Bay are romantically linked with Calgary, Alberta, not because the people were evicted there but because Colonel J F Macleod of the Royal North-West Mounted Police wished to honour his hosts after an enjoyable stay at Calgary House. Buzzards and golden eagles can often be seen circling the hill tops and kestrel hunt in the lower woods.

Torloisk (G — burnt hill) was the home of a famous pirate, Alan of the Straws, so called because immediately after his birth he grasped a handful of straw. His fiery temper led him to clash with his stepfather and so he joined a band of piratical Danes, earning much respect and fear for his prowess. A scheme by his stepfather to turn him against the MacQuarrie, laird of Ulva, failed when Alan was softened by the old man's charms and he instead drew his sword against his treacherous relative, finally settling down within sight of his old friend's island.

Dr Johnson and Boswell enjoyed hospitality on Ulva (ON ulv + ay — wolf isle), though not in the famed but now destroyed Adam house built by later Lairds. Present-day tourists are not so fortunate as all access to the island is forbidden. However, one of its famous sites, the shelf of basalt columns on its northern slopes, can clearly be seen from across the water. The sad tale of the eloping Chief of Ulva and his bride, who drowned at Ulva Ferry while fleeing her parents, is romantically captured in Thomas Campbell's poem, 'Lord Ullin's Daughter'. Thomas Campbell (1777-1844) was a Glaswegian who came to Mull as a tutor and achieved sufficient fame to merit burial in Westminster Abbey. Ulva was also the home of MacArthur's piping college, founded when MacQuarrie's brillant young piper completed his studies under the MacCrimmons of Dunvegan (see Skye).

The scenery across the water of Loch na Keal is often heightened by the sultry light caught under the clouds of Ben More. Grey herons contrast with the rusty seaweed and white cascades of water — all seen at their best during a walk along the rocky shore. The most spectacular of Mull's waterfalls, Eas Fors, can only be seen from below and traditionally hides a cave used by pipers for practising their compositions in preparation for the prestigious competitions.

Joining the road to Iona, one is confronted by a large sign advertizing a mausoleum cared for by the National Trust of Australia. In the wooded estate of Jarvisfield is a monument in honour of **Major General Lachlan Macquarrie (1761-1824)**, the first Governor of New South Wales for twelve years from 1809, and esteemed as one of the fathers of that country. The modest and subdued neo-Gothic building neatly counters the extravagant claims of his epitaph.

The tiny offshore island of **Inch Kenneth** was named after one of St Columba's followers and served Iona as a granary when the population of Iona became too large. The kings of Scotland and Ireland were traditionally buried on Iona, but on many occasions when the weather was too ferocious their bodies were laid to rest on Inch Kenneth. The islet thus preserves a marvellous collection of medieval carved gravestones by the ruins of the ancient chapel; especially notable is that of Sir Allan Maclean.

The road cuts across the headland of **The Burg**, rising above the lush coastal plane to hills with almost alpine vegetation, but explorers on foot should not be distracted from the shore. **MacKinnon's Cave**, described by Dr Johnson as 'the greatest natural marvel he had ever seen', penetrates so far into the headland that no one has ever been able to measure its depth (mind the tide). Linked with stories of a Skye cave (see Skye), legend recounts how a party accompanied by MacKinnon, the piper and a dog began to explore when they met an evil fairy who killed them all except MacKinnon. She promised that his music would save him if he could play until he reached daylight. He failed and shore observers found all the bodies in the gloom. Only the dog survived, denuded of hair. **The Burg** is in the care of the National Trust for Scotland because of its spectacular basalt forms. The famous fossilized McCulloch's tree, caught in the flow of lava, and standing to a height of 40 ft (12 m), has been vandalized by curio-hunters and is now protected by cement around its base. Look out for the wild goats.

Folklore recounts how **Loch Scridain** (G — loch of the waterfalls) was carved out by the Devil when he fell off Ben More after losing an argument with St Columba. Every ledge marks a stage in his descent and his final tumble caused such a cleft that the loch was formed. The little road to **Carsaig** winds over the moor until it reaches the back of beyond and rises sharply through dense woods — a sense of adventure develops and suddenly you are face to face with a red telephone box, with no house in sight. This was featured in the film 'I know Where I'm Going'. The road drops sharply down to a small picturesque stone pier, built for the herring fishers of the last century and surrounded by vertical cliffs — an awe-inspiring but inhospitable scene. A hard walk under the cliffs reveals, two hours later, the famous Carsaig arches and stacks. The caves were used as quarries by Iona's monks, who found the soft stone easy to sculpture into ornamental graveslabs. A sill of sapphires can be seen beyond the caves, still there because they have no commercial value.

At **Penny Cross** there is a monument to the Beaton family, famous physicians who learnt their skills from the monks of Iona and found favour even with James VI before he inherited the English crown. 'Bonnie' **Bunessan** (G — foot of the little waterfall) is a fiction promoted by the Tourist Board, being only a convenient shopping village, but **Ardtun** (G aird-tunna — cape like a cast) has much to recommend it, with good views of the Burg and Staffa, basalt pillars lying in all directions and extensive fossil beds. The road leads straight on to **Fionnphort** (G — white port), the ferry point to Iona, whose 'airport' cage copes with each summer's flood of visitors. There are several nice sandy beaches along the headland facing the holy island, sheltered by the pink granite rocks. Ruined quarries can be seen at **Torr Mor** — a good place to find newts.

Glen More, vividly described by R L Stevenson in *Kidnapped* as his hero David Balfour tramps to the ferry at Craignure, does not always present such a savage image, although even the sun cannot dispel its potential for desolation. The Forestry Commission has created nature trails in Ardmore woods. **Loch Uisg** (G — loch of water) is a beautiful inland loch with a column commemorating Queen Victoria's Jubilee. Under **Ben Buie** (G — yellow mountain) is the medieval square tower of **Moy** (unsafe and therefore closed to visitors), commanding an excellent view down Loch Buie. The old village burial ground is by the sands. Inside the 19th century church is a Celtic cross, and close by are several unspectacular stone circles.

Medieval pilgrims crossed over to Mull at Grass point and many of the drove cattle left here to cross to Kerrera, as this is one of the narrowest points of the Firth of Lorn. On a clear day there is a mirage of mountains and water reminiscent of Chinese watercolours, livened by the many yachts of summer sailors. The old inn has recently been converted into a tea-room.

Duart Castle (G — dark height) (open May — Sep: 10 — 6 Mon-Fri) was the home of the chief of the Maclean clan, built on a crag in the 13th century so that it could watch all movements in the Sound of Mull. It is a typical garrison stronghold, but without the expected Victorian additions for it fell into disrepair in the 18th century and was only restored this century by Sir Fitzroy, the 26th Chief, a grand old man whose hundredth birthday was commemorated by the planting of a rowan (mountain ash) tree in the courtyard to ward off evil spirits. Impressive from a distance and with spectacular views, it is disappointingly hollow inside, with little atmosphere, only a few family trophies. The 27th Chief, Sir Charles, has added an exhibition on scouting and his unobtrusive figure can be seen haunting his domain.

Torosay Castle was designed by two eminent Scottish architects, David Bryce (1803-76) who planned the house, and Sir Robert Lorimer (1864-1929) who landscaped the terrace of the garden descending to the shore. It has all the feel of a family home (four generations are still in residence), and visitors are treated as house guests, encouraged to enjoy the comfortable Victorian rooms, browse through the game registers, admire the portraits and stag heads, stroke the cats and wonder why today's fancy dress is nothing like that recorded in the photograph album of the Diamond Jubilee Ball. Boys realize that this is the home of David Guthrie James, a POW who escaped from Colditz, and can read his school reports and other adventures, perhaps even meeting the hero. The gardens are currently being restored by his stepfather, and are being extended beyond the formal trim terraces and walk with its 18th century Venetian statues to water gardens. A steam railway is planned along the shore to Craignure and the stable block will eventually house an enlarged 'Mull Little Theatre'.

Salen (G — small sea) is a pleasant village built by Major General Macquarrie, and claims to have witnessed much preaching by St Columba. There is a large herd of tame goats outside the village and a flowershow is held close by every August. **Aros Castle**, once the seat of the MacDonalds, Lords of the Isles, was last inhabited in the 17th century and is now in a sad state of disrepair, the ruins probably dating from the 14th century. The woods of **Aros House** now belong to the Forestry Commission who have cut picnic areas and walks through the grounds; they face Tobermory, with good views of its brightly coloured houses.

Accommodation:
Tobermory:
Carnaburg Guest House (tel Tobermory 2479)
Mishnish Hotel (tel Tobermory 2009)
Springbank Guest House (tel Tobermory 2023)
Staffa Cottages Guest House (tel Tobermory 2464)
Suidhe Hotel (tel Tobermory 2209)
Western Isles Hotel (tel Tobermory 2012)
Dunard House (tel Tobermory 2360)
Tobermory Guest House (tel Tobermory 2091)
Ulva House Hotel (tel Tobermory 2044)
Elsewhere:
Bellachroy Hotel, Dervaig (tel Dervaig 225)
Druimnacroish Country House Hotel (tel Dervaig 274)
Kinloch Hotel, Pennyghael (tel Pennyghael 204)
Ardfenaig House, Buressan (tel Fionnphort 210)
Argyll Arms Hotel (tel Fionnphort 240)
Craignure Inn, Craignure (tel Craignure 305)
Isle of Mull Hotel, Craignure (tel Craignure 351)

Craig Hotel, Salen (tel Aros 347)
Glenforsa Hotel, Salen (tel Aros 377)
Salen Hotel, Salen (tel Aros 324)
B & B and self catering available — details from Tourist office, Tobermory.
Youth Hostel, Tobermory.
Camping — free range; Calgary Bay is popular, beside Dervaig church and conveniently close to a pub.
Car Hire:
Macgilk's Garage, Tobermory
Craignure Garage
Bicycle Hire:
Browns, (Ironmongers), Tobermory; and some hotels.
Sea Angling:
Hebridean Ventures, Tackle Shop, Tobermory (tel Tobermory 2458).
I Morrison, Penmore Mill (tel Dervaig 242).
Fresh water fishing permits:
Details from Tourist office, Tobermory.
Pony trekking:
S Morgan, Ormsaig (tel Fionnphort 297)
Mrs Elwis, Erray Estate (tel Tobermory 2052)
Golfing:
Western Isles Hotel (tel Tobermory 2012)
Wildlife Safaris:
R Coomber, Staffa Cottages Guest House (tel Tobermory 2464).
Banks:
Clydesdale Bank, Tobermory, normal hours.
Harbour Master:
Contact Caledonian MacBrayne Ltd, Pier Office, Tobermory
Tourist Office
48 Main St, Tobermory (tel Tobermory 2182); open Apr — Sep: 9 — 5 Mon-Sat.
Events:
July: Highland Games, Tobermory; Regatta, Tobermory.
August: Salen Flower Show; Buressan Agriculture Show.
September: Whiskey Festival, Tobermory.
October: Car rally.

Staffa
(ON staf-ey — isle with the staves)

Connections:
By sea: from Fort William: catamaran service; Wed, Fri, Western Ferries Ltd.
From Oban; catamaran service (weather permitting) Wed, Fri, Sat.

Western Ferries Ltd (tel Oban 3949).

From Oban: ship via Iona; Tue, Thu. Caledonian MacBrayne Ltd (tel Oban 2285).

From Mull, Croig: boat, by arrangement (weather permitting). I. Morrison, Penmore Mill (tel Dervaig 242).

Staffa was officially 'discovered' by Sir Joseph Banks in 1772. Banks had accompanied Captain Cook on his 1768 exploration of the South Seas as the ship's naturalist, and so was not unused to extraordinary phenomena, but his delight in and praise of this island could hardly be greater: 'Compared to this, what are the cathedrals or the places built by men . . . mere models or playthings.'

Less than ½ mile (1 km) long, Staffa stands flat-topped and ringed by cliffs. Uninhabited for over two centuries, it is now famous throughout the world for the hexagonal basalt columns that form its edge, similar to the Giants' Causeway in Ireland. Caused by an unusual pattern of the cooling of the molten lava, almost all these columns stand vertically — great pillars and stepping stones, stacks of giant pencils painted by seaweed, salt and algae, but generally grey and somber under their green sheep-grazed capping.

Dr Johnson and Boswell sailed past, could not land and remained unimpressed. The natives recognized a potential gold mine and charged accordingly: by 1800, the price for an excursion was two bottles of whiskey and 15 shillings.

Keats managed to negotiate a trip whilst on a tour to re-establish his health. He landed and explored the island, but failed to find the words to describe the wonders to his satisfaction. He was especially bewitched by Fingal's cave, the legendary home of Ossian's father, a name given by Banks. The cave penetrates far into the island, lined by monumental columns shaped in an almost Gothic form. Entering is easy at low tide but by high tide and in storms the force of the waves compresses the air which on escaping echoes the report of a cannon, and can be heard on the neighbouring islands. This 'singing' of the 'gigantic organ' challenged the young Mendelssohn on his successful visit in 1829 to write his 'Hebridean Overture'. Turner visited Staffa in bad weather and most of the party failed to land, but the island was crowned as a Victorian tourist spot when visited by the Royal family in 1847. Victoria was suitably impressed and left a number of indifferent sketches.

Modern tourist swamp the awe-inspiring scale of the rocks during their brief hour-long visits. In order to enjoy the island to the full, it is best to camp, bringing enough food for several (possibly stormbound) days.

Iona
(G i thonna — isle of the waves; also known as Icolmkill — Isle of Columba)

Connections:
By sea: from Oban: summer, Tue and Thu; day trips. Caledonian MacBrayne Ltd (tel Oban 2285). From Fionnphort, Mull: frequently; crossing 20 mins. Caledonian MacBrayne Ltd (tel Fionnphort 203).

Iona is the famous home of the Celtic church, fathered by St Columba whose missionary zeal made it so famous throughout Europe that it did not even hesitate to quarrell with the Bishop of Rome about the date of Easter — a dispute it finally lost. St Columba was born of a royal Irish family in 521, when Ireland was ruled by a scattering of kings. Even as a child he showed dedication to the church. His playmates gave him the nickname of Columicill — column of the church, and as a young man he founded several famous monasteries including Derry and Kells. His proud nature caused him to clash with the High King of Ireland and although the threat of excommunication was not enforced, Columba, the victor, was advised to leave his native shores in 563. Sailing northwards he refused to settle within sight of his homeland and so finally stopped at Iona.

Although other Irish missionaries had come to these waters before him, Columba's royal connections and foreceful nature ensured that his authority affected the Scottish kings. When the king of Dalriada died, Columba consecrated one of his own relations, Aiden, whose successful line had a vested interest in upholding the Columba legend, and soon the holy isle became the intended resting place of all Scottish kings. Although the island was repeatedly ravaged by Viking bands, Columba's memory instilled in his monks the courage to return and the Abbey was greatly expanded in the Middle Ages as the flow of pilgrims across Britain increased.

The iconoclasm of the Scottish Reformation caused havoc, and the buildings fell into ruins, but a visionary minister from Govan, Glasgow — George Macleod — survived the First World War to develop the idea of a modern community, which would help the Church to meet the needs of our modern society. A team of six craftsmen and six ministers began to repair the Abbey ruins in 1938 and as soon as some rooms were habitable their numbers increased dramatically, all sharing a common life both during short sojourns at Iona and in their home communities.

Each day of the summer their number of around 200 is swelled by modern pilgrims and tourists paying respect to the achievement of Columba's monks, past and present. The flood of people off each ferry may be off-putting, but most stay only a few hours and visit a few sites, although every knoll, bay, cairn and well has its legends. Any visitor planning to stay will find *Iona* by Marian McNeill a sympathetic and imaginative account of the island.

The ferry docks at Martyres Bay where traditionally the first Viking raiders slaughtered the monks in 798. The first ruin encountered beyond the touristy village is the **Nunnery** built in a Norman style at the turn of the 12th century by Reginald, Lord of the Isles, whose sister was the first Abbess of Icolmkill. Nunneries were often associated with, yet separated from monasteries, and the buildings of the chapel, chapter house, refectory and kitchen can still be seen. Many high ranking Scottish ladies chose to be buried around this chapel as late as the 18th century — the most notable tombstone is that of Prioress Anna (d 1543).

At a bend in the road, where Columba rested on the last day of his life, is the magnificent medieval **Maclean's cross**, probably commemorating a 15th century Maclean of Duart, Mull. The fine shaft is intricately carved with interlacing patterns around a crucified Christ, and behind there is a picture, probably of the warrior Maclean himself. Many of the **Tombs of Kings** have been removed from the graveyard where even rival sovereigns (in total 48 kings of Scotland, 7 of Norway and 4 of Ireland) chose to be buried beside Columba's original resting place, and placed in the **museum** for safe-keeping. Over a hundred carved slabs provide an easily assimilated study of the evolution of the style of Scottish carving, even if the atmosphere is distinctly creepy. Legend records that the first burial here was of Oran, one of Columba's original followers. Hearing that the success of the mission depended on one sacrifice, he offered himself. He was buried alive but on the third day his master opened the tomb. The martyr was still alive and recounted, 'Death is no wonder, nor is hell as it is said.' Columba would not tolerate this heresy and replied, 'Earth, earth on Oran's eye, lest he further blab', now a popular Scots proverb.

Once, there were over 360 sculptured crosses on Iona. Now there is only a handful but the remains of three fine examples stand in front of the abbey church. **St Martin's cross** stands entire, commemorating the 4th century saint honoured at Tours, France. Dating from the 10th century, it is decorated with several groups of religious figures intertwined with serpents and basses. To the left of the main door is an ancient oratory honouring St Columba. Tiny inside and over-restored, it is the only corner of the complex that retains a sacred air on busy days. The Abbey Church, a cathedral from 1508 until the Reformation, dates mostly from the late 15th century although evidence of the earlier building can be traced in the ornamental features of the late Norman and Gothic styles. Grotesque monsters and beasts peer down from some of the capitals, and there are two pleasant 15th century tombs of former abbots placed in the Sanctuary. Modern craftsmen have imaginatively restored the **cloister**, carving the capitals with simple renderings of the flowers found on the island.

Any visit to this isle should be completed by a walk along the shore or up one of the hills, to capture the peace enjoyed by the early monks. The island but not the buildings is now in the care of the National Trust for Scotland.

Accommodation:
Argyll Hotel (tel Iona 334)
St Columba Hotel (tel Iona 304)
B & B and self-catering — details from Tourist Office, Mull or Oban. Many Christians take up the community's invitation to 'discussion, worship and recreation', staying in the Abbey.
Transport:
Only one taxi and no bikes, but no distance is too great to walk.
Specialities:
Iona marble

Lismore
(G lios mor — big garden)

Connections:
By sea: from Oban: two a day, Mon, Tue, Fri, Sat; one a day, Wed, Thu; cars; crossing 1 hr. Caledonian MacBrayne Ltd (tel Oban 2285).

From Port Appin: summer, nine a day; winter, three a day and by arrangement; crossing 10 mins. Ferry House, Port Appin (tel Appin 217).

Lismore raises its green back out of Loch Linnhe, curiously flat and fertile, and watched on all sides by heather mountains. A happy farming community takes full advantage of its potential and little ground is not grazed by sleek cattle. Unexpectedly, like Iona and Colonsay, Lismore is one of the holy isles, though mercifully ignored by pilgrims, having been chosen by St Moluag (523-92) as the centre of his mission which extended north and east to Ross-shire and Banffshire. A contemporary of Columba, Moluag came from similar Irish origins and would have achieved similar fame had he established a thriving monastic community here. Since he did not, he sank into obscurity, until a 12th century bishop of Dunkeld failed to learn Gaelic. Isolated from half his vast see by language barriers, he decided to create a Bishopric of the Isles, and the first Bishop in turn decided to take up St Moluag's cause, establishing his seat at Lismore. His choice of this island in preference to Iona was partly determined by weather and communications, for Lismore is rarely cut off from the mainland.

The present parish church is the chancel of the 13th century cathedral and many charming embellishments to the stonework can

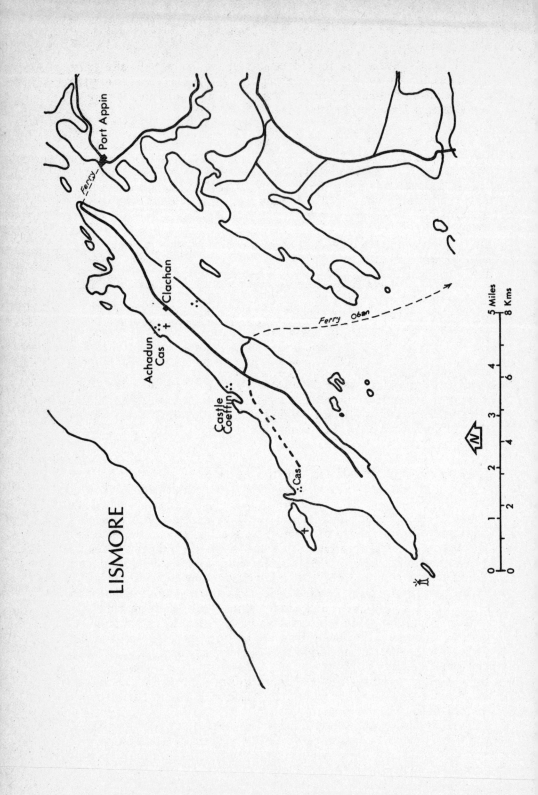

LISMORE

Port Appin

Ferry

Clachan

Achadun
Cas

Castle
Coeffin

Cas

Ferry   Oban

N

0   1   2   3   4   5 Miles
0   2   4   6   8 Kms

be spotted, as well as beautiful pesina and a curious sedilia — a canopy of arches under which the priests' seats would have been placed. There are several fine medieval tombstones in the graveyard where St Moluag is reputedly buried. A relic of his staff is even today held in custody by the Livingstone family, who were given the grounds of Bachuil in payment for this service.

In the 13th century, the bishops built themselves **Achadun Castle** on a rock facing across the loch to Duart Castle (see Mull). This was allowed to fall into disrepair in the 16th century when the bishops were moved to the more comfortable quarters of Saddell castle in Kintyre, but the thick curtain walls remain standing to an evocative height. Castle Coeffin, the medieval fortress of the Macdougalls of Lorn until they were defeated by Robert the Bruce, is even better sited, incorporating a tidal fish trap on the shore. Traditionally of Viking origin, the picturesque grass and lichen ruins have challenged many artists to catch their mood. On the hillock behind the castle are the remains of the largest cairn of Argyll, now just a heap of stones. From here it is possible to spot seven castles on a clear day, a good explanation as to why the island was chosen as a stronghold. On the eastern shore is a much older fortification, **Tirefour Castle**, a very well preserved and picturesque broch perched on a cliff, with its double walls and galleries still obvious.

Since medieval times the islanders of Lismore have become steadily more parochial, relatively undisturbed from their food-producing efforts. In the early 19th centuary, St Moluag's briefly attracted the Highland Seminary of the Church of Rome, training priests to win back the Gaelic speaking regions, but island life proved inconvenient and within a few years it left for the mainland. The lighthouse at the southern tip of the island was built by that energetic lighthouse engineer, Alan Stevenson.

Accommodation:
B & B — details from Tourist Office, Oban.

Kerrera
(ON Kjarbar's island)

Connections:
By sea: from Gallanach, Oban: winter, six a day; summer fairly continuously 9 am — 6 pm and by arrangement; no Sundays; crossing 5 mins. Ferry House, Kerrera (tel Oban 3665).

The tail of Kerrera protects Oban's harbour from the waves whipped up in the shallow Firth of Lorn and is often used to harbour Oban's fleet of yachting visitors. Yet the island remains a world apart,

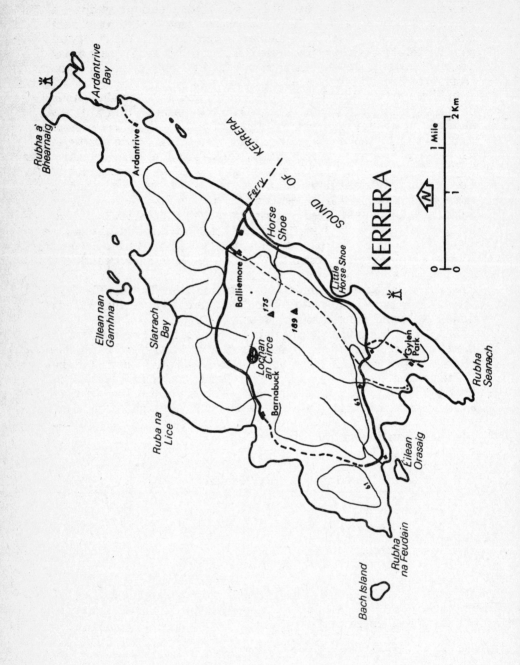

KERRERA

Rubha à Bheàrnaig

Ardantrive Bay

Ardantrive

Ferry

SOUND OF KERRERA

Horse Shoe

Little Horse Shoe

Balliemore

175 ▲

169 ▲

Eilean nan Gamhna

Slatrach Bay

Lochan an Circe

Barnabuck

Gylen Park

Ruba na Lice

61

Rubha Seanach

Eilean Orasaig

19

Rubha na Feudain

Bach Island

N

0   1 Mile   2 Km
0

though so close to the bustling touristy ferry pier. It makes an excellent picnic escape, while its hill provides a rewarding climb through shrub woodland to the views Oban is deprived of.

The fairytale Renaissance castle of the Macdougalls, Gylen Castle, is perched on a rocky promontory at the southern end of the island. Still standing to roof height, the L-shaped towerhouse is ornamented with turrets. The castle was besieged and finally burnt by General Leslie and his covenanting troops in 1647, but there are still some characterful carved heads peering out of the walls and a now undecipherable inscription, possibly reading 'Trust in God and sin no more; my son, do well, and let them say'. The Lorn Lobster Industry has a packing factory by Horseshoe Bay.

Accommodation:
Self-catering — details from Tourist Office, Oban.
Specialities:
Lobsters

Seil
Easdale
(G eas + ON dal — waterfall valley)

Luing
(G Luinge — Ship)

Connections:
To Seil: by bridge from B844 at Kilmner.

To Easdale: by sea from Seil crossings as required; 5 mins. MacFadyen, Ferryhouse, Easdale (tel Balvicar 338).

To Luing: by sea from Seil; frequent service; crossing 5 mins. Ferryman's House, Easdale (tel Balvicar 252).

Visitors arrive on these islands by crossing a steeply arched-backed bridge — 'the bridge over the Atlantic', designed by Thomas Telford in 1792 with almost classical splendour. On its stone work grows the rare fairy foxglove. In the 18th century, the wayside inn would attend the clansmen returning from the mainland as they changed from trousers back into the kilt forbidden after the '45.

The landscape is deceptively similar to the mainland — lush woods and pastures dropping steeply to the waterline, roadsides carpeted with summer flowers and walls smoothed by their autumn burden of brambles. However, for almost 300 years, these islands supported a great industry — slate quarrying, commented on by even the earliest travellers such as Dean Munro. Originally, in the 16th century, the slates were chisled out below the high waterline by the tenants of

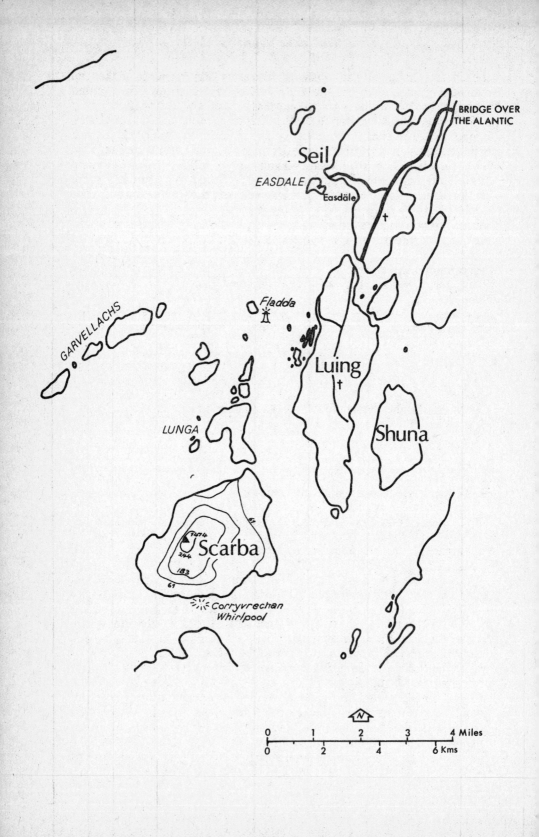

BRIDGE OVER
THE ALANTIC

Seil

EASDALE

Easdäle

GARVELLACHS

Fladda

Luing

Shuna

LUNGA

1474
244
Scarba
183
61

Corryvrechan
Whirlpool

N

0   1   2   3   4 Miles

0   2   4   6 Kms

Lord Breadalbane. Although the workers received a pittance for their labours, they were saved from famines by ever increasing demand. The fourth earl built picturesque cottages for his workers in planned villages. Gunpowder was introduced and the quarries began to alter the shape of the landscape, causing great cliffs and hillocks of rubble, but the men continued to quarry below sea level and by 1880 had reached a depth of 250 feet (75 m). In November 1881 an unusually wrathful gale whipped up mountainous waves which breached the protective sea walls and drowned 240 men, their machinery and their livelihood. Hence the need for a ferry to take visitors across to the village of Easdale today.

The quarries are now closed, but a new museum in Easdale portrays the slate industry and life a hundred years ago (ask the ferryman for opening hours). The modern industry now seems to be tourist traps, of which there are some choice examples. The Harbour Tearooms have republished a fascinating report prepared by the outgoing minister 'for guidance of the new incumbent in July 1843', which captures the mood of a simple life in these white and yellow cottages dwarfed by man-made crags. If this village looks familiar, it is because it was the location for much of the film 'Ring of Bright Water' by Gavin Maxwell.

Kilbrandon chapel, commemorating another 6th century Irish missionary, St Brendan of Clonfert, has some interesting medieval graveslabs, as does **Kilchattan Church** on Luing. This was abandoned after 1685, but sometime before that date some of the stones were covered with graffiti — galleys, crosses and other symbols. Another exceptional tombstone was erected in memory of Sandie Campbell and carved by himself, advertizing his quarrels with his neighbours and with the fashions and ways of the world: 'leave as a dying many my testimony against playactors and pictures . . . against women that wear Babylonish garments . . . against the volunteers of Banff . . . and also the big ships that keep their course in spite of the weather, that presumptious sin Psalm XIX, 13 . . . against men that have whiskers . . . against Quakers, Tabernacle folk, Haldians, Independents, Anabaptists . . .'

Accommodation:
Isles of Sea Guest House, Luing (tel Luing 230)
Tigh an Thuish Hotel, Seil
Willowburn Hotel, Seil (tel Seil 276)
B & B and self-catering — details from Tourist Office, Oban
Specialities
Slate jewellery

Garvellachs — or Isles of the Sea
(G garbh aileach — stone house)

Connections:
By sea: excursions organized by L MacLachlan, Jubilee Cottage, Luing (tel Luing 282), and J MacAlister, Cuan Ferry (tel Balvicar 317).

This scattering of little islands in the Firth of Lorn is now completely uninhabited but, as the BBC television commentator James Hogg discovered in 1975, you can arrange to be left there to camp. His enchantment wore off before his planned fortnight was up and he was glad to return to the conveniences and smog of London.

On Eileach an Naoimh are the remains of a tiny church and a cluster of beehive cells, reputedly the monastery of St Columba's uncle. Celtic monks did not live communally: instead, each one would build himself a circular hut where he lived independently, joining his neighbours only for worship. One of these huts has recently been restored.

Colonsay
(ON koln-ey — Columba's isle)

Connections:
By sea: from Oban: summer, one a day, Mon, Wed, Fri; winter, one a day, Mon, Thu, Fri; cars; crossing 2½ hrs. Caledonian MacBrayne Ltd (tel Colonsay 347).

St Columba's isle has preserved the sanctity of island life, untroubled by the hordes of summer visitors that flock onto more accessible islands. A trip here usually means either a glance from the pier, or a three-day sojourn. The island also boasts a remarkably peaceful history, for even the 19th century brought no evictions. The then laird, John MacNeill, introduced such enlightened agricultural policies that clearances proved unnecessary and even today farming has a healthy air. The geology is perfect, being the lower strata of Torridon sandstone, and the weather is kind with much sun and relatively little rain.

Visitors may roam the island freely. Even the gardens of the laird's home are not out of bounds, Lord Strathcona being distracted by matters of defence in London. Around Colonsay House, built in the early 18th century from the stones of Kiloran Abbey, are exotic gardens of magnolias and rhododendrons, with peaches and figs ripening in the sun. The native flora provides healthy competition, the 500 species including blood-drop emlets and rock samphire. The

COLONSAY

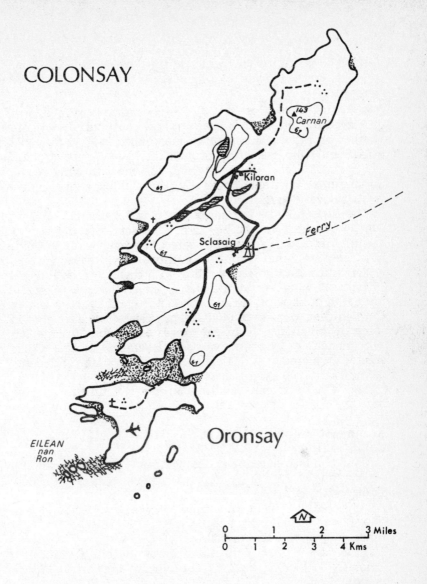

original Lord Strathcona, who pioneered the Canadian Pacific Railways, thought that the climate would be good for rearing decorative wildfowl; indeed it was almost too good, for they ate too much and so the flocks were reduced, but black swans and flamingos can be spotted among the many other varieties of birds populating the six lochs (good fishing) and extensive shore.

Colonsay is littered with archaeological sites — standing stones, circles, duns and hill forts. A complete list is available from the hotel. On the dunes of Kiloran Bay a Viking boat grave was discovered in 1882, with a 9th century warrior and his horse placed underneath

225

the hull. On the north coast are many caves and **Kilcatrine Chapel**, supposedly used by St Columba and certainly by the 13th century convent.

South of **Carn Mor** (440 ft/134 m and an easy climb with views of Islay, Jura and Mull) is the dune **golf course** (18 hole) animated by swarms of rabbits misguidedly introduced 200 years ago by some bright soul who wished to provide fresh meat throughout the year. The lack of predators make them the most thriving of the island's populations, unrivalled even by the Colonsay duck (eider duck) found in every bay.

The little island of **Oransay** (Oran was a disciple of St Columba) can be reached by wading across the sands during the two hours around low tide. It should be visited by every visitor to Colonsay, for here are the quiet ruins of a monastery, disbanded before the Reformation and now crumbling with dignity in its lonely solitude. The lancet windows of the chapel are still complete, with intricate interlaced foliage patterning. The monks of Oransay achieved fame through their carving of medieval graveslabs (see also Islay and Iona), some of which still mark the graves of notable if forgotten figures. The pinacle of these carvers' achievements is Pria Colin's cross, erected in memory of Malcolm MacDuffie, a late 15th century Lord of the Isles.

The islet of **Eilean nan Ron** is now a nature reserve, as it has a breeding colony of grey seals.

Accommodation:
Colonsay Hotel
B & B and self-catering — details from hotel (tel Colonsay 316).
No camping
Transport:
Post bus around island three times a week.
The 'London Taxi' from hotel.
Bikes — contact A McConnell.
To Oronsay — boats, dinghies, from hotel; D McGillivray (tel Colonsay 319); F Nicholson (tel Colonsay 354).
Sea Angling:
F Nicholson
Fresh water fishing permits and golf:
Contact hotel.

Jura
(ON dyr-ay — αeer ısle)

Connections:
By sea: from Port Askaıg (Islay): about 12 a day, Mon-Sat; three a

day, Sun; cars; crossing 10 mins. Western Ferries Ltd (tel Port Askaig 208).

When looking at Jura across the narrow straight from neighbouring Islay, one is immediately struck by the domination of hill, heather and grass. Little else can be distinguished except two small houses, one backed by weather-clipped trees — a sight to please many a sportsman, and they will not be betrayed.

On Islay the islanders talk in awe of how the red deer swim the fast-flowing sound, being swept several miles before reaching the southern tip of Jura. This would be easy to dismiss as a local's yarn but it is true. Jura is not only famous for its deer but dedicated to them. A temporary inhabitant, George Orwell, bitterly compalined that 'Everything is sacrificed to the brutes.' Not much else grows well here for the underlying rock is metamorphic quartzite. The Forestry Commission has experimented with some plantations but deer can be spotted grazing even within the high fencing, wreaking havoc upon the young trees. Thus, at least since Viking times, the island economy has revolved around its 5,000 head of deer.

At present, the island is divided up between five proprietors who cultivate the beasts as intensively as any farmer does his crops. The annual cull of one-fifth is partly achieved by renting out the stalking. Visitors who wish to wander over the island *MUST* ask permission first, for their own safety — high velocity rifles are used on the hill. The easiest way to find out who to contact is through the Isle of Jura Hotel: do not be surprised if walkers are not made welcome in the autumn.

A walk from the ferry at Feolin to Inver Cottage along the pebbly beach leads to the largest heronry on the island, perched in the trees. A conveniently situated mound forms an excellent viewing platform from which to look into the nests. These dignified grey birds can be found fishing in the seaweed all around the island's shores. Jura's only road closely follows the eastern coast of the island and is almost always deserted, except at ferry times. Deer 'scouts' can be seen on the skyline, watching for predators and ready to warn their herds — hence the skill in stalking. There are about fifteen pairs of golden eagles resident on Jura. They can often be seen circling on the air currents above the hills, besides many other birds of prey, such as the polygamic hen harrier which hunts on the lower ground.

Jura does not claim many antiquities due to her inhospitable nature, but does possess a fine standing stone known as Camus Stack, 12 feet (4 m) high but hard to see against the surrounding heather. On the small islet off the coast, An Fraoch Eilean (G — heather island) are the remains of a major MacDonald fortress, used as a guardhouse and prison against intruders entering the sound and commemorated in their family war cry, 'Fraoch Eilean'. The sands of the bay below Jura house 'sing', being formed of tiny pieces of

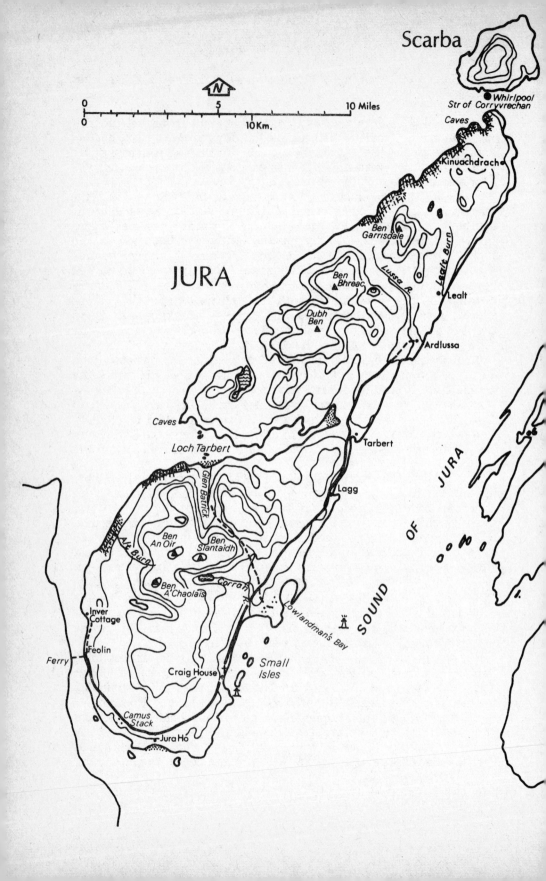

Scarba

Str of Corryvrechan
Whirlpool
Caves
Kinuachdrach

JURA

Ben
Garrisdale

Lussa R.
Lealt Burn
Lealt

Ben
Bhreac

Dubh
Ben

Ardlussa

Caves

Loch Tarbert
Tarbert

Lagg

Glen Batrick

Ben
An Oir
Ben
Slantaidh

Allt Burn

Corran

Ben
A'Chaolais

SOUND

Lowlandman's Bay

Inver
Cottage

OF

Feolin

JURA

Ferry

Craig House
Small
Isles

Camus
Stack

Jura Ho

quartzite which grate when moved either by the weight of a foot or by strong storms. In the little sheltered bays of this shoreline common seals play or rest, hauled out on the skerries in the sun.

Craighouse is the capital and heart of the island, housing most of Jura's 250 inhabitants around a remarkably ugly if architect-designed distillery (visits can be arranged). Palm trees and nurtured flower gardens make a pleasant change from the deer grass and remind the visitor how moderate the west coast climate is, once out of the wind. Here are the only shop, garage, summer restaurant and a comfortable hotel, whose public bar is popular with locals and tourist alike. A string of small islands shelters the anchorage where there are two piers, the older pebble-curved one built by Thomas Telford in 1814 (as was the less impressive Feolin ferry one), while the 'new' piled pier remains popular with cruise boats even if no regular ferry continues to call here.

The single track road continues north, twisting round the coast over the hills, above the whitewashed cottages by the waterline — the homes of keepers or stalkers. From here there are beautiful views of the famous Paps of Jura: Ben Siantaidh (G — holy mountain), Ben an Oir (G — mountain of gold) and Ben a'Chaolais (G — mountain of the sound), conical in shape. Climbers will be rewarded by the spectacle of water and land seen through 360°, and by the variety of alpine plants found on the upper slopes — the best approach is up the Corran River. The only tracked walk on Jura begins 1 mile (1.6 km) beyond the river and climbs up over the shoulder past Loch na Fudarlaich and down Glen Batrick to Loch Tarbert. This serene and beautiful sea loch almost succeeeds in dividing Jura into two, and is lined by raised beaches, a favourite haunt of mergansers and divers. The caves on the northern edge are well worth exploring. In one, John Mercer, a local historian, found 'over a hundred poorly made crosses' scratched onto the walls, signs of an illegal Catholic chapel well hidden from inquisitive eyes.

The inhabitants of Jura claim to be long-lived. In Inverlussa cemetery there is an old gravestone to Mary MacCrain who saw 128 summers, while a modern headstone in the Craighouse cemetery claims that one Gillouir MacCrain spent 180 Christmases in his own home. The road becomes less passable beyond Ardlussa Houe, but if you wish to pay homage to George Orwell proceed to Lealt, to the neglected yet still habitable farmhouse where he and his sister lived for two years after the Second World War. Here among the alders beside the twinkling stream, Orwell composed his visionary novel 1984. A healthy walk or drive by Landrover up the road/track reaches the last cottage, Kinuachdrach, over 30 miles (50 km) from the ferry. A large herd of tame white goats is kept at the house while some escaped long-haired black ones have turned feral and haunt the wood-covered slopes, providing German marksmen with some demanding sport. Other nationalities seem to prefer the deer.

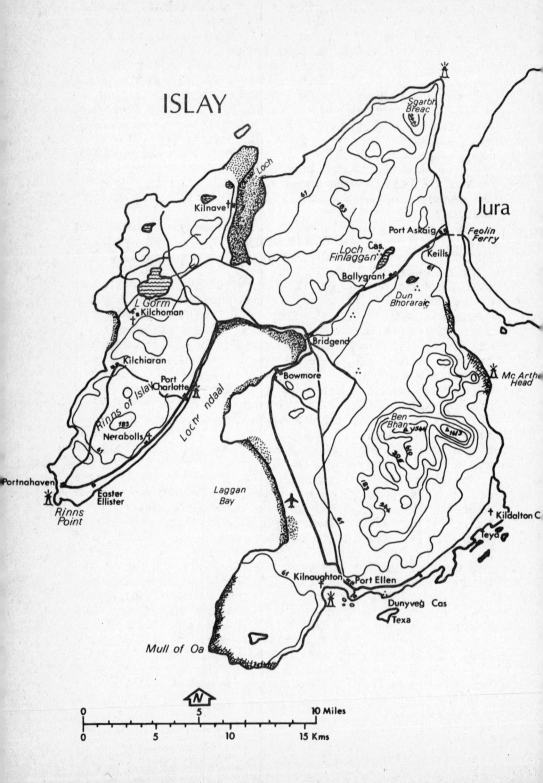

ISLAY

Jura

Sgarbh
Breac

Loch

Kilnave

Port Askaig

Feolin
Ferry

Loch
Finlaggan

Cas.

Keills

Ballygrant

Dun
Bhoraraic

L Gorm
Kilchoman

Kilchiaran

Bridgend

Port
Charlotte

Bowmore

Mc Arthur
Head

Rinns of Islay

Loch Indaal

Ben
Bhan

Nerabolls

Portnahaven

Easter
Ellister

Laggan
Bay

Kildalton C

Teya

Rinns
Point

Kilnaughton

Port Ellen

Dunyveg Cas

Texa

Mull of Oa

N

0   5   10 Miles

0   5   10   15 Kms

The Straits of Corryvrechan, dividing Jura from her uninhabited neighbour, Scarba (ON skarf-ay — cormorant's island) are famous among mariners and in folklore for their whirlpool which will swallow any and everything; even Orwell nearly lost his life there. They are unspectacular except when the outward tide is fought by an Atlantic gale, but the view from the headland of Scotland's inland sea is unparalleled anywhere in the world, as the long arms of the sea lochs penetrate far into the mainland and small islets litter the open water. On the west of the headland are many deep dry caves, often sheltering deer.

Accommodation:
Jura Hotel
B & B and self-catering — details from Tourist Office, Bowmore, Islay (tel Jura 243).
Sadly, camping is not permitted by any of the landowners.
Transport:
Consult the hotel. A bus meets the 'school' ferries every morning and evening.
Stalking and Fishing:
Write directly to the estates — Ardfin, Ardlussa, Forest, Inver and Tarbert. Some offer an all-in package including accommodation.

Islay

Connections:
By air: from Glasgow: two a day, Mon-Sat. Loganair Ltd (tel Port Ellen 2022).
By sea: from Kennacraig to Port Askaig: at least one a day; cars; crossing 2 hrs. Western Ferries Ltd (tel Whitehouse 271).
From Kennacraig to Port Ellen: two a day, Mon-Sat; one a day, Sun; cars; crossing 2 hrs. Caledonian MacBrayne Ltd (tel Port Ellen 2209).
From Feolin, Jura to Port Askaig: about 12 a day, Mon-Sat; three a day, Sun; cars; crossing 10 mins. Western Ferries Ltd (tel Port Askaig 208).

Islay is renowned for its whiskey. Indeed, there are eight malt distilleries actively enhancing its fame and contributing more to the Exchequer per capita of population than any other port of Britain. But Islay's prestige is based on something far more substantial than whiskey, for here was the seat of the Lords of the Isles.
The evolution of the kingdom of Scotland did not run smoothly, and competing claims could only be endorsed by force. By the 6th century Islay was part of the Kingdom of Dalriada ruled by the Scots

— a people from the North of Ireland, and by the 9th century their king, Kenneth MacAlpin, had succeeded in imposing a token on the loyalty of the other three kings. But then the Vikings swept down the west coast, causing chaos and dividing up territories like cake. In the mid-12th century, a Scots leader with a remarkable amount of Norse blood, Somerled, carved himself a kingdom in Argyll and proceeded to defeat his brother-in-law, Godred, the Viking King of the Isles, in 1156. He made Islay his capital, farming its fertile plains and vigorously defending its coast against all comers, founding the Macdonald clan and establishing the domain of the Lords of the Isles for the following three centuries. At times the Lords were sufficiently powerful to treat independently with foreign sovereigns. An episode that would have interested Shakespeare concerned Lord Donald's treaties of friendship with Richard II. Spotting a rising star, he changed his loyalty to Henry IV, but some months afterwards a 'beggar' arrived on Islay looking remarkably similar to the deposed Richard. Known as 'Islay's Mammet' (puppet) this man, whoever he was, found no friendship, just a miserable existence in the prisons of Stirling Castle, and was finally buried in Blackfriars churchyard, Stirling.

Today, although large areas of the island are given over to beds of peat, the visitor will find sizeable windbreaks of natural woodland, and emerald green fields grazed by the milk cows who produce Islay's second export, cheese. Most of the houses are kept sparkling white, with the curious island characteristic of painting only the inner edges of the windows in bright colours.

Port Ellen, named after a fair lady forgotten in the mists of time, is typical of Islay's villages, a 19th century planned settlement curving around the bay with a small collection of shops and pubs. Whiskey is no longer free of excise on the island but the distillery employees are still given a daily measure and so great quantities are consumed, the few teetotallers praising the window-cleaning qualities of their share! A local artist has decorated many of the pub walls with scenes populated by the regulars.

The south coast is littered with distilleries, enormous white warehouses and drying kilns with painted red or black roofs and a few associated neat cottages on the seashore. Most can be visited by arrangement. Lagavulin organizes daily trips to baffle the curious with complicated explanations of the process and a chance to sample the final product. The carefully cut peats used to heat the stills and the channelled peaty streams providing the water have nothing to do with the final colour which comes from the sherry casks, but leave a strong mark on the taste.

Dunyveg Castle (G — fort of the little ship) stands a gaunt ruin on a promontory, watching over the distillery. Dating from the 14th century, it was one of the main strongholds of the Lords of the Isles, convenient because ships could be pulled within the barrack walls to be repaired. It was successfully held against the crown as late as 1615. By 1670 it was deserted and the stones put to other uses.

Kildalton is a pleasant estate with an unusual gatehouse, built of quartz. You can often find a dump of clamshells under the fine oak forest beside the roadside. The grave of Princess Eila can be found by Loch a' Chunic, marked by two large stones on the left of the road and smothered by summer bracken. Legend maintains that Princess Eila was a Danish princess who carried a basket full of stones from her homeland (though why, is not explained). As she wandered, some fell out, forming Ireland, Rathlin,Texa and other little islets off the shore. She finally collapsed by the loch, exhausted, and died. This is a good corner to watch waders and divers, and sometimes even seals, enjoying the sheltered water.

Kildalton Chapel (G cil-daltan — the disciple church) is remarkable for its high Celtic cross, whose arms are surrounded by a ring. This is the finest in Scotland, dating from c 800 AD. Made of local blue stone, slightly worn, and standing 9 ft (3 m) high, it is a very eloquent design, the strong interlacing patterns representing fternity, and the tiny figured scenes on the arms the Virgin and Child and angels, and David and the Lion. Kildalton was probably founded by a monk from Iona, which would explain the presence of this masterpiece and the large size of the now ruined pre-Reformation chapel, which shelters a magnificent 15th century grave slab, carved in high relief and depicting a warrior in full armour. Other recumbent slabs pave the graveyard, many clear enough to be rubbed.

Opposite **Trudernish** farm there is a picturesque collection of old baths dumped by the roadside. **Claggain Bay** is a pink pebbly beach with fine views of Gigha and the Mull of Kintyre, a popular picnic and bird-watching spot. On the hills behind, buzzards may be seen playing on the air currents above herds of grazing red deer.

There are many pre-Reformation chapels on Islay, most situated in scenic spots and surrounded by a web of history and folklore. **Kilnaughton chapel**, dedicated to a St Naughlan, is no exception, nestling by the shore with a couple of beautifully carved medieval graveslabs. **The Oa** is the wildest corner of Islay, a bleak moorland worth traversing to reach the cliffs and their view of Ireland; on fine days, the Giants' Causeway can be spotted. Goats and choughs enjoy the solitude of a setting more appropriate to the Devon coast, and dominated by a crude imitation of a lighthouse, a memorial to the 266 American soldiers drowned on HMS *Tuscania* and *Oranto*.

The long straight road to **Bowmore** (G bot-mor — big mound) runs across a sultry black peat moor. The peat piles are evidence of the skills of the professional cutters who must keep the distilleries supplied with fuel. The comfortable luxury Machrie Hotel has its own farm and offers visitors an exotic range of bar lunches and a championship golf course by the sands.

Bowmore was founded by the laird of 1767, Daniel Campbell, as the island's planned capital, and it is now Islay's administrative and shopping centre. Killarrow had previously been the centre of island life, its importance being confirmed by an annual fair, and it was only through wholesale bribery that the laird managed to ensure that his new town usurped its position. The width of the main street running up from the harbour is witness to his pretensions, lined by large (for that time) town houses — some still with their original signs, leading to his church, built by a French architect in the round 'so the Devil could find no corners to lurk in'. Much of the original furnishing is still in place, awkwardly arranged around the central pillar required to support the roof and conveniently hiding the laird's pew on the balcony from the eye of the preacher (added c 1850). The octagonal spire, though not high, can be seen all along the Rinns of Islay across the water. Another curiosity of the town are the onion domes capping the drying kilns of the Bowmore distillery, established in 1779.

Bridgend has the mood of an estate village, settled around the walls of Islay House, carefully guarded from view by a screen of trees. Privacy was considered so important that a cart bridge was even constructed to cross the main road, but at least the gatehouses can be spotted — two Victorian follies, one round, one square, with canons in place. The long pebbly shores of Loch Indaal are browsed and investigated by armies of waders, enjoyed by picknickers in the summer, by migratory duck in the winter, as a welcome refuge from the gales.

Port Charlotte, named after another mysterious lady, is a charming fishermen's village, created at the turn of the 18th century by Rev Malcolm Maclaurin whose concept of neatness made every house identical, measuring 30 ft x 22 ft (9 x 7 m). The road passes between the two rows facing the small stone harbour and so some of the cottages are reached by bridges into the upper floor. The enterprising hotel is well frequented by locals and organizes diving to wrecks and sea angling off the coast. In the redundant old Free Kirk is the Museum of Islay Life (open 10 — 5, Mon-Fri, summer Sun 2 — 5). Comprehensive displays of the island's past are lucidly explained. Among the most interesting are a farm's medicine box, a set of copper works tools and an illicit still. Run by enthusiastic volunteers, the museum also produces several useful leaflets on local antiquities. Milk tankers herald the existence of the Islay Creamery which can be visited most weekdays, though the cheese is not easily found in local shops.

At **Nerabolls** are two ancient burial grounds, about 100 yards (90 m) apart, containing some of the finest medieval graveslabs to be found in Islay, or indeed Scotland. Carvings of a galley, stag and hounds, and other animals are all indications of the importance of the people buried, but time has hidden the names and today we can create only a shadowy picture of their interests and wealth, and wonder whether they were priests or warriors. 2 miles (3 km) beyond is a series of manmade ponds populated by exotic wildfowl, and more can be seen by the farm of Easter Ellister, for this is the Rodney Dawson Memorial collection, first begun in Lincolnshire and transferred to Islay to benefit from the longer summer daylight hours in 1974. Rodney Dawson died in 1977, a year before his longtailed ducks successfully bred, for only the second recorded time in captivity. Kept in pens fenced against cats and foxes, the ducks, geese and swans exhibit plumages from fiction, so bright and imaginative are the colours.

Portnahaven seems to have been left behind by this modern age. Single-storey cottages are anxiously grouped round the natural harbour which once protected the fisherfolk's boats but now is empty, except for a few pleasure vessels. Most of the small homes are now holiday houses, facing a lighthouse built by Robert Stevenson on Orsay, shadowing yet another medieval chapel. The tidal race is very fast through the narrow sound and advice should be obtained from the locals before a crossing is attempted.

A gentle rural road with a parting of grass round the Rinns of Islay leads to Kilchiaran (G — cell of St Ciaran). St Ciaran was St Columba's tutor in Ireland, and died in 548 AD. Why tradition should associate his grave with Islay is not clear, although there are stories of Columba removing a handful of earth from this spot to save his boat from the whirlpool of Corryvrechan (see Jura) on his return to Iona. The font is worthy of note and so is the beach, well sheltered and full of potential Barbara Hepworth sculptures. The neighbouring farm-steadings have attracted much attention for they are semi-circular in plan.

The present church of **Kilchoman** (G — church of St Comman) is a sad sight, in an unhealthy state of repair. Comman was the nephew of an abbot of Iona and at an early age was sent as a missionary to Islay, not principally to convert the heathen but, as with most Celtic missionaries, to remove him from the distractions of family life. He chose this beautiful spot under the steep green cliffs for his cell and soon became renowned for his piety. A fine late 15th century cross stands among a floor of carved grave slabs, rivalled in its intricacy by St Martin's cross on Iona. Much of the dedicatory inscription has been worn away but what remains suggests that one Patrick had it carved in honour of his father and his own wife. The indented hollows on its base have been caused by visitors turning a stone clockwise whilst making a wish.

Loch Gorm is edged by swamps, the refuge of thousands of swans and geese during the winter months. Highland history is not always concerned with pleasant tales of saints. In 1598, a fierce battle between the Macdonalds of Islay and the Macleans of Mull confirmed the Macdonalds' ownership of the island, even though their chief had not survived the route. The fleeing Macleans sought refuge in **Kilnave**

(G — church of the saints) on the seashore, waiting for the storm to die down sufficiently to enable them to escape. A Macdonald spotted their hiding place, set fire to the roof and burnt them alive. The ruin stands complete to roof height even now, painted yellow with lichen, with a very early Celtic cross still vertical outside. Although this was created only 50 years before the Kildalton cross, the Celts had not then mastered the art of stone carving, and so it appears to be a fragile yet evocative tribute to their early efforts. The many neglected farms of this area make it a good brambling spot at the end of September. At Ardnave Loch, a little island close to the southern shore has the traces of a crannog — a circular Pictish island dwelling, oddly juxtaposed to a Victorian castellated farm.

Beyond Ballygrant is Loch Finlaggan, the most important site of the Lords of the Isles, for on one islet they had a strong keep and on another they held their 'parliament' of chiefs and ecclesiastics. However, since permission to visit the loch cannot be obtained, it is better to study the aerial photographs in the Museum of Islay Life. Around this area are traces of the extensive lead mines worked in the 19th century, best identified by the piles of slag associated with them.

Dun Bhoraraic is a Pictish fort, or possibly a broch (a more sophisticated form), surrounded by extensive earthworks, and guarding both the Rinns of Islay and the Sound of Jura. At Keills there is another pre-Reformation chapel in ruins, with a Celtic cross. Port Askaig underneath the wooded cliff is a ferry point and little more. However, the hotel claims a long record of hospitality and the fishermen are happy to sell lobsters from their varnished boats to departing tourists.

Accommodation:
Bowmore Hotel, Bowmore (tel Bowmore 218)
Imperial Hotel, Bowmore (tel Bowmore 330)
Lochside Hotel, Bowmore (tel Bowmor 265)
Bridgend Hotel, Bridgend (tel Bowmore 212)
Abbotsford Hotel, Port Charlotte (tel Port Charlotte 264)
Port Charlotte Hotel, Port Charlotte (tel Port Charlotte 219
Port Askaig Hotel, Port Askaig (tel Port Askaig 245)
Dower House Hotel, Kildalton (tel Kildalton 225)
Islay Hotel, Port Ellen (tel Port Ellen 2260)
Machrie Hotel, Machrie (tel Port Ellen 2310)
Tighcargaman Hotel, Port Ellen (tel Port Ellen 2345)
White Hart Hotel, Port Ellen (tel Port Ellen 2311)
B & B and self-catering — details from Tourist Office, Bowmore
Car Hire:
McMillan, Port Ellen
Laggan Engineering, Port Ellen (tel Port Ellen 2344)

Sea angling:
Port Charlotte Hotel (tel Port Charlotte 264)
Machrie Hotel (tel Port Ellen 2310)
Freshwater fishing permits:
Trout and salmon available — details from Tourist Office, Bowmore.
Riding:
Mrs Dawson, Easter Ellister Farm, Port Charlotte
Golfing:
Machrie Hotel (tel Port Ellen 2310)
Diving:
Port Charlotte Hotel (tel Port Charlotte 264)
Tourist Office:
Bowmore (tel Bowmore 254); open Apr — Sep: 9.30 — 7.30 Mon-Sat;
Jun — Sep: 3 — 6 Sun.
Specialities:
Whiskey, medieval graveslabs.

Gigha

Connections:
By car ferry: from Tayinloan. Caledonian MacBrayne Ltd (tel
Stornaway 2361).

A small island, lying lowbacked at the southern end of the Inner
Hebrides, Gigha was christened 'Gudey' (the Good Isle) by King
Haakon of Norway in the 11th century. Today it is one of the most
thriving of the Scottish islands. Golden sands sheltered by rocky
outcrops and the quiet mood of the island entice many nature lovers,
for Gigha is rich in wild flowers and birdlife (notably the great
northern and black throated divers). There is safe mooring for yachts
in Ardminish Bay (coastguard: Mr Henderson, tel Gigha 238).

From the highest point, Creagbhan (330 ft/100 m), there is an
enchanting view northwards up the Sound of Bura, and far across the
open sea to Ireland, the birthplace of many of the Celtic missionaries
who converted the Hebridean folk from the 7th century. The less
energetic can take a short amble from the roadside to the **Ogham
Stone**, a granite standing stone with a Dalriadic inscription (the
notches on the north-west edge), possibly spelling out the name 'son
of Coiceili', an Irish warrior.

The ruins of Kilchattan Chapel take up the island's history. It was
built in the 13th century, from random rubble — dark red and coarse
yellow sandstone, now covered with a ghostly beard of lichen.
Incised Greek and Latin crosses can still be traced on either side of
the east window. The chapel stands among an evocative collection of
carved tombstones of Celtic warriors of the 14th century, the more

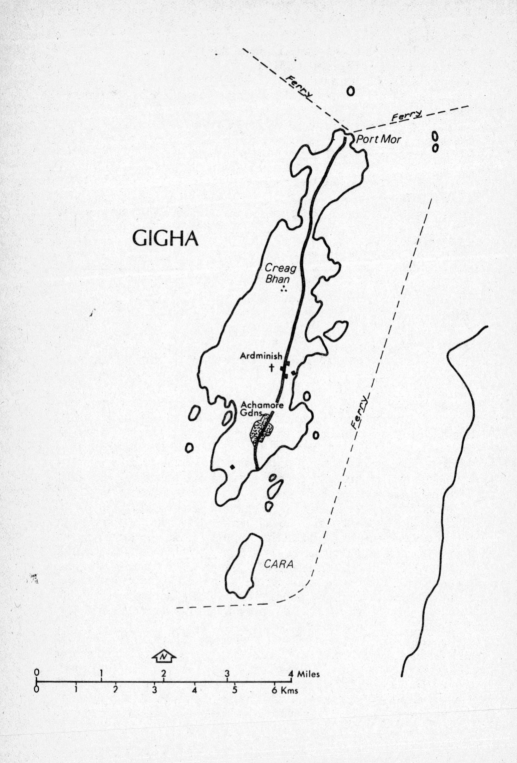

GIGHA

Creag
Bhan

Ardminish †

Achamore
Gdns.

Port Mor

Ferry

Ferry

Ferry

CARA

N

0   1   2   3   4 Miles
0   1   2   3   4   5   6 Kms

peaceful craftsmen of the 18th century, and the crofters of this century, which conjure up the changing nature of island life far more clearly than any history book.

The octagonal rough-hewn font of the Celtic chapel has been moved to the **Parish Church** (Church of Scotland: services at 12 noon, Sun), a typically simple building of 1923, housing an exceptional collection of modern memorial stained-glass windows. Especially notable are those designed by N Wilson, RSA, for Rev Kenneth Macleod (rich with relevant island details, including a Gigha cross, similar to a Maltese cross), and for Sir James Horlick, of the Horlicks drink, Gigha's greatest benefactor.

Sir James bought the island in 1944, and in the grounds surrounding **Achamore House** (available for lets: enquire at the hotel), he carved out 'rooms' among the trees to shelter his collection of rhododendrons and azaleas. Being warmed by the North Atlantic drift and protected by the spine of the island, the **Achamore Gardens** are ideally suited to these exotic shrubs, which are seen at their best in May and June. Sir James extended his collection each year both in size and in species, cultivating the famous Horlicks hybrids. He used to drive through the gardens in a motorized tricycle with dragon ornings, and is still very fondly remembered. Sir James gave his plants to the National Trust for Scotland in 1962, and the gardens are now open from April to the end of September.

The famous **Gigha cheese** (available from MacSporran General Store) is another product of Horlick initiative. Sir James and Lady Horlick persuaded the dairy farmers of Gigha's 900 fertile acres (360 h) to work in co-operation to supply the **Creamery** (visitors welcome), and thus ensured that the island is protected from the decay of depopulation. Today, an immediately apparent air of well-being welcomes visitors to the bluebell woods, green pastures and whitewashed houses.

Accommodation:
Gigha Hotel (tel Gigha 254). This old inn has recently been rebuilt and enlarged, winning the 1977 Award of the Association for the Protection of Rural Scotland. It now makes an ideal retreat, while also catering for day visitors, with a restaurant using local produce. Laundry and washing facilities are provided for yachtsmen.
Bicycle Hire:
Gigha Hotel
MacSporran General Stores/Post Office
Cars are not recommended, as no point of the island is further than 3 miles (5 km) from the pier.
Specalities:
Cheese

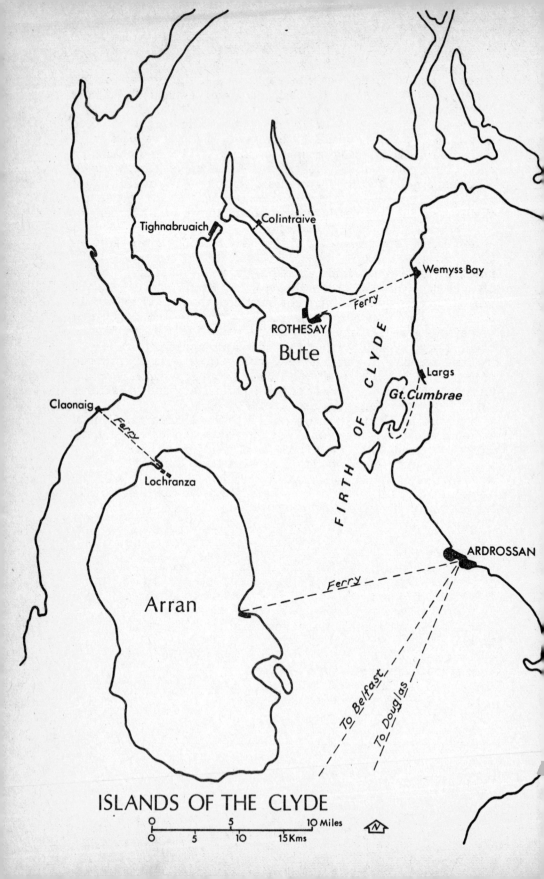

Tighnabruaich

Colintraive

Wemyss Bay

Ferry

ROTHESAY

Bute

Largs

Gt. Cumbrae

Claonaig

Ferry

FIRTH OF CLYDE

Lochranza

ARDROSSAN

Ferry

Arran

To Belfast

To Douglas

ISLANDS OF THE CLYDE

0 — 5 — 10 Miles

0 — 5 — 10 — 15 Kms

N

Part 5
The Islands of the Clyde

Boat enthusiasts will know of the paddleboats' and steamships' daily races around the Clyde, distracting the Glaswegian gentlefolk from the industry of that city and transporting them to pastoral havens of island life. Holiday towns developed on the shores of the islands, became fashionable and were then neglected. Since the Second World War, they have again become holiday isles, offering facilities and variety for all the family, but remaining uncrowded away from the coastal ringroads.

Bute

Connections:
By sea: from Wernyss Bay: approx 7 a day; cars; crossing ½ hour. Caledonian MacBrayne Ltd.

From Colintraive: frequent service; cars; crossing 5 min. Caledonian MacBrayne Ltd.

From Tighnabruaich: sea taxi on demand. Peter McIntyre (Clyde Ltd), Rothesey Pier (tel Rothesey 3171) and Ardmaleish Boat Building Co Ltd (tel Bute 2007).

Bute, nestling in the heart of the Clyde, is easily ignored as simply another of Argyll's limbs breaking free towards her island neighbours.

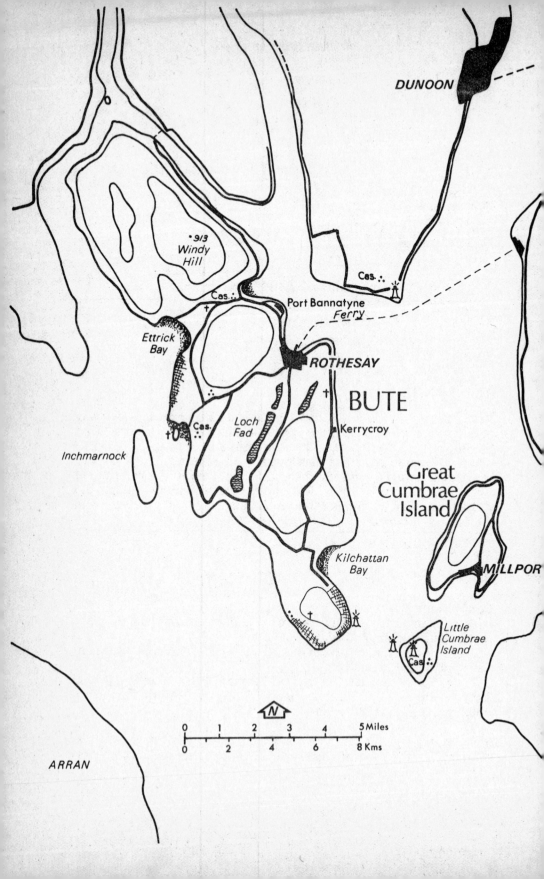

Originally she may have begun this way, but a clear ¼ mile (.4 km) of water alienates the mainland and gives Bute a very individual quality. Like mainland Scotland, the island is divided across the centre by the Highland fault, with igneous moorland-covered rocks in the north, and the younger sedimentary old red sandstone and slate, covered by grassy green fields in the south.

But Bute offers much more than even this startling contrast, attracting over a million visitors each year from the smog of Glasgow to Rothesay (G rath + ON ay — isle of the fort) with its festive holiday air. Sadly, no longer do visitors have to queue to pass through the turnstiles admitting them to the fresh air (this toll has been added to the ferry charge). Made popular in the mid-19th century by the fashionable gentry folk of Glasgow's industries, Rothesay's appeal was soon extended down the social scale. Great fleets of paddle-steamers raced around the Clyde for customers and prestige, often missing stops to save precious minutes, entertaining their passengers with the music of German bands. The *Kyles of Bute*, queen of them all, even engaged the Berlin Philharmonic Orchestra in 1902 to accompany its torchlight and mystery cruises. Along the shore developed a promenade typical of England's south-coast towns, hotels and guest houses strung out along the front, gaily decorated with extravaganzas of cast-iron ornamentation and a rainbow of colours, now slightly worn and peeling with a gently decaying air. Set above a tier of terraces above them all is the grandiose Glenburn Hotel, the old Hydro, where Victorian ladies wallowed in luxury while being 'cured' in the special cold water baths. As fashions changed so did the 'baths', later housing an aquarium, a dance tea room and a museum. The town was originally built on the site of a Napoleonic fort, and the canons were thriftily converted into bollards on the pier. The elaborate ornamentation of the pier and bowling green are also carefully maintained, brightened by baskets of flowers, and even the dowdiest of streets has traces of fashionable glory — in Russell Street there are twisted sugar canes of drainpipes. Victoria Street takes the prize for decorations with its twelve apostles assessing new arrivals from above the first floor windows, and intertwined lamps lighting the street beside the Winter Gardens, once a famous venue for Glaswegian comedians.

Rothesay castle was built in 1140 by the great Norse king, Magnus Barelegs, on the site of an earlier fortress, in the imposingly solid Norman style. The residential tower block is surrounded by a circular wall protected by round corner towers. Temporarily won by the Scots crown in the late 12th century and handed into the custody of the Royal Steward, one Walter Fitzallan, it was soon alienated in the entangled quarrels of the Norse, Scots and English kings. It was won back by Robert the Bruce, who awarded this important stronghold to his royal steward and son-in-law, Walter Stewart, whose son, Robert II, began the line of Stewart kings. His heirs and successors enjoyed their summer house until the Union of Crowns, but in the Civil War Cromwell's troops breached the walls and in 1685 it was burnt by the Earl of Argyll. The Marquesses of Bute, whose family had become hereditary keepers of the stronghold, partially restored it this century and gave it to the safe keeping of the D of E (open daily). The moat and surrounding gardens are pleasantly populated by summer families of ducks.

Little of the old town has survived except for the **Old Mansion House** in the High Street, built in 1687 and briefly occupied by the Bute family. Legend recounts how a former earl took his new bride, a daughter of Argyll, to reside in the new house. She complained about its size and so he took her to the window and showed her the castle which her father had destroyed. The house has recently been restored and is now used as offices. It has a curious example of an outside sink placed in one of its walls.

The **Bute Natural History Museum** (open Apr — Sep: 10.30 — 12.30, 2.30 — 4.30; Oct — Mar: 2.30 — 4.30) provides an excellent record of local history, from prehistoric sites to photographs of the Clyde puffers, with a splendid array of the weights and measures of the Royal Burgh (Rothesay's Charter dates from 1401) and a display of the shells to be found on the island's shores. The school kids collect the seasonal flowers to help visitors identify the large range of species growing on Bute, and members of the museum society have compiled nature and motor trail leaflets for the island.

Bute proved very popular with early monastics and their cells and churches litter the island. In the **High Kirk of St Mary and St Bruoc** is a fine collection of tombstones. The effigies set into the wall of the old chapel are probably of Walter Stewart and his wife, parents of Robert II. Two other tombstones commemorate Napoleon's niece, Stephanie Hortense Bonaparte, and Robert Thorn — one of Rothesay's great cotton mill owners. He realized that this 18th and 19th century industry could not be expanded without an increased water supply and so tried to divert waters from the west of the island overland to Rothesay, but despite his efforts, the industry died at the turn of the century. The municipal gardens of **Ardencraig** are wonderfully exotic, populated with cockatoos and canaries, justifying Bute's claim to be the Madeira of Scotland.

The underlying geology of Rothesay is mostly red pudding rock, but curious dykes of basalt emerge out of it, forced through cracks by volcanoes. Ascog church and cottages, designed by David Hamilton in 1845, in a severely classical if country style, contrast sharply with the elaborate fantasia of the town, backed by a picturesque ruin, not of a castle but of a salt kiln. Many of the grandiose houses built here for prosperous Glaswegian merchants have now been converted into holiday centres for the less fortunate members of our society: please drive slowly and enjoy the juxtaposition of Bute's woodlands with Glasgow's chimneys across the water.

The bay at Kerrycroy, popular with swimmers, is ringed by an English village of half-timbered houses and white stone cottages. There is even a red and silver maypole standing in the centre of the village green lined with sycamore trees. Designed by the first wife of the 2nd Marquess of Bute, at the gates of the Mount Stuart Estate (private), this was once the main ferry point for Largs. The present mansion house, rebuilt in 1876 in an elaborate Gothic style, is open only on special occasions (details from Tourist Office). To preserve privacy, the road swings away from the coast between two beautifully kept beech hedges and windbreaks. Many of the trees in this extensive collection were planted by the 3rd Earl, George III's tutor and the first Prime Minister, who was also actively involved in developing Kew Gardens. Looking due south from the summit of the hill you can spot 'the Sleeping Warrior' (Arran's profile), while on Suidhe Hill the shape of a crown is delineated by larch in a plantation of conifers, planted in Elizabeth II's coronation year of 1953.

Kilchattan Bay is a curious terrace of townhouses facing the sea, a late Victorian overspill from Rothesay, now quiet in its solitude except when the shining sun brings tourists to the beach.

St Blane's Chapel, nestling among the trees on a saddle of the hill, is one of the best preserved Celtic monastic sites of Britain, dating to the 6th century. Both gable ends of the chapel are still standing, decorated with simple carving on their arches. It was used until the 18th century when a gale blew off the roof. A circular stone building close by, known as the **Devil's Cauldron**, was once a popular place of penance. Above the shore is the prehistoric Iron Age vitrified fort of **Dunagoil**, posed on a crag. Traces of iron workings were found on the pebbly beach below. This area of Bute is remarkably unspoilt by the pressures of visitors. Neatly kept dairy farms, their purple and white signs claiming them as tenants of the Bute estate, are not deviated from their business of providing milk for the Bute Creamery (cheese is sold anonymously even if claimed to be a prize winner), and provide no rival distractions for Rothesay, except the charm of rural ways. Access to the less popular beaches is permitted, though usually a donation for charity is requested.

By the quarry of **Tormore Hill** is one of Bute's best viewpoints, from where one can look across to Dunagoil and Duntrone forts and down the Firth to the Heads of Ayr. Below the road is one of Robert Thorn's canals, built to take water round the island to Rothesay, but now dry and covered by gorse and bracken. A text-book example of a raised beach with cliffs can clearly be seen above the foreshore, caused by the melting of the last ice age which reduced the volume of water and so lowered the sea level. On Quien Loch (fishing permits required) is a crannog, a man-made island where a dwelling was erected for safety. This is a good place for spotting swans and little grebe.

The offshore island of **Inch Marnock** commemorates a very forward young Scots lad who pestered St Columba on one of his mainland journeys. Attendant monks tried to quiet the boy but St Columba blessed him and prophesied that he would become a great teacher. Nothing now remains of this saint's chapel except a few crosses, removed for safe keeping to the museum. Bronze Age cairns and cists at the north end of the island gave up great treasures, including 135 beads of a lignite necklace dating from c 1500 BC. On the peninsula pointing to the island is St Ninian's Chapel, excavated in 1953 though little was found there. The famous cockle shore was habitually raided to provide shell lime for Bute's fields until the island was evacuated during the last war so that it could be used as a testing ground for live ammunition. Two farming families have since returned but the island remains a peaceful haven for birds, especially popular with wintering greylag geese.

The 16th century castle of **Crowners** is a grim reminder of a time when landlords handed out their own justice, but is now thankfully only a scenic ruin in the woods. **Dunnalant** fort is Bute's most impressive Iron Age fort, dominating the south horizon from Ettrick Bay, and emerging out of the trees. Its ramparts are still distinct on the south-west side. By the bridge of **Glenmore Burn** are weird concrete frames, used by troops as practice landing crafts for D-day, and by crofters who could not afford to build themselves boats. The shore road north, though unsuitable for cars, is a walker's delight, through bluebell and bramble woods and with views across the narrow passage of water once swum by cattle on their way to market from Tighnabruaich.

The church of **Croc-an-rar** (kept locked most days) was built in 1836 with the unusual feature of a permanent communion table running down the centre of the church (see also South Uist). **Kames Castle** was originally begun in the 14th century by Gilbert Bannatyne, the royal ballie (rent collector) of the island, and has been inhabited continuously ever since. Some unfortunate additions were removed this century and it is now a perfect tower house, surrounded by cut lawns and a park of trees, and enjoyed as a holiday home for spastics. The road north gives easy access to the moorlands and is an excellent bird watching place, especially for gulls and herons.

Fort Bannatyne is a sleepy fishing village, now linked to the straggling outskirts of Rothesay. Brightly painted and more homely than the town, it has several boat yards and is a popular anchorage for summer yachts. The string of yachts across the bay converts every turn of the road into a beauty spot, much appreciated by one of Bute's famous visitors, Edmund Kean. Kean was a very successful Shakespearean actor of the early 19th century whose private life incurred his public's wrath. Fed up with this moral censorship, he walked out of a performance of *Richard III* at Greenock to escape to his newly acquired house by the edge of **Loch Fad**. His rejected wife was not so enamoured by this retreat. The house, **woodend**, is closed to the public but can be seen among the trees across the loch, and its lodge gates are capped with busts of Shakespeare and the greatest Shakespearean actors.

Accommodation:
Licensed hotels in Rothesay:
Ashburn Private Hotel (tel Rothesay 2106)
Bayview Private Hotel (tel Rothesay 2339)
Craignethan Hotel (tel Rothesay 2079)
George Private Hotel (tel Rothesay 2198)
Glenafton Hotel (tel Rothesay 2809)
Glenburn Hotel (tel Rothesay 2500)
Grand Marine Hotel (tel Rothesay 3145)
Haven Hotel (tel Rothesay 3996)
Invercraig Hotel (tel Rothesay 2323)
Isle of Bute Hotel (tel Rothesay 3473)
Palmyra Hotel (tel Rothesay 2164)
Regent Hotel (tel Rothesay 2411)
St Eliba Private Hotel (tel Rothesay 2683)
Guest Houses in Rothesay:
Alamein House (tel Rothesay 2395)
Argyle Guest House (tel Rothesay 2424)
Avion Guest House (tel Rothesay 3285)
Blairbank Guest House (tel Rothesay 2277)
Craiglea Guest House (tel Rothesay 3776)
Glendale Guest House (tel Rothesay 2329)
Kinnell House (tel Rothesay 2669)
Morningside (tel Rothesay 3526)
Rosslyn Guest House (tel Rothesay 3092)
St Fillans (tel Rothesay 2784)
Sunnyside Guest House (tel Rothesay 2351)
Unlicensed hotels in Rothesay:
Ardynen Private Hotel (tel Rothesay 2052)
Commodare Private Hotel (tel Rothesay 2178)
Esplanade Hotel (tel Rothesay 2032)
Fernycraig Private Hotel (tel Rothesay 3739)
Glen Royal Private Hotel (tel Rothesay 4403)
Madeira Private Hotel (tel Rothesay 2217)
Riversdale Private Hotel (tel Rothesay 3240)
The Laurels Private Hotel (tel Rothesay 2348)
Elsewhere:
St Blanes Hotel, Kilchattan Bay (tel Kilchattan Bay 224)
Kingarth Hotel, Kingarth (tel Kingarth 662)
Crown Hotel, Port Bannatyne (tel Rothesay 2129)
B & B & self-catering — details from Tourist Office, Rothesay.

Camping — permission must be obtained from Bute Estate Factor, Rothesay.
Taxi:
McKirdy and McMillan Ltd (tel Rothesay 2317)
Radio Taxis (tel Rothesay 2065)
Car Hire:
Bute Motor Co (tel Rothesay 2330)
Bicycle Hire:
Calder Bros, Rothesay
Yacht and Dinghy Hire:
Contact Isle of Bute Sailing Club, Rothesay
Sea Angling:
Macleod Marines (tel Rothesay 3950)
G Pellegrotti (tel Rothesay 3625)
Freshwater fishing permits:
Bute Estate Office, Rothesay
Golf:
Courses at Rothesay, Port Bannatyne, Kingarth
Bowling:
Greens at Rothesay, Kingarth, Craigmore and Ardbeg
Pony Trekking:
Rothesay Riding Centre (tel Rothesay 4718)
Ettrick Bay Trekking Centre, Ettrick (tel Rothesay 2473)
Tourist Office:
The Pier, Rothesay (tel Rothesay 2151); open Jan — May: 9 —1, 2 —6, Mon-Fri. Jun —Aug: 9 —8, Mon-Sat; 10 —1, 2 —6, Sun. Sep: 9 —6, Mon-Sat; 10 —1, 2 —6, Sun. Oct —Dec: 9 —1, 2 —6 Mon-Fri.
Specialities:
Tearooms; Ritchie's Fish Shop, Rothesay; *The Buteman* — weekly newspaper.

Great Cumbrae

Connections:
By sea: from Largs: approx seven a day; cars; crossing ½ hr. Caledonian MacBrayne Ltd.

Great Cumbrae is easily neglected by travellers of the Clyde, competing neither with the Victoriana of Bute nor the wildernesses of Arran. And yet this small fertile island has at least been discovered and enjoyed by Glaswegians. The ferry arrives at a bus stop (every ferry is met by the round-island bus) and the traffic of bicycles could rival Holland. Cumbrae has a long low circular coast road and one hill route, making for easy cycling with superb views of the shores of the

248

Clyde and of Arran and Bute. All manner of gaily painted granny seats mark every special spot, some signifying no more than a particularly good brambling or paddling place. One local curiosity is the Lion rock, best seen from the north: a dyke of basalt breaks through the old red sandstone covering most of Cumbrae to take on the shattered profile of a lion escaping over the hill.

The Universities of Glasgow have a Marine Biological Station on Great Cumbrae to support their scientific experiments. The museum and aquarium are open to the public (9.30 —12.30, 2 —5, Mon-Fri and summer Sat). Students have made a fascinating model of the depths of the sea around the Clyde and the south-west coast of Scotland, and have mounted a series of clear, simple charts, explaining the movement of currents, both worldwide and local, and local ecological chains. The small aquarium, stocked locally, houses some surprisingly exotic fish and plants — pink Norwegian lobsters, coral sea anemones and sea-mice, slug-shaped with fluorescent hairs, to name just a few.

Millport, sheltered between Port Achur and Farland Points, was discovered and enlarged by Victorian holiday-makers before Bute but to a lesser extent, and its architecture is calmer and less grandiose. Solid residences watch the modern visitors sport in the bay — wind-surfers, rowboats and fishing lines liven the scene. The old County Building (still used for local administration) is a delightful subdued Scottish baronial lodge, complete with a display of ponds and flowers in front, an active funfare behind, and tennis courts and paddling pools at the sides. It is lit up at night by strings of coloured lights. The museum downstairs (open 10 — 4.30) has a small collection of local curiosities, ranging from the mayor's chains to the shoemaker's tools, steamer routes and a large collection of old photographs of Millport's school teams.

Set back from the bustle of holiday-makers is Britain's smallest collegiate cathedral. In the 1840s, the 6th Earl of Glasgow, then the Hon G F Boyle, went to study at Oxford where he became heavily influenced by John Keble and the Oxford Movement. Fired with enthusiasm he envisaged founding a college which would stimulate the church both by training future leaders and by encouraging theological studies. He chose Cumbrae for its location because of long-standing family ties and the island's isolation. William Butterfield, the preferred architect of the Cambridge Camden Society, was enrolled to design a building to suit these aspirations. Although tiny, the church is set above terraced gardens (from where the building stone was quarried and extended into the associated collegiate buildings, producing an imposing horizontal emphasis countered by the fine 123 ft (37 m) pyramidal spire. Inside, the stark nave contrasts sharply with the highly ornate chancel, covered with the Butterfield mark of brightly coloured tiles. In the Lady Chapel are the remains of Celtic crosses found locally and donated by the 6th earl. His money ran out, but the project was saved by Bishop Alexander Chinnery-Haldane of Argyll and the Isles in 1886. Only recently has its collegiate nature been restored by the Community of Celebration, who share the church with the Episcopalian community.

The high road climbs up the gently wooded slopes, past herds of black and white cows, to superb views over the island. On the left is an old curling pond, now overgrown with weeds but a reminder of the time when almost every estate encouraged this winter sport. A charming semi-circular roadside mineral well is now crumbling into disrepair.

Accommodation:
Angus Hotel (tel Millport 397)
Claremont Hotel (tel Millport 797)
Mansewood Hotel (tel Millport 379)
Millerston Hotel (tel Millport 480)
Royal George Hotel (tel Millport 301)
Woodend Hotel (tel Millport 391)
Westbourne Hotel (tel Millport 423)
B & B and self-catering — details from the Tourist Office, Millport.
Camping — permission must be obtained from the Bute Estate Factory, Rothesay, Bute.
Bicycle Hire:
Mapes & Son (tel Millport 444)
Bremner Stores (tel Millport 309)
A & W Morton (tel Millport 478)
Horse Hire:
C McCulloch, Upper Kirkton Farm (tel Millport 689)
Boat Hire:
S MacIntyre, Cumbrae Yacht Slip
D Wilson, Glasgow Street
A Wright, Marine Parade
A Roberts, Glasgow Street
Freshwater fishing permits:
Mrs Hill, Tobacconist, Stuart Street
Golf:
Millport Golf Course
Flagpole Crazy Golf Course
Millport Development Association organizes lots of fun competitions for all ages.
Tourist Office:
Millport (tel Millport 312); open 9 —1, 2 —5.

Arran
(G aran — a kidney)

Connections:
By sea: from Ardrossan to Brodick: approx five a day; cars; crossing
1 hr. Caledonian MacBrayne Ltd.

From Claonaig, Kintyre to Lochranza: May — Oct only, seven a
day; cars; crossing ½ hr. Caledonian MacBrayne Ltd.

The heart of Arran is as untamed as any part of the Highlands. Great
mountains rise steeply from the shore, within a few hundred feet
casting off their mantle of woodlands, mainly oak, to soar upwards,
gaunt and stark, painted by the moody brush of changing light and
challenging climbers and hill walkers to venture ever higher. Arran's
peaks are more free of cloud and mist than most island ranges. The
other more superficial character of Arran is that of a holiday pleasure
ground. The encircling coastal road is populated with hotels and tearooms, craftshops and tourist centres, granny seats and kiddy swings,
perfect foils for the leisure wants of everyman. To appreciate the
range of distractions to the full, join the multitudes in the Tourist
Office, Brodick, and collect the rainbow of free coloured leaflets
covering archaeology to zoology, camping to adventure holidays,
cycling to spinning.

Brodick (ON breior vik — broad bay) is a patchy town, the
Administrative centre of the island but lacking any individual essence,
a random development from the original estate village for **Brodick
Castle**. Glimpsed by the arriving Ardrossan ferry, the red sandstone
castle occupies a site first used by Viking settlers who yielded it to
the MacDonalds, Lords of the Isles. Robert the Bruce claimed the
fortress as royal property but the frequent inter-dynastic quarrels of
the following centures caused it to change hands many times. It was
eventually given by James III to his nephew James Hamilton in 1502,
and was then held almost continuously by the Hamilton family until
it was inherited by the Duchess of Montrose, daughter of the 12th
Duke of Hamilton in 1895. On her death in 1958, it was bequeathed
to the safekeeping of the National Trust for Scotland, together with
the gardens and also Goat Fell and Glen Rosa.

The fine drive twists round the back of the castle, giving only a
slight indication of the Victorian Scots baronial mansion watching
the bay below (open Easter — Sep: 1 — 5 Mon-Sat, 2 — 5 Sun;
gardens, 10 — 5 all year). The interior projects a distinct feeling of a
rarefied yet family home, sporting trophies in suitable multiples,
portraits recording appropriately aristocratic alliances, and an
enviable collection of furniture, china and ornaments collected by
successive dukes. A small exhibition on George Forrest, an early 20th
century botanist who brought vast collections of specimens back
from China and Tibet, scarcely prepares the visitor for the brilliance

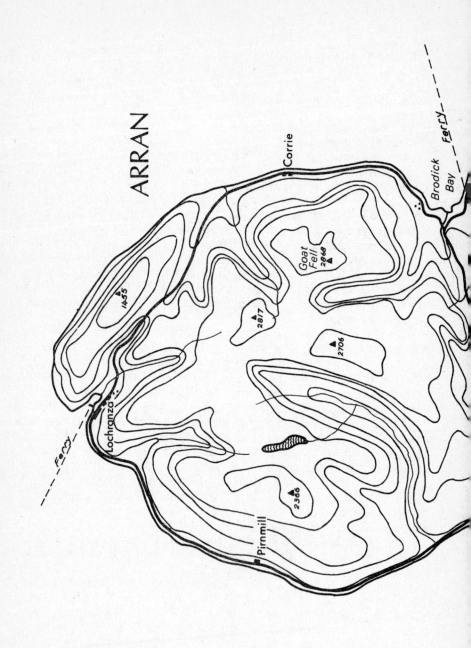

ARRAN

Corrie

Goat
Fell
2868 ▲

1455 ▲

2817 ▲

2706 ▲

Lochranza

Ferry

Brodick
Bay

Ferry

2366 ▲

Pirnmill

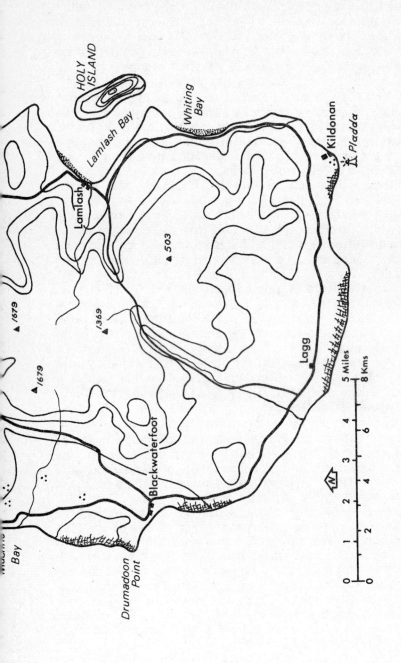

HOLY ISLAND

Lamlash Bay

Lamlash

Whiting Bay

Kildonan

Pladda

▲503

▲1369

▲1679

▲1679

Blackwaterfoot

Drumadoon Point

Bay

Lagg

N

0   1   2   3   4   5 Miles

0   2   4   6   8 Kms

of the azealeas and rhododendrons (best seen in May but flowering
Jan — Aug) which cover the terraces and line the walkways falling
away from the front of the castle. Until the First World War, scrub
woodland overran the wild garden, but the Duchess of Montrose,
helped by eastern explorers and a faithful son-in-law, converted the
jungle into an exotic garden; splashes of vivid oranges, reds and
whites lighten even the darkest corners, the plants thriving on Arran's
mild climate. The collection has been extended to include science
fiction specimens from every continent, and a water garden, while
tucked into one corner is a weird Victorian summerhouse, decorated
inside with patterns of pinecones. Recently the National Trust have
been introducing new plants from the collection of Achamore (see
Gigha), given to them by Sir James Horlick.

Brodick Nature Centre has an excellent bookshop with a good
selection for children, complementing the mood of the centre and
aimed at visiting young naturalists who help to keep a nature log.
Trails are organized around Arran to look for golden eagles or for
geological features. Arran is a geologist's paradise, but for the layman
this wealth of phenomena is a mystery easily unravelled by the
language of children.

The Roseburn Hereitage Museum (open May — Sep: 10.30 — 1,
2 — 4.30, Mon-Fri) presents a lucid display of an Arran cottage, 60
years before electricity but with some home comforts, such as wood
panelling. The 18th century school was converted into a smithy in
the 1850s and although it closed for business in the 1960s, the three
furnaces and all the tools are still in place, used fortnightly in a
demonstration of the art of horseshoeing. The stable houses a
collection of local antiquities, recording archaeological finds,
displaying Scotland's largest collection of thimbles lent by Margaret
Stewart, and frequently used by local craftsmen to exhibit their skills.

The road north follows the rocky coast to the charming hamlet of
white-washed houses at Corrie (G coire — a cauldron), one of the
least spoilt in Arran, although its beaches are popular with sandcastle
builders and swimmers. A local curiousity is the 'Doctor's bath', cut
out of the sandstone by Dr McCredy at the beginning of the 19th
century to provide 'cures' for bored ladies. North Sannox was the
site of a barytes mine, objected to because of its ugliness by the 11th
Duke of Hamilton but reopened and mined until the Second World
War; the minerals were used in paint manufacture and the scars still
remain. A walk around the coast to Lochranza passes the fallen rocks
— a scatter of vast boulders tumbled from the hillside in an avalanche,
and onwards to the Cock, whose silhouette once resembled a crowing
cock with spread wings; like so many birds, it lost its head and is no
longer so spectacular. In this inaccessible corner, Daniel MacMillan,
founder of the international publishing company, spent his early
years.

The road climbs up Glen Sannox , past a tiny graveyard, the resting place of the Goatfell murder victim, Edwin Rose. Rose, a London clerk, came for a walking holiday to Arran in 1889, and met John Laurie. They spent several days together before taking up the challenge of **Goat Fell**, where Laurie, tempted by Rose's holiday funds, pushed him off a crag. He spent 41 years in Perth Prison for his crime. Goat Fell may seem an appealing climb, but do not venture upwards unless you are properly prepared.

Lochranza has a gentle old-fashioned air. Every large house is a boarding house, all sitting serenely round the loch guarded by the solid 14th century keep, a hunting lodge of the Scottish Kings and now a picturesque ruin (maintained by the D of E). It stands in the middle of the bay on a long grassy promontory, surrounded by fishing and pleasure boats, although the fleet of 400 herring boats has long since gone. An enterprising lady offers classes in spinning, and this is a good village to find wool for Arran jerseys. This was the village where Burn's 'Highland Mary' was in service to the local minister.

Catacol (ON — ravine of the wild cat) commemorates one of Arran's most famous heroes, the legendary Fingal, who with typical Celtic loyalty rebuffed a Viking raid led by Manos, heir to the King of Sweden, to prove his manhood. A terrace of twelve tiny cottages is known locally as the Twelve Apostles. The road traverses the raised beach of pebbles under the oak woods, tempting to campers with its views along the length of Kintyre (the farmer's permission should be obtained first). **Pirnmill** was once the centre of an active industry, providing pirns or bobbins for Paisley's cotton mills. Demand outstripped the supplies of pinewood and the locals turned to tourism for employment.

Around **Machrie** is a group of seven stone circles, all lying within sight of each other. Although none are particularly spectacular, this was obviously a very important site during the Bronze Age (approx 2,220 BC — 1,000 BC). A few contained burial cists, but for modern lay observers the most interesting are the fallen stones which were partly shaped into millstones but then left abandoned near their original standing position. A walk along the boulder-strewn shore leads to the **King's Cave**, a large dry cave penetrating the cliff face for 100 feet (30 m). Traditionally this is where Robert the Bruce sat in despair, ready to abandon his attempts to seize the Scots throne, when he chanced to see a spider struggling up its thread. The little creature's determination inspired Robert and he prepared a final and successful campaign to claim the crown. The cave was excavated in 1902 and proved to have a much longer history, as engravings of hunting scenes were found on the walls. These are now hard to decipher beneath the vandalism of modern graffiti. Nearby caves have also been linked with the royal visit and appropriately the royal fern grows on all in great profusion. Many of these caves along the west coast have since been associated with illicit whiskey stills and black market smuggling from Ireland, like so many others around the Scottish shores. Drumadoon Point is capped by the remains of an Iron Age fort.

The String leaves Blackwaterfoot to cross Arran, moving up the fertile valley into the brown moorland. A scattering of teahouses assures intrepid adventurers that they have not totally left civilization as they rise over the moorland to drop down suddenly into Brodick. This road was designed by Thomas Telford in 1817 and given its name by sailors, because its sharp descent can clearly be seen from miles off.

A second road crossing the mountains, The Ross, takes a more picturesque route, following Sliddery Water to its head through a steep green valley, and then taking an easier descent down to Lamlash. There are fewer granny seats along this road, and the terrain is slightly more hospitable.

Lagg (G — a hollow) is a beautiful village settled in a woodland of beach and palm trees by Kilmory Water, supposedly haunted by a laird who sold his soul to the devil, and by a young couple mistaken for smugglers by coastguards and shot while they wandered in the woods; but these transparent spirits are chased away by the heartiness of the patrons of the inn. The creamery, producing the special Arran cheese so remarkably like all other Scottish cheddars, accounts for the sleek black and white milk cows on the fertile southern shores of Arran. Small farmhouses and well-maintained hedgerows make this corner take on a tamer lowland feel, affording a brief relief from the awesome giants dominating the rest of the island.

From among the **Kildonan's** jumble of farms, holiday cottages and trees, emerges the suggestion of a ruined castle, dating from the 14th century; only a corner now remains. There are superb views from here of the flat lighthouse island of **Pladda** and the cone of the volcanic cave of Ailsa Craig in the misty distance.

An easy walk up **Glenashdale** through the forest leads to views of a spectacular waterfall, dropping 200 ft (60 m) to splash onto the rocks below. **Whiting Bay** (named after the fish!) could almost be tucked under the escarpment of the South Downs, its wooded lanes running in rabbit warrens around the slopes. Local initiative has developed a crafts trail which takes in all the craft shops hidden away in this maze. Many delightful hours can be spent searching them out on foot — it is best to drop in at the gallery first, to pick up the map.

Kingscross Point is the place from where Robert the Bruce, in his final attempt to claim the crown, watched the Ayrshire coast for a sign that his supporters were ready. Seeing a glint of light across the water, he presumed that this was the arranged beacon and set sail. When he arrived, he found that his supporters were totally unprepared, but he managed to overcome this setback and finally won the kingdom. Traces of a Viking grave can also be found on this headland and there are marvellous views of Holy Island to be enjoyed. **Holy**

Island (ferry from Lamlash) was the chosen residence of an Irish saint, St Molios, who lived in the cave now named after him. This was not as uncomfortable as might first be imagined, for there is a fireplace and a drain cut into the rock. St Molios established a habit of peacemaking and next to the cave is a sandstone table, round which are cut four seats, where the saint would settle local disputes. Somerled, Lord of the Isles, established a monastery here in the 12th century to venerate this holy man. Now owned by a university federation, Holy Isle is a naturalist's delight with flocks of wild goats and soay sheep grazing the steep slopes, and a multitude of birds nesting there each year. The hillside seems daunting to climb, but easy routes can be found from the south.

Lamlash owes its fine protected anchorage to Holy Isle's steep slopes, and was developed as a harbour early in the 17th century. It was the home of Donald MacKelvie, who used its rich soil to develop the famous seed potatoes commemorating the island — Arran banners, etc. Craft shops, ships' chandlers and inns supply the wants of visiting yachtsmen.

Much can be said of the beauties of Arran, wearing its spring greens or autumn golds, and its summer hedgerows of flowers, but essentially this is a holiday island, catering for the needs of any family with a touch of professionalism yet without the mercenary attitude of most other resorts.

Accommodation:
Blackwaterfoot:
Blackwaterfoot Hotel (tel Shiskine 202)
Greannan Hotel (tel Shiskine 200)
Hamilton Arms Hotel (tel Shiskine 333)
Kinlock Hotel (tel Shiskine 286)
Rock Hotel (tel Shiskine 225)
Brodick:
Altanna Hotel (tel Brodick 2244)
Auchrannie Hotel (tel Brodick 2234)
Belvedere Private Hotel (tel Brodick 2397)
Douglas Hotel (tel Brodick 2155)
Ennismar Hotel (tel Brodick 2265)
Glenartney Hotel (tel Brodick 2220)
Gwyder Lodge Hotel (tel Brodick 2377)
Heathfield Hotel (tel Brodick 2204)
Hollybush Private Hotel (tel Brodick 2267)
Invercloy Hotel (tel Brodick 2225)
Kilmichael House Hotel (tel Brodick 2219)
Kingsley Hotel (Brodick) Ltd (tel Brodick 2226)
Hotel Ormidale (tel Brodick 2293)
St Elmo Hotel (tel Brodick 2229)
Allandale Guest House (tel Brodick 2278)

Dunvegan Guest House (tel Brodick 2273)
Oakbank Guest House (tel Brodick 2283)
Tuathair Guest House (tel Brodick 2214)
Glencloy Farm House (tel Brodick 2359)
Catacol:
Catacol Bay Hotel (tel Lochranza 231)
Corrie/Sannox:
Corrie Hotel (tel Lochranza 273)
Black Rock Guest House (tel Lochranza 282)
Heathfield Guest House (tel Lochranza 286)
Kildonan:
Breadalbane Hotel (tel Kildonan 284)
Kildonan Hotel (tel Kildonan 207)
Kilmory:
The Lagg Hotel (tel Sliddery 255)
Lamlash:
Aldersyde Hotel (tel Lamlash 219)
Bay Hotel (tel Lamlash 224)
Glenisle Hotel (tel Lamlash 258)
Kilbride (tel Lamlash 319)
Lamlash Hotel (tel Lamlash 208)
Marine House Hotel (tel Lamlash 298)
Whitehouse (Hotel (tel Lamlash 278)
Altachorvie (tel Lamlash 286)
High Trees Guest House (tel Lamlash 470)
Lilybank Guest House (tel Lamlash 230)
Myrtle Bank Guest House (tel Lamlash 354)
The Lookout (tel Lamlash 352)
Tighaniar Guest House (tel Lamlash 240)
Sanyu Monamhor Glen (tel Lamlash 257)
Westfield Guest House (tel Lamlash 428)
Lochranza:
Bute Lodge Hotel (tel Lochranza 240)
Lochranza Hotel (tel Lochranza 223)
Caber Feidh Guest House (tel Lochranza 284)
Kincardene Lodge Guest House (tel Lochranza 267)
Pirnmill:
Clisham Guest House (tel Pirnmill 278)
The Anvil Tearoom (tel Pirnmill 240)
Whiting Bay:
Burlington Private Hotel (tel Whiting Bay 255)
Cameronia Hotel (tel Whiting Bay 254)
Craigielea Hotel (tel Whiting Bay 245)
Eden Lodge Hotel (tel Whiting Bay 357)

Grange House Private Hotel (tel Whiting Bay 263)
Invermay Hotel (tel Whiting Bay 431)
Kiscadale Hotel (tel Whiting Bay 277)

Royal Hotel (tel Whiting Bay 286)
Trareoch Hotel (tel Whiting Bay 226)
Whiting Bay Hotel (tel Whiting Bay 247)
Stanford Guest House (tel Whiting Bay 313)
B & B, self-catering and camping — details from Tourist Office, Brodick.
Youth hostels at Brodick, Lochranza and Whiting Bay.
Cycle Hire:
Howie Hires, Brodick (tel Brodick 2460)
Mrs Glen, Brodick (tel Brodick 2444)
Mrs Rogers, Brodick (tel Brodick 2314)
Corrie Craft (tel Corrie 661)
Stanford Hires, Whiting Bay (tel Whiting Bay 313)
Mrs Hislop, Lamlash (tel Lamlash 441)
Horse Hire:
Glenrosa farm stables, Brodick (tel Brodick 2380)
Cloyburn Trekking Centre, Brodick (tel Brodick 2108)
Kelvin Laugh Trekking Centre, Whiting Bay (tel Whiting Bay 424)
Cairn House, Blackwaterfoot (tel Shiskine 256)
Sea Angling:
Details from Tourist Office, Brodick.
Freshwater fishing permits:
Details from Tourist Office, Brodick.
Diving:
Arran Diving Centre, Brodick (tel Brodick 2272)
Golf:
Courses at Blackwaterfoot, Brodick, Corrie, Lochranza, Lamlash.
Mountain Rescue:
Lists of walks available from Tourist Office, Brodick (tel Brodick 2300 and 2340)
Tourist Office:
Brodick (tel Brodick 2140): open Jun — Sep: 9.30 — 7.30 daily; Oct — May: 9.30 — 5 Mon-Sat.

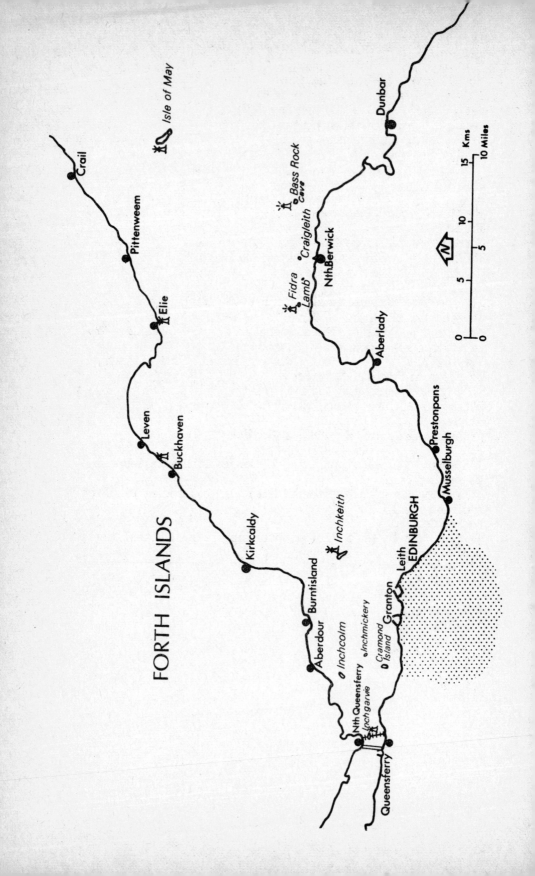

FORTH ISLANDS

Crail

Isle of May

Pittenweem

Elie

Bass Rock
Cave
Craigleith
Fidra
Lamb
NthBerwick

Leven
Buckhaven

Aberlady

Kirkcaldy

Prestonpans

Inchkeith

Musselburgh

Burntisland

EDINBURGH

Aberdour

Inchcolm
Inchmickery
Granton
Leith
Inchmickery
Cramond
Island

Nth Queensferry
Inchgarvie

Queensferry

N

15 Kms
10 Miles

10

5

5

5

0   0

Part 6
The Islands of the Forth

These little islands scattered in the Firth of Forth are not as insignificant as their size would suggest. Several were important spiritual and intellectual centres in the early Middle Ages when monastics chose to live apart from ordinary men, and today several are important bird reserves (access is often restricted). No self-respecting island hopper should ignore them.

Inchgarvie
(G innis garbh — rocky islet; but also from garvies (sprats), which are caught in plenty off the rocks.)

Standing in the centre of the Forth between North and South Queensferry, Inchgarvie was first recorded as fortified when John Dundas of Dundas built a castle for the protection of boats — a square tower keep, similar to that on, Loch Leven. Succeeding fortunes saw it demolished and rebuilt through the following centuries (traces can still be seen) and even used as a detention centre during the mid-17th century, until the Dundas family sold it to the Railway Board for £2,700. They wanted it as a foot for the **Forth Railway Bridge**, which was begun by Sir Thomas Borch. The Tay Bridge disaster alarmed the Board who subsequently commissioned Failer and Baker to design the present construction. Acclaimed as an engineering masterpiece, this bridge is 8,296 ft (2,558 m) long, took seven years to build (1883-90), is fixed by 8 million rivets — the last tightened by HRH Edward Prince of Wales, and cost £3½ million and 57 lives. Originally, many of the stones of the fortifications were used as ballast, but these were replaced in the Second World War by the most amazing stationary concrete battleship. There is no access and the islet is best seen from above on a train heading north.

Inchcolm
(G — isle of Columba)

Connections:
By sea: details of availability of boat from the Abbey Custodian (tel Dalgety Bay 823332).

This small islet, 1 mile (1.6 km) off the Fife coast, was named after a 6th century hermit, possibly somehow associated with the founder of the Iona Monastery, who realized that he could live off its fertile pastures while remaining undisturbed from his contemplations (fresh water came from the 40 ft/12 m deep holy well). By the 12th century the island had achieved such fame that not only was the Danish king defeated by Macbeth buried there, but Alexander I chose it as a site for his Augustinian canons c 1124. Successive kings continued to patronize the Monastery, giving it much land in Fife and often using the priors as diplomatic envoys throughout Europe. The size of the Abbey today vouches for its importance. The chapel, chapter house, dormitories and cloisters are still standing, and are now in the care of the D of E (open Apr — Sep: 9.30 — 7 Mon-Sat, 2 — 7 Sun; Oct-Mar: 9.30 — 4, Mon-Sat, 2 — 4 Sun). An excellent guidebook records the history and architectural development of the site in detail.

In 1335 an English ship attacked the monastery. It made off with all the monks' treasures, including the statue of their patron saint, Augustine of Hippo, but then ran into a sudden storm. This was seen as God's reprisal and everything was returned. Unfortunately for the monks, subsequent raids were not hampered by superstition, but they continued to lead a life of distinguished learning, nevertheless. A Scottish history, *Scotichronicon*, was composed on the island by Walter Bower and decorated by other monks. By the 15th century the monks had taken the precaution of fortifying their fertile isle, but by 1578 the canons had lost another battle — against John Knox's Reformation.

During the following century the buildings were used as a house but the island was soon deserted. It was subsequently used only for occasional fortifications, eg at the east end during the Napoleonic wars, and as a place of quarantine for plague ships.

Inchmickery
(G innis na ghicaire — isle of the vicar)

Connections:
By sea: private hire from Granton or Port Edgar.

Rising only 48 ft (15 m) out of the Forth, Inchmickery has long been established as a site of religious importance, for on its north side is the 14 ft (4 m) high 'cow and calves' neolithic standing stone, whose precise significance can now only be guessed at. In the 19th century it was ringed with valuable oysterbeds, but now only a profusion of seaweeds, lichens and mosses covers its rocks. The isle has been declared a Bird Sanctuary to protect its large and vulnerable tern colony. Landing is forbidden May — July; at all other times permission is needed from the RSPB, 17 Regents Terrace, Edinburgh (tel 031 556 5624).

Cramond Island

This is the only Forth island affording easy access, as it can be reached by foot across the cockle sands (1 mile/1.6 km), within two hours either side of low tide. Cramond was first recorded as an important Roman station, 'Caer Almond'. In 1004, Constantine IV, a rival of Malcolm II, was murdered by Malcolm's brother whilst hiding on the island. The 19 acres (8 h) were divided between medieval monarchs and ecclesiastics into King's Cramond and Bishop's Cramond, though why is not clear, but this fertile pasturage continued to be used into the 19th century. A homestead for the herdsman still stands. This man made a fortune because of the famous oysterbeds surrounding the island (now over-fished and polluted).

Inchkeith

Connections:
By sea: as for Inchmickery.

A ¾-mile-long (1.2 km) arrow pointing to Portobello and commanding tremendous views of the valley and Edinburgh, this rocky outcrop was known even to Ptolemy in the 2nd century AD as the city of Alavia. Bede named it Urbs Guidi after Gareth (=Keith), the Pictish king who made this the capital of his kingdom of the Lothians and Northumberland. In the 7th century it was famed for its 'school of prophets', no doubt a collection of missionary monks. In 1010 it was given to Robert de Keith, Earl Marischal, by Malcolm II for services aginst Viking raiders. In quieter times, James IV — in the true spirit of scientific enquiry — placed a dumb woman on the island with two babies, to see what was 'the original language of the human race'. Apparently they were found to speak Hebrew! Mary Queen of Scots came to inspect the fortifications of her French allies and a commemoration stone inscribed MR 1564 is now built into the lighthouse. This was designed by Thomas Smith in 1804. A grey stone building, it stands 55 ft (17 m) high, 23 ft (7 m) above sealevel, and can be seen for 23 miles (37 km), its white 167,000 candle-power paraffin light flashing every 30 seconds.

Inchkeith's defences continued to be developed up until the Second World War, when vast earthworks of trenches and enormous blockhouses and barracks for 600 men transformed the island. It now houses an extraordinary number of gulls. Visits are possible but intending visitors should arrange their own transport (tel 031 554 5261 for permission). Beware of sunken reefs when approaching the island.

Craigleith

Connections:
By sea: from North Berwick, Mr Marr, by special arrangement (tel North Berwick 2838).

A rocky barren crag, rising sheer to 168 ft (51 m) out of the Forth, Craigleith is a gull's paradise.

The Lamb

So called because of its shape, this is another bird rock. All landings are forbidden (and dangerous), except an annual landing by the RSPB to count the birds, mostly guillemots, razorbills and cormorants.

Fidra

(N — feather isle)

Connections:
By boat as for Craigleith.

On the northern arm of Fidra, over a natural arch, are the remains of a hermitage connected to the Cistercian Order at North Berwick, founded by Duncan, Earl of Fife in 1154, and later removed to Newbattle, Midlothian. A chapel dedicated to St Nicholas, then the patron of sailors, kept a light burning in the altar window to warn his wards of the rocks. For their troubles the eleven monks earned £20 a year (a lot). The custom was revived by the Northern Lighthouse Board who built a lighthouse in 1885 — it flashes every 15 seconds. The name probably comes from the eiderduck who breed on the rocks in large numbers.

The Bass Rock

Connections:
By sea from North Berwick, Mr Marr (tel North Berwick 2338). Independent travellers must obtain landing permission from Sir Hew Dalrymple, North Berwick.

In the late 1960s the Bass Rock was brought to national notice by a poor black-browed albatross who persistently courted a gannet to no avail. The albatross has since left but the gannets remain — about 7,500 pairs. These birds were a popular medieval dish, though not with Charles II who found them as repulsive as the Solemn League and Covenant.

A volcanic cave, the Bass rears 350 ft (110 m) out of the sea. A curious tunnel 170 yards (155 m) long, bores through its centre, in an east-west direction (reachable at low tide), with many other caves penetrating its core.

Legend records that the first inhabitant was St Baldred, an Irish missionary linked to the Columbian Church, who died in 606. Halfway up the rock is a ruined chapel dedicated to his name and built in the 16th century, perhaps on the site of his beehive cell. The island played many a dramatic part in medieval politics, helping Black Agnes, Countess of March and Dunbar, hold out against the English siege of Dunbar Castle in 1338 by supplying food and wine. In 1405 it sheltered the King's son, James I, who later imprisoned his enemies there. It is said that the enemies of Mary Queen of Scots wished to place her on the island, but as the Lauders refused to sell it, they kept her in Loch Leven Castle instead. In 1671 it was sold for £4,000, and used as a prison for the Convenanters and then for some Jacobites who turned the tables by capturing the garrison and bargained for their freedom. In 1701 the fortress was dismantled, and the island was sold to Sir Hew Dalrymple (whose family still hold it). Sheep were grazed and the gannets harvested, but the buildings crumbled and it remained deserted until 1902 when the lighthouse was constructed. This now flashes 'six white every 30 seconds'.

The island is a seabird's paradise. Besides gannets, fulmars, shag, herring gulls, kittiwake, razorbills and guillemots are packed onto its curtain of ledges, while puffins burrow into the cap of turf, and blackbirds, hedge sparrows and rock pipits dance over the ruins. 45 species of flowering plants have been recorded on the Bass, including the Bass mallow (Lavatera arborea), a biannual growing to 6-10 ft (2-3 m) around the buildings, with rose coloured flowers in July; this is also found on Ailsa Craig and in south-west England. Seals can sometimes be seen swimming around or basking on the rocks.

Isle of May
(Celtic maigh — plain)

Connections:
By sea (May — mid-Sep): from Anstruther: Capt Anderson (tel Anstruther 215); Mr Thorburn (tel Kircaldy 52242).
From Crail: James Smith (tel Crail 484).

The Isle of May is the outermost island of the Forth and the largest, measuring 1 mile by ¼ mile (1.6 km by .4 km). It is ringed by cliffs, some reaching 160 feet (50 m), except on the north end. Legend records how St Mingo was abandoned as a child on the beach of Aberlady, rescued by a fish and taken to the May in 516. Near the south-east corner are the remains of a chapel dedicated to St Adrian (a hermit killed by the Danes and buried here), built by a Benedictine monastic settlement endowed by David I to pray for the souls of his forebears. Nothing could be done to protect the fertile island from raiders and it was soon abandoned by the monks for Pittenweem, but it remained a place of pilgrimage until the 15th century — hence the local names of pilgrim's well and pilgrim's haven. The monks made much money through harvesting the numerous rabbits for their skins.

The caves of the South Ness were used in the 17th century by 'wreckers' and smugglers, who even had a still there; later, the Fife fishermen hid from the Press gangs in the 'Press Cave'. In 1658 permission was given for money to be collected from vessels to pay for the first lighthouse, a coal-burning beacon kept alight by three men and 400 tons of coal a year. Its efficiency varied with the direction of the wind and the wreck of two ships in December 1810, mistaking a limekiln fire of Dunbar for the beacon, led to the construction of the existing lighthouse in 1814 (one flash every 20 seconds). The 'low light' of the north end was made redundant in

1934, and the buildings were given to the British Trust of Ornithology. In 1956 the island was declared a National Nature Reserve. It is now run by the NCC who have a small hostel for scientists monitoring the large colonies of seabirds and the visiting species that use the island as a migratory resting place; the island also supports numerous plant communities — over 60 varieties of sea-weeds have been found.

Accommodation:
For scientists only (Apr — Oct). Booking Secretary, Nature Conservancy Council, 12 Hope Terrace, Edinburgh (tel 031 445 2481). The NCC also produce a booklet.

Maps

All maps drawn by Alastair Gillies.

Index to Islands

abbreviations: Cd — Clyde Islands; Fh — Forth Islands; IH — Inner Hebrides; OH — Outer Hebrides; Oy — Orkneys; Sd — Shetlands.